LACANIAN COORDINATES

LACANIAN COORDINATES
From the Logic of the Signifier to the Paradoxes of Guilt and Desire

Bogdan Wolf

LONDON AND NEW YORK

First published 2015 by
Karnac Books Ltd.

Published 2018 by Routledge
2 Park Square, Milton Park, Abingdon, Oxon OX14 4RN
711 Third Avenue, New York, NY 10017, USA

Routledge is an imprint of the Taylor & Francis Group, an informa business

Copyright © 2015 by Bogdan Wolf

The rights of Bogdan Wolf to be identified as the author of this work have been asserted in accordance with §§ 77 and 78 of the Copyright Design and Patents Act 1988.

All rights reserved. No part of this book may be reprinted or reproduced or utilised in any form or by any electronic, mechanical, or other means, now known or hereafter invented, including photocopying and recording, or in any information storage or retrieval system, without permission in writing from the publishers.

Notice:
Product or corporate names may be trademarks or registered trademarks, and are used only for identification and explanation without intent to infringe.

British Library Cataloguing in Publication Data

A C.I.P. for this book is available from the British Library

ISBN-13: 9781782202806 (pbk)

Typeset by V Publishing Solutions Pvt Ltd., Chennai, India

To Livia,
To Weronika

CONTENTS

ABOUT THE AUTHOR — ix

CHAPTER ONE
The debris and the new discoveries — 1

CHAPTER TWO
New coordinates of psychoanalysis — 21

CHAPTER THREE
Of the truths and lies of *logos*: Lacan meets Heidegger — 51

CHAPTER FOUR
The signifier, the letter, the voice, and the subject of certainty — 79

CHAPTER FIVE
Two sides of repetition — 115

CHAPTER SIX
The drive and its satisfactions — 129

CHAPTER SEVEN
Superego and the logic of guilt   165

REFERENCES   189

INDEX   193

ABOUT THE AUTHOR

Bogdan Wolf became the editor-in-chief of the Psychoanalytical Notebooks, a publication of the London Society in the Lacanian Orientation, after receiving his PhD. from Warwick University in the 1990s. He has authored several articles and book contributions in English, French, Spanish, and Polish; co-edited the widely acclaimed collection *Later Lacan* (published by SUNY Press in 2006); and translated numerous texts. He is a member of the New Lacanian School and of the World Association of Psychoanalysis. He has lived and worked in private practice in London for over twenty years.

CHAPTER ONE

The debris and the new discoveries

Knowledge in psychoanalysis

What does psychoanalysis do? If there is anything psychoanalysts may have in common, it is their diversity in which is recognised the work of loss, failure, and impossibility in the practice of psychoanalysis. It will be of no use, if only of pretence, to try to agree on these *in principio* and *a priori* without passing through an experience we call psychoanalytic. It is on the basis of this recognition that the analyst becomes authorised to capture his psychoanalytic experience in a form of a definition. How to define psychoanalysis, Lacan asks, if no one knows what psychoanalysis is. And since no one knows what it is, psychoanalysts can only speak about it on the basis of particularity, what it does, and to whom.

There is no point, I suppose, in launching a critique against the academics, philosophers, scientists, and other "psychoanalytic theorists" when they take a swing, and sometimes a stab, at psychoanalysis because there is no one, including clinicians, to suppose them of such a knowledge. "No one knows what psychoanalysis is" implies anyone can say about it what gives them pleasure. The measurement of knowledge may imply some form of a proof of what does not deceive, as Lacan said early on. But a knowledge of psychoanalysis does not give itself to measurement in the same way science would and does. Psychoanalytic knowledge can be found as situated in the structure of the discourse as a produce of analysis. Therefore, psychoanalytic knowledge is not so much measured as produced as a result of the analytic process. In the end of analysis we only know what we say or what we choose not to say, which gives us an inkling about desire, which in the case of those who followed Lacan's desire gives them some indication about theirs. It may only be pertinent to note that whatever the *qualitum* of the analytic experience, psychoanalytic knowledge produced in effect derives at the beginning from what the subject wants to know and not from spoken and written productions referred to, which sometimes eclipses the subject's desire in relation to knowledge.

The question therefore shifts towards the one concerning the practice of the symptom and of who listens and with what kind of ears. Does one listen because what is said easily slips into common beliefs, prejudices, agitating our well-worn yet overblown affects to resist and protest or does one listen to that which remains incomplete, enigmatic, unknown, and allusive? Sooner or later in the course of the analytic process we come to realise that in psychoanalysis we do not deal with meanings or units of information communicated, or ranted to and fro for better or worse, of the agitated prejudices of the ego. We realise this because precisely it had originally prompted us to seek in analysis an answer to the question of the subject: what do I want? Why is life so difficult? Why must I die before coming to know what life is? How much more of this sometimes unbearable solitude? Why does love never last long enough? Why did I agree with what other people wanted me to do to come to question what they expected of me? And so on. These traces of desire and obstacles to it at the same time constitute the indication in question—it is always what I want to know and from whom that will determine the product at the end.

Whatever the degree to which these questions differ from one subject to another, they already highlight a conflict and a struggle, alluding to what might be at stake and vaguely pointing to the paradoxical satisfaction that kept the subject hostage to these assumptions—for they are questions only in so far as they suppose an answer, namely an other who may have it. Analysis comes to existence out of this supposition. What is expected of the analyst and how to bear the enigma of that desire with which the subject comes to analysis to ask about it in any way he can, nostalgically, depressively, aggressively, persistently, until ….

The hysteric "knows" it from the start, without knowing it, and Freud must have known it if he founded the practice of psychoanalysis starting with transference to his hysterics. But every subject is a hysterical subject, it is just that some do not want to know this and others only come to know it much later. There is no knowledge about the subject's suffering, the malaise that turns him into evil-conceited actor or a compensation seeking victim, other than that which comes from the Other's desire and the satisfaction called jouissance. The idea of knowledge called abstract, and therefore absolute to the extent that it is all alone, separate from any other, falls under the scope of the ideal rather than truth. One suffers for truth in order to be duped by it and to realise one has suffered for a lie. But let's not reduce this lie to a whiff of vanity—this would render the truth worthless and the subject cynical. Lacan placed the two in the most intimate proximity when he said "I, the truth, lie". And for those who listen badly, he added: "there is no way to tell all of it, the whole truth". Why not to say some of it, not-all-of-it or not-every-one but only the relevant one, the one that led the subject by the nose to land a blow at the end of it? This is the kind of truth Lacan would tell us, not giving a toss to the question what to speak about to his students and followers, but following what insists and imposes itself on the subject.

Freud started with the hysterics because, being one of them, he also shunned the absolutist and totalist claim of philosophy to knowledge, assigning it from the start to the desire of the master who was obviously not without desire *for* the master. That's why it is not to everyone that we would give a just produced article for comment. Just as it is not everyone that we would ask about the analytic experience or the everyday life of the Greeks.

Psychoanalytic experience revolves around the body that does not have a body and around the real knowledge of that lack. How many times can the subject tell the truth? Every single time he speaks as there is no way to say it all. It is not an infinite number, for those who like to count, but it is not countable in advance either. Lacan made this link in *Television* connecting the satisfaction called jouissance with the uncountable number.

In the article "A spectacular health" (2008), M. Focchi tries to give psychoanalysis an autonomous place by way of eliminating the functions it serves together with other practices, like those of producing therapeutic effects, for example, or its utilitarian value or its function in the market, etc. In the end he is left with a remainder that can no longer be found in all those functions psychoanalysis purportedly shares with other psychotherapies and therapeutic services. This remainder cannot, of course, be defined in the same way as its use value or therapeutic function. As a doctrine and a practice, Focchi writes, psychoanalysis is an "extra factor" that relates to the object of psychoanalysis and no longer to its use value. This distinction, in slightly different terms, was already isolated by Lacan who, as early as at the time of founding the school of psychoanalysis, distinguished between pure psychoanalysis and applied psychoanalysis. For many critically inclined purists, this distinction in the Founding Act was an opportunity for attacking the term "pure" as they mistook it for an attribute. But with this term Lacan created a category to be distinguished from the category of the applicable or applied. He therefore distinguished analytic formation from applied psychoanalysis, especially in the mental health care institutions, where its functions and uses reflect a mixture of qualities, pure and impure being among them.

Pure psychoanalysis thus leads us towards the area that far from being abstract or puerile, in the sense of solely theoretical, designates what Focchi (2008) called "the object of psychoanalysis", the extra factor that is not shared by or in the field of applied psychoanalysis. And he gives us some indications of what this factor might be when he says that it has to do with jouissance in the speaking being. Jouissance, we could say, points to one side of the object.

The other side has to do with semblance. What kind of satisfaction is jouissance? Let's take a few examples. A boy who, before he turned criminal and abused women, had been systematically beaten by his mother until black and blue; a patient who keeps his shit well within his reach and marks his territory with the marker of loss; a man who constantly provokes his partner, so that she exhibits anger, even fury that serves for him as some kind of assurance and a token of her love; a man who insists on having all as one, a wife who loves him, children who admire him and work where he is respected; a woman who is happy in her marriage but cannot resist gravitating towards another man for a bit of nookie here and a bit of nookie there. Each of these modes of satisfaction called jouissance constitutes a unique mode of being in the world of discourse, and a paradoxical choice one makes without knowing it or wanting to know it. Getting in, getting out, and making use of objects, instruments, enduring suffering, relishing the idea of another satisfaction, and so on. Precisely in this sense these are also the objects of knowledge we do not want to know anything about. In the end we will, one by one, know something about it. Psychoanalysis inevitably comes to this point: you will know what you want to know, whether you are careful or not, but not in the way you imagined it to come or not to come. We will need to examine these modes of repetition in due course.

Metaphors of the unconscious

But even these instances or insistences of jouissance do not exactly convey the foreignness of the libido filling the space of speech by the speaking subject. The subject speaks, and there are no other means, Lacan stated early on, through which he can transmit what he says. An analytic session, a pure analytic session because it does not apply to anything, rests on these experiences and acts of speech. In the analytic session we try to say the impossible, to speak about jouissance as close as possible to *it* speaking. But how close is "as close as possible"? The uninterrupted flow of words, the tears that flood the trail of discourse, the rhythmically punctuated statements, the repetitive utterances, sometimes accompanied by the movement of hands, the momentarily raised voice and the blind passion of some deep and unfathomable frustration that propels the movement of the subject, will sooner or later be derailed by a direction of the signifier the analyst isolates. These clear enough indications of a gruesome and recurring hurt are not the end of it or all of it, which would be another mode of jouissance. While showing that something had been done to him, some irreparable damage, a traumatic blow to one's being in the mist of the past or in the maze of the present, all these, as soon as they begin to emerge and hit the air, start to mark the contours of the subject and make any therapeutic techniques, any advice or programme oriented treatments, any instructive and informative and descriptive comments, useless. And yet these indications of the satisfaction called jouissance with which the subject is imbued, hit the core of his existence and touch the most frequented passages of everyday life.

Here then we have the "extra factor", the unique point on the map that orients the itinerary of jouissance of the speaking subject in the analysis called "pure" as it can no longer be left in the hands of array of therapeutic reactions. But is this what Lacan called pure psychoanalysis? The recurring question keeps imposing itself on us again and again in the era of regulation and passing talking therapies through the sieve of application value as determined by unexamined ideals and prejudices of the officials. Here it is indeed to do with a purification of practice and of therapeutic relations that are left at their purest when never entered into. The question of analytical formation that interests me lies elsewhere. It arises nowhere else but where the demand for analysis becomes articulated, by mistake, flip of a tongue, dream, parapraxis, in short by way of the unconscious.

When the Freudian unconscious came into ex-istence, it was first heard in the stories of psychoanalysis. Initially, the unconscious was presented through diverse metaphors that primarily included that of archaeology, of ruins, of architecture, and of the dark and hidden sides. A theory, and psychoanalysis was no exception, needs an interpretation, and the literary one is always nearest as it makes the best use of the imaginary means. Freud himself admired Schliemann, who discovered Troy under several layers of other urban ruins—and after initially giving up on the original site only to return to it following his coordinates—and we started to discover Freud. This marked the beginning of Freud's discovery that was also his discovery of sexuality in everyday life.

As we know Freud invented psychoanalysis while working with the hysterics, which in his time meant hysterical women. Something puzzled him about them and he started to listen to them closer and closer. It was through the discourse of the hysteric, as we would say with Lacan, that he found the unconscious. How he discovered it has not ceased to puzzle us. Just think about this: the blabber as the cornerstone of psychoanalysis, yapping, moaning, and complaining as a foundation of the unconscious. And then, why not? If he had closely followed the cascade of words and the libido flowing through them, it was only to grasp that something of the order of the infinite was at play in that blabber, something continuously imposed itself on and between words, grimaces, surprises, laughter. And very quickly Freud discovered that the hysteric does not know what she is talking about. This was a crucial point. This blabber was indestructible, unstoppable, and somewhat like the drive, blind. It already had some of the characteristics of "our" unconscious, as Lacan elaborated it after founding his school in 1964. But it was not without the recourse to this inaugural discovery of Freud that Lacan came up with his own definition of the unconscious couple of years later, which for me is the most beautiful and intriguing one. Quite simply, the unconscious is "what we say it is".

That the unconscious is what we say (it is) follows from another statement Lacan made some time earlier, namely that language is the condition of the unconscious. If it were the other way round, as Laplanche wanted it, what would have Freud been listening to? Philosophical ideas? And who would we have today in the analyst's chair, Žižek? As if an idea, and a concept, were not part of language and part of the demonology of the obsessional. As if Lacan did not say that the concept of the unconscious is included in the unconscious. Freud continued to prick up his ears not because language was performing phonetic acrobatics before him but because he found a real satisfaction at the heart of the hysterical blabber. If the unconscious was constructed as an effect of language, the satisfaction was produced alongside it. We call it phallic jouissance.

Now, what exactly did Lacan have in mind when he said the unconscious is what we say? His assertion seems to imply that the unconscious is flat and even superficial. And that it is right there before our noses. So we waited all these years since Freud's discovery to find that the structure of the unconscious is constituted as a surface? How disappointing it must have appeared to those who did not follow to realise that psychoanalysis is no longer a reflection of the "oceanic feeling" or an oracle of infinite meaning or a veil of profundity unknown to mankind. Gone with the wind went the archaeology of the unconscious, gone the architecture of depth, and gone the metaphors of castles and palaces, undergrounds and vaults, of Alhambra and of Schliemann's Troy, of glimmering light in the distance and of the dark side of the moon. Gone but testifying to fantasies of their authors who like Dwelshauvers gave us several definitions of what the unconscious is not. We should add to it Hartmann's *opus magnus* on the philosophy of the unconscious.

The unconscious as a surface and the dignity of the subject as captured in relation to the Other on the surface—this was indeed something radically new. It led Lacan to grasp a new reality where appearance is no longer the opposite, or a sign, of essence but enmeshed in it just as rose that appears as a rose is a rose. "A rose is a rose is a rose", Gertrude Stein said not knowing she, too, was a Lacanian. With the difference between the appearance of a rose and its essence disappearing in Plato's library, we were left with the truly incomprehensible knot of the real and the symbolic, being and its manifestation, that comes to existence in the analytic process is never the way you have imagined it. The appearance as essence and the essence as appearance, inseparable, like two sides of a band or inside and outside of a hole. The unconscious is just that kind of a rose.

Love and terror

The terrorism of today, which should be described as a destruction without time for negotiation, remains *our* failure—"our" in so far as violence is responded to violently. Terror, indubitably, emerges as a form of love, the most violent love we have come to witness, that appears as perplexing, indeed. It is a love to death but not without love of death. The act of destruction does not go without a subject whose saying is measured not to resonate back to him for which some listening of another is needed. That's where the failure lies, in not hearing what may come in reply to violence. This love of death, which Freud called the death drive, has disoriented us as it indicates one way street where only death could catch up with death. This strange love of what Lacan called "dark God" has shaken the foundations of our belief in humanity. The unconscious can have this jolting effect of undermining and reorganising a subject's belief in an instant, which is followed by a tacit mourning of coming to terms with it. The strange thing is that after an act of violence that tears to pieces our convictions, life goes on and a belief in the survival of humanity goes on too, however anachronistic this may seem to some. Love and terror have become neighbours, Christian neighbours who cannot live apart from each other, who love each other to death. How could there be terror without God? The unconscious, where it is not true to human convictions, the unconscious as inhuman, has this trace of being a terrorist, capable of destroying what we love and cling to, the ideals we mistake for the "universal values". With the unconscious rewriting our daily history, psychoanalysis appears to enlighten the terrified ego gripped by the terror of the unconscious. In the dream told by an analysand he appears on a breakfast TV program and is asked whether psychoanalysis can in any way contribute to the debate about "terrorism". "I said yes", he says, "yes, it can, however *minimally*". Perhaps he would want to change something in peoples' perception of him. Perhaps he is gripped with guilt. His wish shows him as meaning well. Like all of us he is a Creon who would banish and condemn the law breakers to eternal hell in the name of good. That's his good, as

Lacan showed us in *The Ethics of Psychoanalysis* (1992). In the dream the subject gives a brief answer to the newsreader—"yes, it can, however minimally" He suffers and suffering is not universal, it concerns the subject, him. And then something awakes him: "We all suffer", he adds, "the terrorised and the terrorising". In theory we do, but the terrorised and the terrorising in the subject intersect at the level of the trauma. They are new signifiers for him, never articulated before, and they will produce new meanings. What's important for him at this moment is what side he is on. This choice would be on the side of sense. To recognise his position where the two sides overlap would be something else and determine what he is for the Other. Of course his dream speaks about where he is in relation to those in his early life who wielded violence. In childhood the violence is language. It is called trauma, and it is a failure to symbolise an act in the act. So we only do it retroactively, after suffering has weighed down on him. Subject's suffering is the royal road to the unconscious, to the master signifier between the terrorised and the terrorising that weighs down on him. And it is not royal at all. Is it true that he sees himself as someone of whom some knowledge can be supposed or does he expect the analyst to tell him this? Yes.

Some days later I open a newspaper and am reminded that the public debate on terrorism is widening and that it is not only my patient's dream that is a constant reminder of it. In its spotlight on this occasion are the politicians, the media, and military experts. Of course nobody invites, it is true, psychoanalysts or psychologists to contribute. It is perhaps partly because this would lead to lessening the effects of the media "terrorism" on our lives. A metaphor provides a detour for this thrust as the excitement of winding one another up would gradually peter out.

The media is just another word for journalism but its ethics are the same—"the public has the right to know", which is followed by what strikes us as a duty to realise this right, to convey the information irrespective of whether the public, and that's you and me, wants to hear it. This ethics appears of interest to us because it contributes to the politics of knowledge which for the journalist is on the side of "military sources", "official sources", "government sources", in short on the side of the master. It is an ethics of how it should be. This master discourse does not contribute an iota to the problem of the cause of terrorism. Can it be that my analysand contributed effectively to locating his own trauma? Clearly he touched on his subjective position in the dream that itself presented him with the dilemma of the good and guilt in the face of violence. What about evil? It is not strictly speaking a psychoanalytic concept as it appears to ignore the death drive of the perpetrator or actor. The good intentions rather contribute to this ignorance.

There is nothing more unforgivable, according to Lacan, and more dangerous than so called "good intentions". This implies that some intentions, as discovered *after* the act, can be forgiven: "I only wanted a bit of fun", says a man about his extramarital affair. At least his lover will know why he is not worthy of her. But if you do not do it out of love, if you do not let yourself be duped by love, then instead of forgiveness there is only time for the good intentions—"I did it for …" implies a bonus for the doer. "One for you and one for me", is the name of the action called good.

"Terrorism", as the word is used today in the media, is unilateral. Its definition precludes "us" or "me" and "you", as there is no time to negotiate between you who terrorises me. It is only based on "them", sometimes on "him", very rarely on "her" although one should never discount the Medeas around us, of the politicians and journalists alike. The third person just happens to be the one that, according to Lacan, does not exist. The Other, the big Him, the One beyond the time for negotiation, the Other as the guarantor of evil, does not exist. Nevertheless, what does not exist does not cease to distribute and shuffle fear in the public domain. That's one way of approaching terrorism as an *effect*. The effect of the unconscious reminds us that no one authorises what we want except for the lack of knowledge about the *cause*. In effect, the unconscious reminds us that what authorises us to speak, and therefore to act, are the things that you and I want for us *qua* your or my neighbour, whether this relation is based on love or on hate or, as Lacan suggested in his late teaching, on both. In the end we ask ourselves how to know the things the unconscious arranges for you *before* its effects become manifest? For now, until the effect is disregarded as an effect of a cause, the unconscious is a terrorist. In "Science and truth" (2006g) Lacan said it of the subject—the subject is a terrorist because what I want always clashes against what is wanted of me, which is where my responsibility lies. My responsibility is my freedom. Psychoanalysis is the only profession—for it is not only a formation but also a profession—whereby the subject's responsibility is an effect of the unconscious. "I am only authorised by what I say" is the Spartan rule of the ethics of psychoanalysis.

So if it is not you and not me, if "I" and "you" are not at the forefront of my relation with the world, who else could it be if not "them" or "him", the other, the unbearable neighbour, the tyrant I take with me to my dreams? What, I am not responsible for my nightmares either? Then I become an object of tyranny and destruction. Poor me. This is what Tony Blair evoked when he said: "No, terrorism is not an effect of our foreign policy but an act against 'our' values and way of life". It is in this sense that the unconscious is a terrorist, as it objects to a deluded judgement, undermines the naivety of good intentions, wrong-foots the narcissistic obsession with "our" values, and rips into pieces the megalomaniacal claims of cultural superiority. And it is always an effect.

Unilateralism appears as the condition for terrorism to have any meaning for "us". Not so with God, whether as an existence or as a faith. When we speak about God, unilateralism is not in question. The question of God, just like that of language, truth, creation, funereal rites, love, and evil in each instance requires a believer, a practitioner. God is therefore a collateral because it is based on the relation to the Other, either by way of subordination or symbiosis, in its most radical form. Psychoanalysis, as Lacan said, cannot do without taking an account of it.

Why to speak about the tenderness of the terrorists, then? Only a psychoanalyst could approach the problem in such a way. We need to make sure we do not take Stalin for anybody else, a man without scruples or mercy, without a doubt, sending people to death without a blink, a "perfect scoundrel". Or Hitler with his obsession of grandeur and supremacy spiced by a hatred of the Other. The scoundrel—whom Lacan distinguished from a fool, an indispensable clown-adviser at every decent royal court and only missing in modern governments—is the one who does not lie and, therefore, does not tell the truth or believe in loss. Thatcher believed in equality—in everyone aspiring to own a Rolls-Royce as the highest social ambition, if not an obligation due to my neighbour already having one. Selling the neighbour for profit became part of her new totalitarian vision of millionaire society. The neighbour in question, let's remind ourselves, was the one who is not for turning—the Lady. Although she failed to turn society she did not believe in into "mass individualism" of plutocracy, she succeeded in turning culture into a shop. Inevitably, in the grand scheme of things, she had to eliminate free higher education, because it was not profitable, and with it those who said they were not for sale. But it was Stalin, the perfect scoundrel, who before her had an idea that those who do not follow the Party guidelines should be deemed mentally unfit and sent to psychiatric institutions. Then came Szasz to say there is no such a thing as a mental illness.

The terrorists do not fit this bill. Millions sent off to Gulags still does not make Stalin a terrorist, as he never put his life on the line for a greater goal. One does not aspire to such an ambition without being first told one is worthless and a failure, and that only a redemption before God could change that. And the greater the magnitude of an act, the more everlasting the redemption. Were not kamikazes brought up in this way, as subordinate to a greater goal, like a country, its glory, and their glory in the afterlife? A belief in redeeming oneself opens the flood gates of destruction, which is an act that can be carried out without a grain of anger or revenge. Idealism has never been more lethal. History is a long procession of idiots and fools like Simon de Monfort, Ghengis Khan, Hannibal, or of scoundrels like Stalin or Judas.

The scorpion and the symptom: is there a philosophy of psychoanalysis?

Philosophers cannot forgive Lacan and psychoanalysis that it dares to transmit the lack—of total and unquestionable clarity, for example—without relying solely on the universality that in philosophy remains the main player. The idiosyncrasy can be seductive as well as irritating, and transference, as we know, can also turn into the negative one.

Succumbing to this dogmatic distinction it is worth noting that the difference between philosophy and psychoanalysis depends on whether the one making it does so following his or her analysis. In other words, the true value of philosophy may be revealed if it appears as a signifier of a very special quality, a master signifier indeed. According to Lacan the subject suffers from the signifier, sometimes from the signifier in relation to the imaginary, and sometimes from the signifier in relation to the real. It is not that psychoanalysis deals with the real and philosophy with the love of truth, as Badiou (2003) conceived it. Both deal with the signifier, and in both there is something real at stake with the imaginary serving as a smoke screen.

"Philosophy", too, can be a symptom, a symptom of the father, which has formed from the subject's response to the unbearable of the real, and therefore acquired a special quality and meaning, for example that of an ideal. And of course, within the field of the ideal a hell, too, can break loose. So where is the subject of the symptom? Once a scorpion asked a frog to carry him across the river. "Oh no, I will not", said the frog. "Why not?", asked the scorpion. "Because if I do you will sting me". "But I will not, I promise", replied the scorpion, "I just want to cross the river". "All right, then, jump on", agreed the frog and took the scorpion on her back. Halfway through the crossing the scorpion stung the frog. "And why did you do this?" asked the frog. "Because it is in my nature", answered the scorpion. The work of the symptom has to do with what we call our "nature". It is not so much a "human nature", as Winnicott called it, but the nature of the symptom in the speaking being that interests us. It has to do with what precedes the subject, with what makes the scorpion before he becomes a scorpion. In other words, the symptom has to do with what acts despite him wanting something else, with what compels him, pushes him, is stronger than him. Somewhere Nietzsche says that not everyone has the right to make a promise. But would it not be equally untrue to make a rule according to which only those who have come to terms with their "nature" can be expected to keep their promises? This is the kind of difference between philosophy and psychoanalysis I have in mind.

Whatever the field of knowledge that precedes entry to psychoanalysis, there arises a question of the cause of a subjective shift in relation to knowledge. But this happens, truly, as a result of transference, because what emerges as an effect of the shift is the very subject, the one who supposedly has knowledge, which only takes him to the analyst to extract it. This knowledge is what opens a path towards the particular. No, it is not a path, it is rather a slide of significations and a spiral or a fall—things will only get worse after the garments, poses, habits of thought, efforts of the body get chucked all the way down to the pit of repression. Some will have survived and transformed to effect new ways for the *ananke*, the necessary. When at the university, my fears were confirmed that it is a place where the difference between the academic knowledge, or what Lacan called university discourse, and the knowledge of experience, which is the discourse of the unconscious, also known as the master discourse, remains unformulated. For Lacan the discourse of the unconscious was a site of intimacy that he called, and for a reason, extimacy. The truth is extimate or internally excluded, which means that its discovery, like that of the unconscious, involves the other, the neighbour, the analyst. The truth befalls and surprises you when you accept an invitation without looking for it. Only the master can allow himself to fall. Truth is not a duty or an obligation with respect to knowledge although this how it is suffocated in the academic research. It must have surprised Beckett when he wrote: "The sun shone, having no alternative, on what was nothing new". To Beckett the same never ceased to shine. My former tutor in philosophy used to go to the toilet in the middle of every tutorial, always at the same time. He did it for years and will perhaps continue for the rest of eternity but it will always be his and nobody else's eternity. The sun shining on Beckett revealed the truth which is always new for the subject. It will shine on my professor one day, too.

Freud did not trust philosophers and did not make much of them. He made exception in two cases: Kant whose categorical imperative he took to embody the superego following the dissolution of Oedipus, and Brentano, an epochal philosopher whose lectures immixed elements of psychology and ancient philosophy, he attended in the 1880s. Freud situated philosophy in the field of *Weltanschauung*, namely as a discipline and practice of presenting a picture of the self-contained world that, by this token, is free from cracks and incoherence. In some way he regarded philosophy as a species of science, at least as not opposed to it, in another way it was part of religion. Freud treated philosophy as a modality of obsessional neurosis with paranoiac traits and, by this token, as being structured like the discourse of religion. In short, they belonged to the order of thought. Freud even said "animistic" thought. This has to do, Freud says, with the "overvaluation" of the words and beliefs when reality takes place in accordance with thinking imposed on it. So it is an obsessional's worldview that Freud gives us as a demonstration of a structure of error as constituting philosophical investigation.

Freud was the first one to consider the great discourses of humanity, religion, science, philosophy, and art, from the perspective of libidinal satisfaction they aim to achieve at the service of the subject. And this meant the failed satisfactions. What bothered him about philosophy was that it covers up the lack, ritualising the process because it does not know what to do with it. Lacan called this lack the lack in being, which is the effect of impact of language on the body and which implies that totality can only be conceived of as the imaginary *Gestalt* as he showed in the mirror stage. For Freud the philosopher overestimates thinking by failing to include the lack into the equation. But that was not everything.

Later on Lacan equated thought to jouissance, condensing Freud's efforts without taking anything away from him. "Thought is jouissance", Lacan says, because thinking, apart from being a process, is also a form of superegoic command. Thought follows the command: "Think!"

"You are from a different mould", I was once told by a philosophy professor when including Freud in an essay on Descartes. There is no point in arguing with that, so I took it as a compliment, having no choice of receiving it otherwise at the time of graduation. *Tempus abire tibi est.* And so I was gone. It was made plain that references to Freud, Camus or Dostoyevsky were not welcome where a common sense would suffice. They did not know how Einstein defined common sense, namely as a sum total of prejudices gathered before the age of eighteen years old. That's a good enough reason to take it as a reference. It sometimes felt like breaking the rules of the game, and Pirandello's eggs were cracking there one by one. Nietzsche, Augustine, Heidegger? Another scoff. It was a foreigner's privilege which I stretched *ad libitum* when necessary. It would be unthinkable, I imagined, for a French university professor to be quite so dismissive when a student were to refer to Dun Scott, Bishop Berkeley or Hume. Of course I could not have known for sure. What could one want from these thinkers who would go for a pee during lectures and not swerve from the comfort of using the works they knew by heart? Obviously I was at the wrong place, reading Freud between classes and refusing to write essays without him. But it was at the right time for all the master signifiers to be learnt and understood. Philosophy is about everything and nothing else.

To think or not to think and the Lacanian session

As a passionate psychoanalyst Freud undertook to work out the function of thought as a compulsion on the basis of the real object missing from the scene of subject's satisfaction. He was working then on the dynamic of the mental apparatus. Psychologists would call this apparatus a "model" but, to be fair to Freud, nothing was further from his mind in the course of constructing the first ever faulty structure of the psyche. Having thus proposed an apparatus at the heart of which lies a fundamental failure he was now in the position to bring in thinking as a reproductive process. The process will attempt to connect—and therefore to patch up the gaps between—the instants of perception, namely establish an identity between a representation perceived from outside and a representation invested by the ego. The insistence of what Freud calls thought-process and a compulsion to think operates as a link between unbridgeable and irreconcilable representations, namely the signifiers. It constitutes an attempt to build a communication vessel between reality and experience. Whether Freud speaks of cognitive (judgement) or practical or theoretical thought the question is always about identity between perception and experience. For Freud these form an essential opposition. Thinking therefore is not on the side of truth—even if, as Lacan says in the seminar on *Ethics*, it is responsible for the process of the search for the object—because it has a different function to fulfil, namely that of bridging subjective knowledge and the knowledge of reality, in other words a knowledge of another subject. This is Freud of 1895, though not without Lacan, my Freud at the time of being at the wrong place. I decided I will not stop arguing with the university philosophers without my master. It was just that I did not yet know that it was not Freud, or Lacan, who was my true master, but the unconscious.

Lacan takes up thinking in several places of his teaching, including, in the late 1960s, that of the relation between "I am" and "I think" as mutually exclusive, which radically differs from the Cartesian formula. Some years later he accounts for the position of the analyst as that of *apensé*. This brings the subject back to where it was, that is to say not to where the analyst interprets but to where the unconscious does. Jacques-Alain Miller's work shows the logic of the end of the era of interpretation. Both positions seemed to me to be linked. There was a logical connection between the unconscious as interpreting, as making a new leap and producing a new sense, and as wanting to be heard, namely to be interpreted, and the position of the analyst as not thinking. By handing the interpretation over to the unconscious, the analyst remains in the position of *apensé*. Lacan's proposition would thus be that the analyst does not have to enjoy the command "think!", he or she does not have to think. And this opens a new dimension, namely that of the lack, of dealing in the work with the subject's history with that which has become, was or has always been missing. That's why the analyst, Lacan says, can be dumb, a *dupe*.

The unconscious interprets thoughtlessly which is one of the points at which we can locate Lacan as an anti-philosopher. An analysand tries to make sense of a separation with his girlfriend and says "It feels like ... my desire wilted". That's the end of the session. Who knows how long it lasted, how many minutes or how many years? The real is marked by this statement, and the cut is its effect. One used to call it a short session. It may be amusing how Jacques-Alain Miller explains that when in conversation with our IPA colleagues, who prefer to work with alarm clocks rather than with the unconscious as timeless, namely with infinity and its interpretation, we do not call the Lacanian session "short" but "variable". This is closer to the truth as no two sessions last the same amount of time. But we should be saying, he adds, that the session is infinite. He thus introduces a paradox of time arising from the timelessness of the unconscious. If the unconscious is timeless, as Freud said, and cannot be reduced to a series of indivisible moments Aristotle thought it was, or to Leibniz's monads, the time of the session is in fact infinite because it is real, prior to any measurement or calculation. Since in analysis we are confronted with the sexual relations that do not exist, the infinity of the session is the condition for the cut. Philosophical analysis of a text is self-perpetuating and produces another text. The analytic session does not aim to produce another session or another analysis. It produces a loss of jouissance, following the cut. It produces a gap, which is the time of wilting. The infinity of the session implies the necessity of subtraction because the infinity in question is not the infinity of adding numbers, as Euclid did. The infinity in question involves taking every series as an infinite one, namely as including the number totalling the infinite series, as Cantor did. The cut, you could say, is a mark of infinity but not only that. Lacan's infinity was made of the real, of jouissance without limits. The infinity of adding numbers involves the limit, so a higher number can be added. But the session can only be infinite by subtraction, which is the effect of the intervention of the symbolic.

So it was not a few minutes, as the analysand returns to the statement some years later, I lost count of how many. "My desire wilted ... because ... I willed it". The flash of the unconscious, its sudden opening struck out the infinity in a blink of time. The name of the subject's desire is that of wanting to go where it had taken him, where he wanted in the first place, namely in the time of loss. This return to the time of loss, to the *es war*, constitutes the Freudian ethics. As for Lacan's ethics the secret jouissance of "wilting" remained linked to what he called giving up on one's desire. But what opened the field of desire by bringing it back to the subject was not so much the "I willed it" as the fall of the said jouissance.

Thinking—that which mediates and seeks identity between subject's knowledge of the unconscious and the knowledge of the Other, otherwise known as a battery of signifiers—gives way to the object *a*. "Enjoy your thinking" is the dancing clown in whom hides the horror, and the error, of that little real that comes from beyond which is here and now. Where there is thinking, we have a horizon of the object. From *pensé* to *a*. Then back to *apensé*.

Being, lack, and Freud on narcissism

> It is not up to psychoanalysis to account for philosophical error for the benefit of philosophy, as though philosophy thereafter would be able to "realise" or account for itself. There can be no such thing, since to imagine it is precisely philosophical error itself. The subject is not wrong to identify with his consciousness, as you have me put it, God knows why, but in being compelled to miss the topology which makes a fool of him in that identification. (Lacan, *Television*, 1990)

This is Lacan responding to philosophy students at Vincennes in 1966. There is more to quote. And more. A philosophical error—which consists in that paranoiac effect of causally linking being and thought, and making no room for illusion—can only be accounted for, Lacan is saying here, by the subject. Whether the subject identifies with being a "philosopher" or a "thinker" is of no consequence to the fact that the type of error involved cannot be corrected. To establish a causal link between thinking and being, after the work Freud conducted with the hysterics, was for Lacan one of the areas he approached with a measure of suspicion. When I think, I cannot *be* at the same time. If I am, and you just let me *be*, and I drift on the sea of the other, as Blanchot (1981) dreamt of, does this constitute thinking?

The act of thinking, in so far as it builds a mediation between the subject's knowledge and the sesame's of signifiers on the side of the Other, puts being into question by this very stroke. There is nothing to fall back on once I go where "it thinks". Thinking is a balancing act, a tightrope crossing with anguish under the feet. Let's take an example. When the subject hears the clocks ticking, only three or four in the collection of over forty, she evokes a hide and seek game in her childhood which she played with a boy hiding in the wardrobe with the clock in his hands. But what awakes her, what brings her to analysis is the dream of a bomb going off in the wardrobe. She is suspended by the mystery of non-being whose name is anxiety to the extent that it is aroused by the other wanting, what if not something called "me". The violently opened gap in language makes this move all the more filled with trembling.

The order of being—despite everything Heidegger said concerning *sein* all this time when he was in love with Hanna—is revealed as a lack in being and, therefore, as wanting to be. I want to be, and therefore to be this or that, constitutes the law of identification. Lacan's modification on the subject of being and thinking leads him, therefore—this "therefore" follows for him from the analytic experience—to the following: it thinks where I am not. Being, on the other hand, remains within the field of the gaze and of the instance of homogeneity, namely of the image of the body as a whole.

According to Freud's work "On narcissism" (1914c), the philosophical insight, which is subject to the critical agency of the superego facilitating the compulsion of vigilance, works as a kind of narcissistic gaze into the work of the I-libido. The object of this observation not only structurally belongs to the space of the ego image, as Lacan defined it, but is the very image in its idealised (i.e., self-investing, self-loving, self-aggrandised, in short auto-erotic form). The register of the imaginary is crucial to grasping Freud's observations. In this way, the mode of observation called philosophical, Freud continues, vacillates between what he called the *Selbstgefühl*, "sense-of-self" or "feeling-oneself", and self-criticism. The philosopher is the one who, feeling he is watched, watches himself. Philosophical observation produces the effects of self-observation and self-analysis, given that this *self* names a reflective direction the libidinal investment takes. This is the circuit of Freud's analysis. The true object in this process is the regressive offshoot of the intersubjective failure or, more precisely, the libidinised "me" as the image looked at or, quite simply, the *me*. That's why Freud insists on the paranoiac element in the philosophical observation. I-watching-myself-being-watched is constitutive of equally ideal and paranoiac circuit that is very often accountable for what happens in introspective thinking. This, we could say, is Freud's portrait of a philosopher as a thinking being. One can find it amusing when bearing in mind the heavy guns of philosophical thought *par excellence*. But it also raises the questions of being and thinking which are rarely pursued. What would become of philosophy if the philosopher made a move towards the lack in being rather than towards totality as everything and nothing else? It is the type of the question Lacan was trying to raise. And he did the best he could because there is no answer to this question except at the level of the subject one by one.

Freud's objections remain valid, and have been reinforced by Lacan's work on isolating and formulating the discourse of the unconscious first and then developing other, separate discourses. That's why it is not clear to me, as it was not to Natalie Charraud (1999), why Badiou made psychoanalysis a condition of philosophy. It is possible that what led him to this claim was a supposition that the opposite holds true. It is a view often expressed by the philosophising commentators who aim to give a comprehensible account of what psychoanalysis is by claiming that without the concepts that evolved in the history of philosophy for over two thousand years, there would not be a psychoanalytical theory. One could only say to those who espouse such a view that they could not have got it more wrong than that. There is indeed nothing more plain in Lacan, not to mention Freud, than an instance of experience, on which psychoanalytic clinic was founded, namely that the condition of psychoanalysis, whether at the time of Emma, Dora, the mirror stage or Joyce's *sinthome*, is language. That's why Lacan said that the unconscious, conditional upon language, is what we say.

CHAPTER TWO

New coordinates of psychoanalysis

New coordinates and the school

What are these coordinates? They are points, places on the map that in our practice we work to determine and between which we navigate. As we move from one point to another, chart the uncharted, encounter the uncertainties, these points of reference orient us in our practice. Even to enumerate them—the subject, the signifier, the letter, love and hate, the phallus, jouissance, the Woman, desire and demand, anxiety, object *a*, semblance, shame and guilt, drive, the symptom and *sinthome*, the Real, Imaginary and Symbolic, knowledge, discourse, ignorance—is already to miss what they do. So many yet so few, some to be found not where one expects them, others to be determined retroactively, and others still never changing place. One can neither count them nor discount them but without counting on them we would be adrift. To believe in the unconscious implies just that. Why new then, why this ado? If there is a new one, perhaps two new points on the map of psychoanalysis, it is the object *a*, a strange and elusive creature without which no encounter with what escaped us, compelling us to seek what is lost, would be necessary. And, second, the School that never was before. Having been founded by Lacan, the school is marked and inscribed as a place around which we circle, finding there the work done and to be done, and therefore a point of mooring. It is not an academy of Plato or Lyceum of Aristotle, neither a school of Faust nor a monastery nor a university. And yet it is a place where an encounter with the signifier outside meaning happens and work called knowledge is produced. Not to mention that it is the most vibrant, dynamic, unpredictable, changeable, nomadic, as well as monadic in its indivisibility as One, place that can also function as an object cause of desire. But let's start from some kind of a beginning.

The School exists. It exists to the extent that it was founded by Jacques Lacan with a single stroke of an act. It was founded in 1964, so it has existed for about half a century at the time of writing this. The sole reason for it coming into existence was Lacan's desire in the act called founding. The Founding Act or *Acte de fondation* thus bears the mark of existence. Then there is a history that preceded the act, the de-supposition of Lacan at the hands of his colleagues, the ostracism and the *ex communica* to which he was subjected by the IPA in 1963. First banned from teaching in the IPA, then his students and trainees being asked to make allegiance. And they did, one by one, the best ones staying with Lacan. But why the best ones? Perhaps the most courageous ones, those who took the risk, who had nothing to gain, who had no bonus to expect, who were interested in Lacan? No. Perhaps those, too, but, above all, those who loved him, therefore, the best ones. And why with Lacan? Because he never made false promises, because he always spoke the truth as there was no way to say it all and because he gave us Freud, remained Freudian to the end. That was enough to start an unfinished legacy. Psychoanalysis began with Lacan at that moment. Of course, there was Freud, the father of psychoanalysis, without whose *corpus* nothing would have happened. And there was the psychoanalytic movement of several decades, recorded and archived. But in some way psychoanalysis began with Lacan's School. The history, the movement, and the chronicles—all these had a status of an appendix.

At the time Lacan was founding the School of psychoanalysis, on the other side of the globe a war was raging, Vietnam, my first war. Napalm bombs were falling like rain drops over the dense, dark green jungle. I recall it frightened me. What if there were people living there. The trees would light up like matchsticks in a long succession of fireworks. This was another side of terrorism, remotely controlled from the cockpit or the military bases. Then there was a public execution of a Vietnamese prisoner, thin like a cane, his hands tied up in the back, by a fellow soldier who first ranted something to him and then shot him dead in the head. Today we have Iraq and Abu Ghraib, the new and old perversions that I will come back to later. The US government, under both Johnson and Bush, was condemned by the public opinion for making the hell break loose, and allowing torture and countless deaths. In Paris in the 1960s Lacan was excommunicated for teaching about structure and discourse that determines the elements contributive—but not responsible because only the subject is responsible—to the destruction and terror, which are inscribed in the social bond, in war and in peace. He taught about the subject as a "terrorist", and about the imaginary structure of paranoia. And, finally, shortly before being struck off he devoted the whole year of work to anguish and its causes. He was teaching the wrong things then. With the School just founded, Lacan was building in the place where one no longer condemns to death for corrupting the youth, as it was done to his Ancient epigone. Instead of the goblet of hemlock, there was now a School of knowledge of the unconscious. It did not turn out all that bad in the end. He built it with love and on love but not without anticipation that it would have its underside to unfold, the de-supposition of knowledge he called hatred, raging under his nose as well as in all those war places, in short, the real subject. If there is anything love will show sooner or later, it is the work of the drive, of destroying you whom I love because there is something else and more in you than this. With these words at the end of *Seminar XI* (1977) in 1964, Lacan showed, following Freud, you cannot have one without the other. But we are not expecting that politicians and generals will lie down on the analytic couch. And then an idea crossed my mind. Why not?

Since the Founding Act, the signifier "School" has been inscribed in psychoanalysis. The School became a place of work where everything and nothing happens, but usually it is something much less than that. It became a house for the working community where the cause of psychoanalysis can be advanced, a map of coordinates among which are each and every member as symptoms and as speaking and writing beings in the bond that can be called social because it addresses the Other. It is structurally not possible, whether in Vietnam, Paris or Abu Ghraib, not to take into account some relationship with the Other, whether in destruction or perverse torturing the human object for a "greater" goal. The School became a place of "refuge", if that's the word emerging from the Greek *schole*, to speak to one another with the symptom. What brings the workers to work together is made of transference and ignorance as the latter is no less a passion than the former, and of which the analyst makes a few—four to be precise—uses. To this extent any discourse is possible in the Lacanian School because any of the four modes of ignorance are possible, the master's because it is also the unconscious that is stronger than me, the hysteric's because there is no obsessional's, and that of the university because, since the School is not structured like a university, what would ignorance be without the academic knowledge of it, which is where Aristotle started. But only the analyst, in the discourse where the lack of knowledge becomes dominant, knows, through *his* ignorance, all four. As it is well known, Lacan tried to define the analyst as a saint, albeit for the reasons that are not at all obvious. One of them was the jouissance of the saint, a precarious and enigmatic thing for the observer, baffled by the question what he gets from this. Second, Lacan was possibly the first one to consider the saint as not so much the embodiment of a supreme benevolence and altruism in the religious tradition, as was once assumed, but as kind of an odd one out, an interrogator of the tradition and a maker of an *ascesis* that in practice shows the traits of subversion. Every *Benedictus* has his *Franciscus*. The saint appears as a constant source of anxiety for the master, just as Antigone, as we shall see later, was a thorn in Creon's beliefs. But *ascesis* should be approached here as what it signified for the Ancient Greeks, namely as "exercise", "practice". As for the saint, as Lacan stated, nobody really knows where the saint's desire goes and what satisfies it. The School then was founded not without this unknown real that the fools, idiots, and saints alike keep searching, each one in their own analysis and in relation to the cause of what brought them here. And this is the subject's seal of its relation to the cause. And Lacan proposed, which continues to be passed on as an invitation, that the analytic mould we become, one by one, is then testified to and presented at the end of analysis by means of a mechanism he called the pass—a testimony presenting and accounting for the process and the end of analysis. Let's just say that the place of the School is where the desire for certainty turns into an encounter with the "void of guarantee", which is how knowledge and ignorance topologically overlap. And there is no reason to dissuade anyone from thinking that it is not the same today. Something new and something old.

Psychoanalysis, religion, and Dawkins

One of the breakthroughs of psychoanalysis as invented by Freud was the formulation of the structure of sacrifice. To put it succinctly, self-sacrifice as a common practice in the Christian domain whether in public or in private, does not relinquish the compulsion to cease all satisfaction, called jouissance in psychoanalysis, but refuels it. This is how *ascesis* was understood for a long time. The self-imposition to give up on the enjoyment of life, has an effect of producing more and more jouissance which amounts to wanting comfort out of more discomfort.

This was one of the ways in which Freud tried to undermine and if not rid of religion. Or did he? Religion seeks ways to appeal to the symbolic order to deal with and put an end to the dis-order of the real of jouissance. This attempt to put at rest and to pacify the real involves not only a practice of the subject but also a god or a deity that is supposed to substantiate the reason and provide knowledge for the whole cycle I have just sketched out. And then, is this god or deity not the one where the satisfaction is forever higher, more fulfilling, encompassing and oceanic beyond measure? For Freud religion includes and supports the idea and practice of punishment for deviating from this cycle, once you are caught in it. The commandments are something else, they give direction to anguish, keeping it at bay. Under the pretext of the universal moral order, the commandments regulate subject's relation to his neighbour. Freud was the first one to point out that this cycle and the origin of morality belong to the structure of the unconscious, and therefore its politics, as Lacan took it a step further. The politics of the unconscious revolves around the limits of the subject and, where these limits turn into the practice of rituals, religion is in the offing. Religion belongs to the set of practices where the guarantee can be provided at the moment of need. This guarantee becomes collective when everybody expects the same thing through group identification Freud elaborated. Once the leader, whether in the church or in the army takes up the place, the practitioners are not expected to differ from another one. Psychoanalysis cannot promise guarantees other than to question the promises of love, knowledge, security, and happiness, namely the promises that were made to us in the first place, and it is now too late to ask those who made them whether that they had had the right to do so. We make these promises because they have the same value and function as the commandments, relieving us of the excess of anxiety and keeping the symbolic order in the vicinity. But unlike religion, psychoanalysis puts these promises and their satisfactions, as formed at the basis of our relation with the *Nebenmensch*, into question—the practice very remote from the order of salvation supported by the symbolic order of the Name-of-the-Father. According to the later Lacan, psychoanalytic practice does not adhere to or take its bearings from the sponsorship of the symbolic. It rather takes the side of the disorder of the real and its *ascesis* Lacan called subjective destitution in the sense of the absolute singularity of the subject who is left with the master signifier all alone. At this point the subject no longer has the Name-of-the-Father as an aegis against the real but admitting it in use but not as an existence. To this effect, Lacan spoke of the solitary relation to the unconscious as a real, namely, fragmentary truth. In the end of his teaching Lacan grew interested in the relation between psychoanalytic practice and the Tao and the practice of Zen without trying to eliminate religion as a discourse.

Lacan never thought it would be possible to get rid of religion (2013b), a point stressed by Jacques-Alain Miller. Lacan even spoke of the triumph of religion. He gave obsessional neurosis a legitimate place, unlike Freud who thought the world would benefit from the eradication of obsessionals. He never succeeded in this and ended up making the obsessional the hysteric's partner. There is something deeply precious to what the obsessionals carry around, taking it with them everywhere they go. They never drop it or forget it or part with it even when they do all these things. In the end, nothing will prove to be more valuable in the midst of these revolutions than the image of an irreplaceable life style, "our way of life" and the "universal values" the politicians insist on today. One could call this insistence part of their "good intentions" but it is a defence of the debris of the symbolic order that elevated them to this position. And this is the triumph Lacan anticipated. It is as if he was saying "thank God for the obsessional" but *de facto* he was following the logic of discourse and the essential elements in it. Neither Vietnam nor Iraq would change that, on the contrary. The perversions of the Abu Ghraib confirmed the "universality" of the "dark god" that sponsors the reduction of a human to a thing, which is the case where the "good intentions" of the pious reach an apogee.

Apart from the densely ritualised practices of the obsessional neurotic, Freud referred to religion as an illusion that has a future. And he based this claim on the experience of the ego, an overwhelming feeling, once attributed to the divinity. This was Freud's reply to Romain Rolland's letter and the so-called religious experience. In the recent years we hear of one particular experience called spiritual offered from the hands, or rather arms, of a Hindu woman, nicknamed the "priestess of hugs", otherwise known as Amma. The story goes that for over thirty years she has been travelling around the world to hold in her arms politicians, senators, and celebrities. This priestess has shown unlimited generosity in offering a moment of comfort and maternal jouissance to those who ask for it. As if the body did not need, were not made of, words. And this is perhaps what Freud was talking about when he mentioned "oceanic feeling" of the ego.

In the end Freud approaches religion through the death of Moses (1939a [1937–1939]). Moses is a means to establish the One, first monotheism. Then the question arose for Freud whether there can be the One outside the Judeo-Christian religious tradition. On the other hand, the death of Moses is a prelude to the "death of God". When Freud speaks about the illusion of religion having a long future, he affirms its therapeutic function, perhaps the only one that has some basis in the unconscious. Illusion has a future, then. Does philosophy have a future? According to Nietzsche, yes (1984). According to Freud philosophy is not an illusion.

But let's say in defence of philosophy that it forms a discourse that places thinking in the dominant position while at the same time failing to include what it excludes, namely what it lacks. It is almost as if it had three rather than four elements in the Lacanian discourse I will take this up later. Hence Lacan's remark to the students of philosophy about the object *a*, something which philosophy fails to account for. And hence the striking divide of Lacan, the anti-philosopher, that it is not for psychoanalysis as the discourse of the analyst to correct or alter other discourses, including that of philosophy. For this reason philosophy can be approached as a labour of a thinker who subscribes to what I would call *singularis qua universalis*. If this were the principle of philosophical discourse, it would not be so bad concerning its future. It would even be good enough to enable us to understand why in the case of some authors examining and analysing the culture of today in the broadest sense of the word, they are led in the end to attempt to save philosophy as such an *universalis* even if this term merely affirms the exclusion of what these attempts continue to produce, namely the gap in being. And why not if this is what it has always done? Perhaps with one exception.

Freud was adamant from the start that he was not interested in reading Nietzsche's ideas in order to be able to formulate his own. It was brave of Freud to resist this temptation. And he did not change his mind just because he received Nietzsche's collected works for his birthday present from Ferenczi. It was also Freud's honesty. It was about his subjective position and not about "philosophy". Someone nevertheless insisted, a psychotherapist it appears, that there would not have been Freud without Nietzsche. This author, Ronald Lehrer by name, wrote a book *Nietzsche's Presence in Freud's Life and Thought* (1995) where he tried, based on all sorts of dubious analogies, to reduce Freud's formulations arising from his analytical experience in his work with the hysterics, to Nietzsche's insights. The book tries to construct a dimension of metasubjectivity according to which Freud's ideas can be willy-nilly traced back to Nietzsche's prophetic intuitions. Nietzsche's revolutionary statements about Christian morality led him to believe, and not without paying the highest price when his psychosis finally triggered, that religion had no future at all because God was dead, and since we all killed him, the future that this opens for us is the one of guilt.

Nietzsche's death of God (1974) was his name for the era of the Other that does not exist. How did Freud come to reach this point? Through the death of Moses, through the death of the father, whether primal or real, who nevertheless remains present as a symbolic instrument and a guarantor of peace as an effect of the dissolution of the famous complex. But that's not how Lacan approached Nietzsche's idea of the death of God, not as a patricide but as an unresolved castration. Therefore for Lacan the philosopher's statement was not to be read at the level of a symbolic remainder following a murder of the father. Lacan did not read it as a dissolution of the complex but as its foreclosure. And Lacan went on to say that the death of God was not a true formula of atheism. Lacan tries to find a way to go beyond "belief", which lays foundations to religion, and beyond the collective guilt of "we have all killed him". To go beyond these does not imply for Lacan to resurrect the primal father who Freud describes in his myth and not to re-establish one God as an existence. Seeking a formula of atheism Lacan was opposing it to religion as a collective identification around a certainty of the Other. In the discourse of psychoanalysis it is not the case that there is no God or that the inexistence of the Other can be put to rest on account of atheism. Which is not the case with Richard Dawkins, the self-proclaimed atheist who believes in science and in its future reality. And perhaps for this reason he tries to make his case more convincing when writing about the "magic" of reality. For Dawkins (2006), then, religion and God are different names for the same thing. The therapeutic function, the function of illusion and error, which are not the same, faith and knowledge—all end up in a sort of metaphysical stew from which Dawkins tries to extract an essence of truth, and oppose to it, while at the same time excluding himself from it as a subject who is cooking it, which is what the scientists do, a scientific truth. In this way, he treats science as a cult, and places it on the pedestal of religion. But the future of religion is not a future of science. In psychoanalysis the place of God remains empty because it is always linked to an agency of creation and therefore to some kind of beginning and representation. The atheism of Dawkins is no less spurious than Nietzsche's belief in the death of God as an answer to religion. The reason of this lies in the fact that the belief in science as a replacement of the religious belief authorises one to perpetuate the same error. It is the error Lacan already elucidated in his talk to the students of philosophy. The error Nietzsche warned us against was to take effect for cause. What Lacan punctuates is that the real is treated as a ready-to-hand knowledge, as that which knows, while the object a is simply omitted from this calculation although it guided the subject to this point in the first place. In short, it is the same old story of regarding the means of measurement and logic as a given rather than as subject's construction in relation to the Other and which includes the extimate object. Psychoanalysis does not aim to correct this error because it is already inherent in the structure of the relation with the Other, more specifically in the structure and the elements of discourse. From this perspective it is not surprising to see that the Dawkins' labour revolves around systematic attempts to correct the mistakes of religion by means of science.

This is what troubled Lacan and his atheist discourse: how is it possible, he asks, that the theologians can do without God more than the analyst? Lacan makes this very important statement in the 1970s, in his seminar *Encore*, where he also makes other important statements, for example about the nonexistence of *the* Woman, which is not without relation to the question of atheism. This paradox in the question about the theologian's and analyst's relation with the Other seeks to articulate the fundamental disparity between belief and knowledge, namely between belief and certitude. In classical terms this difference has always been formulated as a difference between religious faith and scientific knowledge. Having a belief, however, as Lacan says more than once, is not a matter of religion. What Lacan teaches us from the start is that certainty is not to be found in reality. He certainly does not give us the answer but marks the coordinates with which to approach the paradox to work his way around it. And one of these indications is the empty grave of the crucified. While the Christ's image gives rise to the everyday perversions supposedly authorising the pain of self-punishment, what remains before the grave is a mantra of the name. The death of God was not a solution for Lacan, and it certainly does not solve the question of the status of Other or of the real that cannot be broken, or mastered by knowledge. Nor can it be solved by replacing one object of belief with another, let alone by desiccating the belief itself. The empty place of the One allowed Lacan to say that the true formula of atheism lies in that God is unconscious. Lacan formulated atheism in this way in anticipation of the triumph of religion and of the future of illusion to come. He wanted to put a wedge between the real that does not exist, the truth of truth, and the real as impossible to put the rein on, yet immixed with the signifier with which beliefs are made. "God is unconscious" implied for Lacan that God belongs to the dimension of what is fundamentally *unrealisable* in the human desire to the extent that we believe in it just as we believe in the symptom without sufficient knowledge what makes up the belief itself for every subject. At the same time we draw, one by one, some satisfaction from it, from the "x" of desire that escapes the subject and eludes even the most enigmatic of dreams. And to show this Lacan chose the dream already commented by Freud, "Father, can't you see I am burning?"

The death of God and the paradox of sacrifice

The position of the analyst becomes manifest as the Other that does not exist. There is no truth, Lacan reminds us, to tell us about the truth. And there is no metalanguage to say it all, however disappointing it may sound to some and be of relief to others. But the nonexistence of the Other is not the only position in analysis, and in particular in the treatment that has no end.

For some this position will make use of the Name-of-the-Father just where God is supposed to be. Unlike an encounter with the man in psychosis, the Name-of-the-Father can have a pacifying function for the subject and no illusion as such to support it. Lacan did not believe that the Catholics, or the Japanese albeit for a different reason, can be analysed as they subscribe to the existence of the Other by not making use of the name in relation to the empty grave. In other words they believe in the Other of the Other. The empty place served for Lacan to designate both a lack and a remainder. In analysis, the lack and the remainder are put into use not only for the sake of truth but as a loss that opens up a gap in being. Whereas the analytical process comes to an end, the monologues in the confessional do not have to. In the early days after Freud's discovery, this served as an analogy between confession and analysis until Lacan spoke of the nonanalysibility of the Catholics. Lacan made the difference clear enough although the analogy held water because early on Freud stressed the cathartic element in the talking cure.

At the end of the confession the priest, unlike the hugging priestess providing the "oceanic" feeling, would state that the sins are absolved, my son, and instruct to say three Maries and off you go. Couldn't the analysand do some housework in the analyst's house if he has no money to pay for sessions? Couldn't he learn a few aphorisms of Freud by heart to "pay" for his mistakes? Or the other way round, when "money is not a problem" why not having more sessions to get it over with? Each of these fantasies touches on the paradox of sacrifice, and with it of guilt and punishment, while saving the Other as the master who commands and imposes jouissance on the believer. For one must believe in the Other to be saved first. But this is nothing else than a fantasy in relation to the object lost. The unconscious knows no punishment for loss and bears no solution to it. The next step would be guilt, which gives us an inkling of desire. When you renounce the latter, Lacan formulated his ethics, the former re-emerges with a double force. The question that emerges with it is: what do you owe the subject, symbolically speaking?

When Lacan takes up the death of God in *The Ethics of Psychoanalysis* (1992) he breaks it down to two stages, and this has always puzzled me. Firstly, God is dead and has always been dead. Secondly, God does not know he has always been dead. Lacan will later say that if there is anyone to know it is the subject. What does the subject know? He only knows what he can accede via the signifier of the Other, provided it is also the signifier of the *lack* in the Other because the big truth about the Other does not exist. The subject only knows what he accedes through the signifier because the latter represents the former, to evoke Lacan's definition, namely represents the subject for another signifier.

The subject's knowledge, therefore, is limited to the larder of the Other where the signifiers are stored. Love is the key to the door of the unconscious but not its condition. What remains of the jouissance of the Other, of life and death *in* the Other, appears as a sign coming *from* the Other, namely the signifier of the lack, which in the Other stands for desire. For this reason the grave will always be empty and God always dead. Lacan found in the signifier of the lack in the Other the true mystery, perhaps the only mystery and secret in psychoanalysis. He said this in his commentary on Hamlet, so he must have considered it to be of value for the obsessional neurotic. If there is anyone who delays *ad infinitum* the step towards opening of the Other's desire, it is the obsessional.

The fall of a supposition that there will always be another to love me, to guarantee that my love for my neighbour may one day be returned all at once, comes under the spell of a belief—for to believe is to be under a spell—in the jouissance that, Lacan reminds us, is not a sign of love. Let's try to distinguish the jouissance Lacan did not believe to be a sign of love from the jouissance implicated in the paradox of sacrifice that simultaneously reduces and boosts jouissance. Is it the same satisfaction or do they differ, Lacan asks. Does the satisfaction I get from sacrificing my satisfaction the same as the one that was sacrificed? How can I know this before I have done it? And if I do know it, does it mean the spell has been broken? Lacan's remark helped me to get closer to the gist of this paradox. The sacrifice of a "pound of flesh" is followed up by the subject reclaiming the signifier of desire, namely the phallus. But if the subject indeed had the phallus—and all the unbound power that imagination could bring with it—why would he want to sacrifice it? Who on earth would want to rid themselves of the most precious master key that opens the doors to the Other's desire and can have an effect of love? The point of course is that it is not the phallus that is sacrificed nor that following the sacrifice of some libido it could then be claimed as a possession. The phallus is nowhere to be found. Which is why Lacan marked it as a minus, a sign of castration, $-\varphi$. Which means that it can be found where it is not, a lack, following a renunciation of jouissance and not its sacrifice. I make this distinction because that's where Lacan takes us. The real at stake in jouissance is not its aim—the satisfaction to be had after the sacrifice, which always remains the same—but the object.

In the paradox of sacrifice, jouissance remained the same and only its place altered. It changed from the subject showing readiness to sacrifice some of his flesh to that of the superego that now commands that I enjoy it. Enjoy your sacrifice! The ferocious superego commands the order of the day: enjoy your sacrifice, enjoy your being and your thinking! This change of place of jouissance does not dismiss the false authority under which the analysand set out to believe in love and work, and which led him to the symptom. This false authority, this so to speak, *phallacy*, comes as an effect of a belief in the jouissance of the Other, in some supposedly real Other, which supposedly forms my suffering. An attempt to meet my neighbour outside the symbolic, which is the school of Marquis de Sade, leads from love to perversion. My suffering may be an effect of an identification with the supposition of the suffering of my neighbour. Not that when a friend tells me of his discomfort this does not discomfort me, which it does, but that when I try to alleviate his discomfort, say his distress at losing a job, I do so by sacrificing some of my goods and possessions. I can only do that if I do not count them or if I am dispossessed of them as the most precious object. In the latter scenario the paradox of sacrifice of replacing one satisfaction with another sets in and nothing has changed as my discomfort and suppositions about its causes linger on. This is the perverse position of trying to encounter the other at the level of experience of the real. What interests Lacan, and what is crucial in grasping the ethics in psychoanalysis, focuses on the first moment, namely on the actual renunciation of the object. That's why the ethics of psychoanalysis is singular, concerning the subject of the unconscious, and goes beyond the compulsions of the superego. If I suffer it is not because of my neighbour's suffering but because I did not dare cross the limit which is the ego's image, the most precious object of all. This limit, which touches on the primary narcissism, was for Lacan the compass of an action, good or evil, because in each case it concerns the other, someone I love and hold dear. The satisfaction arising from my self-image is therefore invested in the belief I exhibit in the world of others. If sacrifice has always been conceived of as a way out of a fault, for the subject the exit plan also involves *culpa* for the fault and the fantasy of punishment. The product of the belief in the jouissance of my neighbour is, in effect, guilt. Sade is constantly confronted with guilt but believes in the absolute jouissance as a way out of it.

Lacan, following Freud, did not fight guilt with sacrifice. He found a sign of desire in guilt and for this reason opposed one to the other, guilt to desire. Guilt is the obverse of desire and in analysis a sign of guilt is usually a signpost to desire. But he only did this after shifting the coordinates of Freud's paradox. What does sacrifice change? Sacrifice, rampant not only in the Christian tradition, fails to account for the subject's fault which the belief in the Other's jouissance is supposed to account and make up for. What gives us access to the Other is desire and nothing else—the contingency of the signifier of desire. No doubt analysis creates conditions where love can go through these vicissitudes of sacrifice more than once, and in effect render the contingency material. Lacan showed us that desire is the matter of contingency, and he never went back on it. I intend to return to this problematic in the course of this study.

Of the origin of morality, love, women, and men

Let's now take up one of the threads of love, one of its vicissitudes as it seems enmeshed, following Lacan's statement in *Seminar XI* (1977), with something more than love, with the real that love keeps bumping to. What Lacan reiterates following Freud, and highlights it, is that love is the sole condition of speaking, whether speaking well or not, which implies addressing the other. But just because the subject is in some way in love, or under the spell of love when speaking to the other, does not imply that he knows how to speak about love. Very few did and Lacan was one of them. And what he said of love has today become part of the collection of his aphorisms. Here is one: "to love is to give what one does not have". What is worth reiterating in this aphorism is that the subjective destitution Lacan points to has not been achieved through sacrifice, which leaves the object intact, but through renunciation of jouissance at stake in the search for the lost object.

The connection between love and speaking could be called a Freudian condition of love to the extent that Freud situated love in the place of a gift, and therefore a giver. This did not prevent him from stripping love bare to a hypnotic effect that was a necessary element for the work of transference both as facilitating analytic process and as being its impediment.

The "sole condition" appears as an evocation and a reminder of the primary act of giving voice to the Other, of calling and demanding, which is not the same as screaming. Freud made a distinction between a scream, which was more on the side of cathartic emission, and a call of demand designating articulation of needs and therefore entry to language. It is interesting that precisely at the point when Freud speaks about the first tokens of love he also seeks the genealogy of morality. When the child's mother, responding to the call, gives the child through her tone of voice, her words, her touches and warmth, the first interpretation, it is in this initial response of the mother, Freud points out, and through the exchange that emerges from it, that there will be marked what Freud will call in one of the letters to Fliess "the origin of morality" (1950 [1887–1902]). Freud is proud to have established this connection. Love and morality—no longer at odds with each other, no longer in an overvalued clash, but one being the sculptor of the other. In this combination, in the relation between subject's love and ethics, we will find a basis for what Lacan teaches us about passion. Tender, aggressive, tyrannical, obsessive passion that would not exist without the most intimate, yet extimate, neighbour, is how Lacan advanced early Freudian enterprise to the point of symptom formation. From love, as a condition of speech, to passion as a symptom, as a human "nature" that stings the subject no matter what, because it is stronger than him—yes, to work with the symptom, to identify with the symptom can also imply to work, to love, to hate, and to ignore with passion. Passion is what is left of being, a remainder of the body's real that does not leave the signifier in peace because it comes from the body of speech. The saint whose desire is touched by a question mark of the one who wants to know as to where it is going, is not without passion. It is more difficult to say a passion for what or whether it is a passion for anything in particular. This is the question Lacan raised. One can love this passion—or hate it like the frog—but it does not change the nature of the scorpion and of the semblance that deceived us. Couldn't we have ever wished for a more compelling partner-symptom than passion? Not between women and men.

A Belgian-born couple therapist Esther Perel, who has lived and worked in the USA, wrote a book, *Mating in Captivity* (2006), that immediately catapulted her to fame. This, at least by American standards, is worth noting. What was the revelation that made nine or so publishers court her until one of them won her hand and a contract? Her claim that love and sex are incompatible. That if you want to keep your relationship, which is where love is, you have to translate sex into seduction and erotic play. Perel is quick to notice that more often than ever before married couples do not want to sleep with each other anymore. Men and women, she claims, need space for themselves alone, and therefore a space that separates them. And once the space of separation is erected between them, and they can go off on holiday without the partner, they can then resume, or indeed commence the game of seduction. The problem, according to Perel, is that we expect one person, a spouse, to provide what an entire community used to give: love, friendship, sex, and other forms of bonding. Go your separate ways, she recommends, and you will be brought together. Many couples benefited greatly from her advice. One couple, for example, in order to sustain their relationship, have been meeting only in motels. Another one make love outside their block of flats when they come back tired after work. Another couple have a very intense social life and pretend not to know each other at the parties and meetings they go to. This is not exactly what Tolstoy recommended when he said that man and wife should abandon sex altogether and live like brother and sister in so far as this would guarantee that the incestuous thoughts leave much to be desired. Perel appears to be Lacanian by following the logic of the non-existence of the sexual relation, keeping love to one side and the modes of sexual satisfaction to the other. The discourse of love and fucking under the stairs are obviously two different things.

There is an artifice present in the examples Perel seems to pride herself on, since after all she succeeds in two things simultaneously: in keeping the couples together and in them not ceasing not to write their relationship. She does not write it off either, and devises in each case a mechanism that would help them to face up to the old "can't live with them can't live without them". What her interventions and good advice seem to touch on has to do with following the nonexistence of the sexual relation, which means an impossibility of writing it, literally. And this then receives a practical twist, almost like a commandment. And this is supposed to open up space for love, namely for the question of how to cope with the lack of satisfaction, given it is the common denominator for the lovers. Now, love can assume, according to Perel, a dimension of pleasure and turn into the pleasure of thinking about another, as Jacques-Alain Miller called it, or of speaking to each other as if the spouses have only just met. In effect, this discourse of love, the pleasure of thinking of and speaking to the other, can sustain the unsatisfied desire where words, and thoughts, serve as signs of love, and where unsatisfaction assumes a (plus) value. Perel is not concerned with a "shortage" of desire but with excesses generated by being together at all possible levels, in other words with the boredom of having it all. So she says: "enough!" which is what a therapist does. She tells the couples, almost literally, that the sexual relation does not exist, and follows what Lacan said, that it does not cease not to be written. This was Lacan's second formula of nonexistence, which in my view should be taken alongside the first one, namely that the Other does not exist. The second statement is correlative to the first one because both imply that the impossibility of writing the sexual relation has to do with the nonexistence of the jouissance of the Other as the Other sex. This is Lacan's underlining claim concerning the nonexistence of the sexual relation, which I will take up later in more detail. Since the jouissance of the Other sex cannot be symbolised nor can the relation with it. Love or sexual relation *or* love and sexual relation can only happen, Lacan seems to say, differently for every lover because they enjoy themselves differently in approaching the other's sexual satisfaction. Why not to say, then, what is impossible to say or write instead of preaching about the truth about the truth which, the position common to religion and science, and which in effect cancels if not disables the desire of the Other? That's how Lacan defined desire. Although it is unrealisable it can be interpreted.

The prohibition of excess, which is an effect of confusion between love and jouissance, may not lead to stopping the excess. This follows the same logic as the logic of self-sacrifice whereby a forced disposal of satisfaction leads to relocating jouissance from one place to another. Lacan already put his finger on this when he said that jouissance of the Other is not a sign of love. It is in this way that he introduced us in his seminar *Encore* to the confusion between love and jouissance. That's because these two, jouissance and love, are often confused in analysis. When a relationship fails and does not live up to our expectations and when the satisfaction of it ebbs away, is it to do with love or with jouissance? Lacan put a wedge between them, separating love, in analysis called transference, from the object of satisfaction. One of the most pertinent questions concerning love is how to speak to the one you love about the one you love? How to speak of love *and* the jouissance produced by the love works, its ascents and falls? That's the question where the psychoanalytic experience may prove enlightening. I will come back to it in due course. Lacan linked love to knowledge, namely that he who speaks about the one he loves, supposes that there is a subject, to wit an analyst, who knows where this is coming from and why it fails. As for the object of jouissance, Lacan links it to the drive before it becomes the elusive, and allusive, object *a*, that causes desire. What is the answer to the question of love if not a place where it intersects with jouissance, and where desire as unfulfilled and unrealisable, glides over. Love, before it becomes a gift of what the subject does not have, wants more love, it wants to enjoy which is never enough. Only the hysteric's desire appears never to be confused because it is always unsatisfied, always supported by the signifier at the level of demand that remains ambiguous. For this reason, on Lacan's map of passions he linked love to ignorance as a junction of the symbolic and real. The lack of satisfaction appears to signify the gap in knowledge. But does it mean that what I want is not to know or that wanting to know supposes a gap? These are some of the questions I want to take up in due course when taking up ignorance in discourse. Now, suffice it to say that the problematic of desire always pushes us towards the unexpected. In the simplest terms this implies that for some subjects the outcome of analysis appears to be on a completely opposite pole to the one where it began. This is so because there is no desire to go to analysis. There is a desire to know, as Lacan indicated by giving transference an epistemological status, but, paradoxically, it does not lead to knowledge as we shall find out. It may be for some, therefore, that these signs of the emergence of desire this can mark for a subject the end point in analysis.

So what does Perel do in her couple oriented therapy? She instructs her patients, not without a reason, to put up a wall between love and sex, between the discourse of love and the sexual jouissance of the relation that does not exist. And in doing so she does not cease in her efforts to save the relationships that are brought to her consultation room in a seriously dysfunctional state. This "does not cease" bears the mark of the order of necessity and reminds us that the analyst works with the symptom. Necessity indicates what does not stop pressing, insisting, being stronger than me, like the scorpion's "nature" that may prove as compulsive as a sexual jouissance. But Lacan calls the sexual relation that which does not cease not to be written. It does not exist because its writing or symbolisation can only but fail to account for the sexual encounter. Unlike in the case of the symptom here we have a double negation. Something insists in the symptom that does not stop being written in the body. But this is not the same as in the sexual relation that, unlike the symptom, cannot be written. What in the symptom is unstoppable can be symbolised. Because it is symbolised, the repetitive work of the symptom is no longer unsustainable for the subject. What in the sexual relation does not cease, cannot be written. Here something insists, like in the system, but fails each time it insists. This not ceasing and failing form the double negation. The lovers' jouissances cannot be added up and written up. The double negation opens the dimension of impossibility. The relation between non-existence and negation is not straightforward. When someone says that God does not exist, does this amount to negating God? And if Valéry says that atheism is a roundabout way to speak about God, does this imply that atheism as a negation of God equals God's nonexistence? Not in Valéry's account although this is the case in Dawkins'. For Dawkins, the negation of God leads to God's nonexistence. As we know Freud introduced negation as a foundation of neurosis. When interpreting a dream I say that the woman in it is not my mother, this indicates that it is indeed my mother. Why? Because by naming what I do not want to exist I name what does. I name the repression in this primary relation to language—it is not x. My logic teacher used to say that unicorns do not exist but the chalk he holds in his hand does. How does he know that that which does not exist is the unicorn? Because it is not in his hand? How can one name what does not exist? If my teacher had children he would know that there are unicorns in the world. The name is linked to an object through belief. But the negation of an object through the name does not amount to rendering the object non-existent. The negation of an object puts into question the relation between belief and knowledge or between belief and certitude. My logic teacher, however, who was an excellent logician, was nevertheless duped by relying on an equation of the real and realism.

Negation, then, which is a judgement of existence, forms a condition of repression. Negation contributes immensely to the question of existence and of nonexistence because both are linked to the register of the symbolic. And repression, as Freud showed us, is a modality of existence given the repressed continues to exist in a latent form, and can return as symbolised at some unexpected point later in life. The repressed belongs thus to the order of being written as Freud already made it the kernel of the symptom. Not so with the sexual relation that insists nevertheless but on what?

That's the question. When Lacan says "the sexual relation does not exist", this does not amount to negating the sexual relation. If the couples do not do it at home they will end up doing it in a motel or in a park at night or with strangers at a party. Perel does not deny this. She seems familiar with the scorpion's "nature". Whatever we do in love,

Lacan says, when a speaking being addresses another speaking being with the words of love, there is a hit and miss, so to speak, as if the aim lied beyond, as if it was a body of jouissance of the Other. This for Lacan encapsulates the act of destruction that he formulated with the following words "I love you but because beyond you I love something more than you, object *a*, I mutilate you". This is how love trips over the fantasy, and how for men a woman appears as an object *a* in the fantasy. So the man approaches this object in the way the woman appears to him, namely as *a*-veil-able. For Lacan the woman has a nature of a semblance, that is to say, of making belief she is what she is not. And Lacan is not the first one to point it out. A man assumes she is the scorpion, making belief she is not. For a man the woman's semblance may appear as a veil because he may think that a veil is a sign symbolising some other woman beyond. But for Lacan the veil assumes another sense. It marks the woman who, wearing it, does not have the phallus. Not every woman is phallic. She can be. For some women the veil can assume the function of covering the lack. In which case it is the veil that is itself phallicised, namely marked by man's desire. For Lacan, however disappointing as this may be for some, beyond the veil there is nothing—not the object but nothing. Hence it is of no avail to try to remove the veil from her to strip her bare because the veil is what she is in essence, the mystery of her desire as caught in man's desire, which makes it often so difficult for him to have ears for her. What is underneath the veil can already be found on the surface. This seems to me to be Lacan's response, his topological answer to the question of the lure of the woman as the Other sex. And it echoes for us Lacan's definition of the unconscious as that what we say. Here the topology of the veil confirms that for Lacan there is no such thing as interiority, that what best historically responds to the mystery of the opposition of the interior and exterior is the mystery of the surface that Lacan found best exemplified in the baroquesqe fold.

The hit and miss game, which is what Lacan left us with concerning love, is another name for the impossibility of the sexual relation. And because the relation cannot be written and remains a failure, Lacan turns our attention to the sexes as absolutely other. Woman and man never meet each other except in infinity. They never enjoy at the same time for who and what would be there to know it? And they never write love letters in the same way which means that they come up with two different jouissances. The "sexual relation does not exist" belongs not only to the order of nonexistence but also to non-negation and impossibility. Impossibility is what we practice to be surprised and taken aback when it turns into the possible. It is called a surprise. It gives way to what remains after the failure. It concerns the field of language where love is made to exist. "Love exists" would be Lacan's ultimate conclusion of his discourse, provided we approach this existence alongside the nonexistence of the sexual relation.

Lacan made love into the fifth element. Love is not only the condition of speaking, it permeates life carrying with it, to our surprise, hatred and ravage. If there is no escaping responsibility from one's subjectivity, there is also no escaping from loving the Other, folded into which lies a fantasy of destruction. And I recall here that this is what Lacan said about God as standing for love. And that's also the reason, it seems to me, why he said that theologians can be more successful in embarking on their pursuits without God than he. Couldn't we say that love is the condition of God to the extent that this love for God is also *a*-theist? Why not to say that Lacan made love into the condition of God? You have a good life, a father says to his four year old daughter, and she replies without a thought: I have a good father. She is far ahead of him and can anticipate what the condition of happiness in her life is. She can already convert this anticipation and this knowledge into a gift of sharing what she does not have.

The story of donkey's ears or the secret of psychoanalysis

Here it is, then, a little sketch in two prologues to the problems I will take up in the course of this study. At the end this brings me to the question of psychoanalysis itself and more specifically of its secrets. On many occasions Lacan illuminated the secrets of love for us. But he also spoke of the secrets of psychoanalysis. Let me start by telling a story of donkey's ears.

Long time ago lived a good and wise king. He was just and fair to his people who loved him in return. One day, when strolling in the forest he met two gods, Pan and Apollo. They were quarrelling as to who is the best musician in the world. When they saw the king they asked him to act as their referee. They took turns and played the most beautiful melodies on their instruments. After the contest the king could not make up his mind who is the best musician in the world. "Who shall I choose?" worried the king, "Pan or Apollo, Pan, Apollo, Pan …?

Let it be Pan," the king eventually decided but not without hesitation. "Pan?!" Apollo cried out: "You think Pan is the best musician in the world? But if you really do, you do not have king's ears but donkey's ears." And with these words Apollo changed king's ears into donkey's ears. The poor king felt so ashamed and embarrassed that he withdrew to his castle and from now on his people only saw him in the castle window wearing a strange long hat. After some time the king needed a haircut. To do that he ordered the court barber to make an oath not to reveal the king's secret to anyone. The barber agreed and was shocked to see king's donkey ears. Shortly after his pledge the barber fell ill. He could not eat or drink or sleep. He called the doctor who after examining him said that there was nothing he could see wrong with him. Perhaps the barber carried in him some deep worry or a despair that made him suffer so much. The barber realised that it was the king's secret that made him ill. But because of the pledge he could not say it to anyone and started to weigh down on him. "What shall I do?" he asked himself, and an idea dawned on him. "If I cannot tell anyone about the king's secret perhaps I could confess it to the ground." And he did what he said. He lied down on the grass near the forest, made sure there was no one nearby and then confessed his secret to the ground by whispering it several times. Then he got up and almost immediately felt much better. He felt cheerful and light and was relieved. "I am cured, I am cured", he shouted and danced (it is what in analysis we call rapid therapeutic reaction). After confessing his secret to the ground, his voice sank deep into the earth. It sank first into the grass, then into the moss and foliage underneath. It then went deeper through the layers of sand and loose rock until deep down it fell on a seed. Later the seed grew shooting through to the ground and above. From the seed grew a reed. As the king was unhappy for such a long time, a minstrel was called to amuse him. A minstrel tried all sorts of entertainment tricks but none worked. The king remained without a smile on his face. In the end the minstrel decided to play music for the king. He cut out a reed, made holes in it and began to play it like a flute. At this point we do not know whether this music made the king happy again. What we know is that when the minstrel began to play one could just about hear a quiet whisper spreading along the sounds of music: "The king has donkey's ears …" And although the king was surprised and asked "Who revealed my secret?" let's just say that somehow he was not so unhappy anymore.

Why not say then that the use of the name (i.e., subscription to the name of the father) is equivalent, logically speaking, to the subscription to the function of the secret in psychoanalysis? If there is a secret in psychoanalysis, this is perhaps because psychoanalysis itself will always be a transmission of a secret.

Psychoanalysis has always been embroiled not only in its own clinical intricacies but also in the social discourse with the counterparts of religion and science. In the era of attempted regulation of talking cures, which amounts not only to an attempt to gag them, what can be expected of the discourse of psychoanalysis? What can those who seek in it a place to confide freely the secrets they would never confide to anyone else, expect of psychoanalysis and make it into? Whatever can be said of the issues involved in the attempts to regulate and standardise the singular encounter with the real, and with it the talking cures in general, one thing remains as certain as it possibly can. The regulation of psychoanalysis would never bring the regulators the expected satisfaction. This is because the analysand, the one who speaks freely of his secrets, having been compelled to confide them to the other lest he becomes "ill", puts into question the nature of the powers of authority that seek a satisfactory conclusion to regulation process. The moment you want to gag the flow of thoughts and words slipping through the underground foliage, as in the story above, the moment you muzzle the confidence of the relation with your confidante the analyst is supposed to be, is the moment when negation becomes confused with nonexistence. And as the lesson with Dawkins and his God of science taught us, the relation between negation and nonexistence is far from straightforward. That's why Lacan pointed to the symptom to give us some inkling about this difficulty. And that's why psychoanalysis and communism are incompatible, as the symptom and an ego ideal are not good bed fellows. What can be expected of psychoanalysis, is to give way to the secret of experience by rendering it less relevant. On the one hand, psychoanalysis remains the guardian of the secret, on the other hand, it creates conditions of knowledge and channels for the signifiers where the secret is confided.

In his teaching, especially in the 1970s, Lacan steered clear of the song of the sirens where the master signifier, heard as a *dominanta* in the discourse of religion and science, aims to make us believe in the truth as supreme meaning. He steered clear of subjecting his listeners to meanings other than the little anchoring points, and introduced to what in the analyst's discourse functions as *dominanta*, namely object *a*. What Lacan was telling us was that since mastery is not foreign to music, it is not foreign to speech either. The king sought appeasement in music but stumbled upon the signifier of the unconscious that became his master. The master says: there is no way to escape mastery. And Lacan noted, as does the king's story, that the unconscious is its most formidable tool. The question for Lacan was not how to overthrow the master's authority but how to make the question resonate to cause the silence to speak. In other words, how to create conditions for the fault, which is there from the start, to emerge. The king's castration rendered these conditions propitious to the transmission of his secret. It is in this sense that the progression of Lacan's teaching, as much as it is available to anyone to follow, is also a progression of a secret. From the secret of the signifier of the lack in the Other to the secret of jouissance that cannot be written, marks the itinerary of the secret in Lacan's teaching.

At the end of analysis, when there are no more secrets left with which we started, we come to a realisation that making unhappiness less relevant and the real less weighty, does not change the fact that a mystery remains. It is a mystery of an absolute singularity of the subject each one is, one by one, that has no interior and no exterior but only a surface. To the extent that analysis aims at speaking about the satisfaction, called jouissance, Lacan's aim was to make jouissance speak. It is not enough to say that the signifier constitutes the difference between the subjects. What makes the difference is how the signifier of the lack in the Other traverses across the body and spits out its images. This fascinated Lacan a great deal, especially in his later teaching, and amounted for him to tying up a knot made of the three I have just mentioned, the real of the body, the symbolic of language and the imaginary that makes them stick. This knot embodied for Lacan the singularity of the speaking subject. I say "embodied" because it is not a representation or a metaphor but a structure as real. If this is the direction, the orientation where Lacan took us, it also stresses that psychoanalysis is to be defined as an experience of language, and of speech in particular, as a de-universalisation *qua singularis*. I was led to conclude with regard to Freud's critique of philosophy that the exercise of the philosopher and his particular variation of mastery revolves around *singularis qua universalis*. It is a particularity to be reckoned with. Psychoanalysis does not stand in opposition to such an effort nor does it negate them. On the contrary, analysis deuniversalises what appears under the universal function of the name as the signifying operator. This signifying operator (i.e., the Name-of-the-Father) both obfuscates the secret of the subject and marks it with a seal of guarantee. That's only the first step. You only do not tell the secret if you know what it is.

What is the *universalis* in psychoanalysis if not a name that facilitates transmission of a failure of the sexual relation to the extent that jouissance is not a sign of love? What the father transmits to the child in the form of the sexual function concerns something of the order of the absolute, the mother as absolute jouissance. On the other hand, the very function of the paternal metaphor opens, like in the case of the king who makes a judgement, a dimension of what cannot be named, what is impossible to say. At the end of his teaching Lacan approached the impossible as interwoven with the sexual relation.

So what is the secret of psychoanalysis? "I am not going to tell you", a little boy says, already a master of his word, "because it's a secret". When we think about a secret we think about the master as its guardian, as a knowledge, namely a signifier, that the master has at his disposal to reveal or not to reveal. But this is not the case of psychoanalysis, and of the discourse of the analyst in particular. In psychoanalysis the secret is not guarded by the speaking subject or the subject of the unconscious. The secret of psychoanalysis, this is no mystery, has to do with the object. We can see this in the analyst's discourse. The secret of the discourse called analyst's has to do with the place of *dominanta*, which is the place of desire as agent, being occupied by the object *a*. It can thus be heard, for those who can hear it, as a syncope because it has an effect of a cut. The syncope interferes with a continuity between *dominantas* by being inscribed as discontinuity. The analyst finds this place to cut in and to mark the space between them. But that's not the only thing he does.

The object a—an introduction

Lacan brings the object *a* closer to love, even inserts it *in* love. He does that, already in *Seminar XI* (1977), which is a new way for love that moves away from the definition of love as always narcissistic. In 1964 Lacan inserts the object *a* in love because in love's heart there is a void, the impossible to give that one nevertheless continues to give as it is what one does not have. And it can only be passed from one to one. Let's take up, for example, castration as the true place of love. The castration the father passes to the child makes up for the fault we are so secretive about. The subject may wonder whether it was not the object from the start that secreted from the drive and led the subject to love. Lacan's object *a* is indeed quite unique as it cannot be replaced with another. It cannot be socially shared, exchanged, substituted by the so-called goods or human values. And it always has to do with that part of the subject that has been forgotten, remains between words, outside the tongue slip and beyond the Other. The object that arises through anxiety to become a product of castration relative to the drive satisfaction, is neither transferable nor exchangeable, just like a last minute one way train ticket. In short, I am talking about the object that is not to be received and must therefore be given away to the Other. What is left of it mobilises desire to act, that is to say prompts to a speech act as an object aiming at the subject. And this is how Lacan marked it in the analyst's discourse, $a \rightarrow \$$. This will allow Lacan to inaugurate, after *Seminar XI*, the pluralisation of the names of the father based on the fact that for each subject there is a singular object *a*. We could say that the pluralisation of the names is a logical consequence of the end of *Seminar XI* (i.e., "I love you but, inexplicably, I love in you more than you—object *a*—and therefore mutilate you").

The indivisibility of the object *a*, together with the fact that it is non-returnable and nonexchangeable, names what we encounter in everyday life as a strange presence of what is not for me nor for you. I can think of many examples. Here is one, it is not for the loved one to say what he is loved for. He does not have to have the knowledge of what causes his lover to fall for him and to claim in some way his "ownership". In effect, the object *a* can produce a division in those who try to make an exclusive claim to it. In other words, it is not me who chooses the object. What is the object *a* if not that little hollow that remains from the satisfaction of the Other, in relation to the Other, that prompts desire to emerge at the point of loss, which confirms the lack, and which nevertheless remains a compass of pleasures in life? In other words, what is this object if not the one that chooses me as the subject? The object *a* chooses the subject, just like in Harry Potter it is the wand that chooses its master. And if it was the other way round, the power of the lover would always be subdued and insincere due to uncertainty of what kind of object he is for the loved one. "The wand chooses its master" is an illustration of the logic of division of the master in relation to the object that supposedly satisfies him. In effect, we can see that the master becomes a divided subject and, therefore, looks for the means of regaining his mastery by means of what if not fantasy?

From this perspective, what an impossible "solution" this could provide to an unsolvable question like that of "ownership" of Jerusalem. But this is how the problem presents itself nevertheless. As the most desirable object that divides its claimants, Jerusalem remains indivisible and unpartitionable. And if it cannot be divided or shared in its entirety, it could nevertheless be passed from one side to another, from one cycle of festivities to another, so that the object could be enjoyed by one party at a time. There is always something one wants to go back to.

In *Seminar XX, Encore* (1998b), Lacan introduces a term that inscribes the object permanently in the heart of love. He calls it *hainamoration*, "lovehate". By doing this Lacan points to the "other side" of love, its lining, or in French *l'envers*, the term Lacan already used in his seminar on discourses. The lining implies that it is the other side of the veil—not beneath the veil but its reverse, its inside out. Hate and ravage are now the modes of the real according to which the object chooses its master, its lover who will recognise it unmistakably on the veil, which is the woman or the feminine subject, as the one for him. The question arising from this new approach to love as incorporating hate, concerns the place of the veil, or its absence, and its phallic value. This appears of crucial importance in some relationships, especially between mother and daughter, but also between man and woman. The veil and the castration as a place of love bring us to privation. It is an early reference of Lacan, from *Seminar IV* (1994), whose relevance to the secret of the object and of *hainamoration* appears to me as paramount. We recall that during this early period in his teaching Lacan worked on a triad of castration, frustration, and privation, and presented the last term as real. Privation is real because it concerns a real gap in the body, and thus requires a mediatory function of the imaginary and the symbolic object. Privation is real just as hate and ravage are real. Privation presents itself as the real lack because it concerns the impossible as such. But since it is real it also points us in the direction of the symbolic plane, and I have already mentioned the phallic value of the veil. The phallic object is not the object *a*. The veil concerns the phallic object, and the beyond of the veil has to do with the object *a*. So we are in the field of desire. The secret of the object lies behind where there is nothing, which is also the void in the heart of love. But it is not without the veil and the phallic object that Lacan approaches the object *a* at that time. And who is to be blamed for there being nothing beyond the veil? It is the father but not just any father. Lacan assigns the mediatory function of the real privation to the imaginary father. What is the imaginary father? Usually it is the one to be blamed for the neighbour's flat being nicer than mine or God who spawned all sorts of anomalies in our life. As Lacan puts it, the imaginary father is the one to take the blame for screwing up our life in general and for not enabling us to speak about the sexual relation in particular. Thanks to privation, at the end, life may turn out to be good and happy. The passage from the real father, as initiating castration, to the imaginary father as, let's call him a patron of privation, is based on the symbolic function of the name. Here, then, we have three fathers in Lacan's teaching.

What Lacan called pluralisation of the names means that each privation bears a different name, and that for each subject there is something else. We could say that the analytic process aims at the secret of jouissance and concludes at "for each subject something else". The question is not whether I know the secret. I always do and sometimes I can tell it and sometimes not. This is how the mechanism of repression becomes introduced, that I am unable to tell the secret knowing it very well. The secret of the object is another matter, which is particular to psychoanalysis. It concerns the question of what object was I, am I, for the Other. And this is where the interrogation of the secret of psychoanalysis has led me. The secret of jouissance, which is not a sign of love, comes from the interrogations of the remainder, of the traces of jouissance left by the absolute jouissance of the mother, the Freudian *das Ding*, as Lacan fished it out from Freud's "Project for a scientific psychology" (1950a [1895]). And since we are dealing with the absolute jouissance, Lacan deploys three fathers each providing a different response—one to take the blame for not protecting the child from it, the second one for saying no to the child who enjoys it, and the third one for saying yes to the symptom the child will form in response to it. In a word, as Eric Laurent put it, the function of the father is to guide from drive to love. Or from passion to desire.

The secret of psychoanalysis is to be found in the object that emerges in this passage. And this may appear as incomprehensible to all the fans of state regulation of talking cures in general, and psychoanalysis in particular. It was Freud himself who warned us against it. Today he is not alone. Bernard-Henri Levi has even gone so far as to say that psychoanalysis is the right to the secret. In the light of technological developments and alternative ways of introducing the sexual function—where neither privation nor the paternal function seem the condition of desire—from adoption through design babies to babies on order, there also emerges a right to the father or the right to the name. In so far as technology is on the side of the state (i.e., on the side of the global oppressiveness of the superego in the structure of subjectivity) psychoanalysis remains on the side of the name of the secret and of transmitting it in and outside the consultation room.

To this end, when a demand for the cure is articulated with all the resonances that come along with it, and the door to wanting to know the secret of desire opens up, how does the analyst respond? He can respond *desecretely*. Having gone this way himself he is unable to do otherwise save a little variation. No matter how hard he would try and even against his worst judgement, the analyst is unable to put forward anything resembling an ideology, a "philosophy", a worldview. On the side of the real, he supports the discourse where in search of true love lost, the subject aims at the nameless object that caused his despair. On the side of the symbolic, there will always be a symptom that brings him back so that he can move on with it. Somewhere along the way there will be attempts to make sense, the creations, constructions, delusions of meaning. Lacan logicised these stages, and I will take them up at the end. As for the non-analytical interpretation the analysts are free to contest what they desire as this was already inscribed for them in the products of their analyses. To escape it is as irrelevant as having to follow it.

Psychoanalytic experience may belong to the subject at the end but in the first place it was the object's and that's how the subject was supposed. What guided it, what pushed it in this direction? Is it a taste, a smell, a glimpse of mystery or a silence that the master signifier will first attempt to subdue it and then give way to the object that says "find me, love me, and drop me"? Lacan added the gaze and the voice to this impossible list of objects, inherited from Freud, that animate subject's desire, and fantasy with it. We will find it in a precise place on his graph of desire. The analytic experience passes through the pathway of desire. Like in the case of the passage from "my desire wilted" to "my desire willed it", the experience relies on seizing the unconscious when it opens. When love rules strong the unconscious closes. When it opens, love is lost, again. So after the passage the speaking subject will not be the same again. One can seize it by taking a chance and by way of contingency. For Lacan the experience of psychoanalysis was contingent through and through. Before we embark on the analytic process it appears as a free choice or a passage that might happen or might not. Then we discover we have urgent things to say to the analyst, which may lead to more important discoveries. Free associations are no longer free but conditional upon the urgency that brought us to analysis. In analysis we speak what we have to say and not what we can. Spinoza was right when he said we don't know what we can. The associations follow the route of necessity not of possibility, and that's the basis for contingency. Once we have embarked on the process there is a moment in analysis where one can only say: it had happened, so it had to have happened. We could say that before this passage the future of the unconscious, or the unconscious as future, was contingent. But at the end, when the effects can be traced retrospectively, the passage appears as necessary.

What Lacan stresses for us is that the subject will never be the same following the shift from the possible to the necessary. This shift occurred as an effect of the subject's division that makes him fall out with being, so to speak. What appeared in that place of loss was what we call retroactive temporality. We could say that the subject subscribes to the unconscious when he is caught by the signifier at the level of the passage from the possible to the necessary.

This is what Jacques-Alain Miller pointed out when he spoke about a confusion between the possible and the contingent. When we speak of the phallus and phallic signification as contingent, we only distinguish it from the necessary. The phallus is not necessary because it does not have to be inscribed and only sometimes is. Therefore it is contingent. But the contingent, in the light of the new definition, is impossible to the extent that at the moment when it takes place there is an effect of surprise and disbelief, which is also the sign of the real: "I cannot believe it took so many years ... to realise that ... wilting ... that I actually willed it ... wanted it." Now, there is no going back ... When the initial surprise subsides the impossible becomes possible. It is possible that in the psychoanalytic conditions such things happen. In psychoanalysis the impossible happens.

CHAPTER THREE

Of the truths and lies of *logos*: Lacan meets Heidegger

From sein *to* logos

I will start with what appears to me to resonate in the rhythm of the analytic practice, however those who venture into it may wish not to be ventriloquized by what nevertheless brings them to it. Courage and hesitation not only go hand in hand but prove an irresistible mixture, especially to those who are drawn by the letter of their unconscious, just as Dupin's gaze was drawn by the corner of the envelope sticking out of the coat pocket. This detail had much less to do with the proverbial devil than with a pursuit of the Other's desire to the letter, which may lead the subject to act. Anyone who has gone through an analytic experience will be able to confirm what effects their own act had on them. As for the one who still hesitates whether to enter or not, as Dante already foretold on the doorstep to the *Inferno*, their approach to psychoanalysis will not be devoid of the presuppositions that appear to be as good a reason not to enter it as to do so despite them. Who knows what is going to happen? Taking a chance, after leaving the hope behind when anguish weighs heavy, may be good enough, if only spiced up with a tinge of English optimism that usually tips the scales in favour, for, after all, it cannot be all that bad. Look what medicine can do to you without you even knowing.

Fortunately, and despite the confusion of reasons and causes which is part of that step of courage when your body actually leans forward, steps out of the river you have been in for too long, psychoanalysis was not written in Latin or Greek even if occasional echoes of antiquity can make you think otherwise. But that is the way some may hear what psychoanalysis has on offer for them. Let's simply ask this: is it not an echo of what is already inscribed in the ear of the unconscious? This ear or ears, should of course be pricked up, provided you know what to do with the signifier, with what is heard, or they might turn into donkey's ears, and you already know the story of how the king got donkey's ears. Given in analysis we learn over and over how to hear, how to read and how to speak, the ear in question turns out to be the ear of the Other, which is the locus of language thanks to which the signifier is distinguished from the sense it produces. And this can sometimes be quite surprising.

The subject goes to analysis with some expectations to receive from the analyst what he thinks he does not know but what already constitutes, as Lacan said from the start, part of the message, which is his demand. Where do these presuppositions come from if not from what is most near and therefore most foreign, from the extimacy of the unconscious itself? And how has psychoanalysis, the place one can only arrive at insufficiently, come to become the site of the rumblings of the unconscious where both religion and science failed? Until this point, until Freud removed it from the pot of ideas that can be imagined and visualised, which was around 1880s, psychoanalysis was caught between the mirage of ontology and the subject's destitution Lacan called *désêtre*. Shall we call it *unbeing* as in *un*doing being? With its unforecast future the question that reposes itself for me is this: how does psychoanalysis manage to distance itself from the ontological presuppositions of the history of philosophy without being trapped in the generalised ideals and concepts to which we no longer lend an ear? In other words, which is Lacan's starting point, precisely because of his borrowings and interest in the dead letters of philosophy: how was the gap of the unconscious sutured? While this question may well lead to many academic a thesis, it may prove useless in analysis where "drop the quote" is the starting point. And then, with the ear of the Other in place, with the Other as a place of language embodied by the analyst, it's over to the unconscious, to the truths and lies of the unconscious. From the beginning of his teaching Lacan was subjected to the generalised ideas of fellow philosophers and scientists, but proceeded to bid farewell to phenomenology of his time. Lacan allowed himself to be drenched by the *universalis qua singularis* of philosophy and science. Then he shook off the excess of the Other of the Other of his contemporaries. Having shaken off claims of the universal truths, he focused on the Other of the signifier and taught what his ear was attuned to best: a particular as such, namely the subject as supposed and spoken, and as a speaking one, whether neurotic or psychotic. It was at this juncture of particularity, through which myriads of reference passed and entered his teaching, where he met Heidegger.

It is somewhat ironic that for Freud philosophy came to incarnate a certain ideal which he later dismissed as narcissistic, while Lacan, who distrusted the totalising tendencies of philosophy, and even called himself an anti-philosopher, made several forays into texts that deserve no other name than philosophical. Why and to what purpose if not to subvert the pretence of truth lovers and question the limits which are not the limits of philosophy but of subjectivity. Psychoanalytical task therefore became marked by the ambiguity of a certain return which aims not at truth, which was after all a philosophical ideal, but at the lies that speak in the name of it. Such was no doubt the fate of Sartre (1956) and Merleau-Ponty (1968) in whose writings Lacan found valuable reference points.

Let's recall the scene when Lacan meets Heidegger in the 1950s, not only in person but prior to it in an analytic session. Frustrated by the analyst's silence, Jean Beoufret, says to Lacan, his analyst, that he had met with Heidegger in Freiburg and told him about Lacan. Without hesitation Lacan asks: "what did he say to you?" Roudinesco (1990) claims that by breaking his silence Lacan fell for it. But Lacan responded at the point where Beoufret's unconscious was pleasing the master and therefore kept the Other silent. Lacan did not ask about what Heidegger said about him, Lacan, but about what he said to him, Beoufret. Of course Lacan knew that Beoufret was at that time responsible for bringing the master of Freiburg over to France to spread his word, which he did with success. But he was obviously less successful in his session having to insist on breaking the analyst's silence. Lacan did not respond to this narcissistic tease but followed his desire by inquiring about Heidegger's—"what did he say to you?" Lacan's interest at the time had to do with Heidegger's reflections on language starting with *logos*.

Lacan did not believe in philosophy which did not prevent him from reading texts like *Sein und Zeit*. But it would not be surprising if he took up this *sein* at the level of the signifier, which is where the unconscious makes it resonate for the subject, to arrive at a completely different sense it produces in French. While Heidegger's attachment to *sein* stretched to a lifelong meditation on its meaning, for Lacan it may have been a passing encounter with a signifier, perhaps not without some amusing effects. Nevertheless Lacan's growing distance to philosophy does not seem to me to be the result of a sense of disappointment one gathers from the fact that among the philosophers, beginning with Plato, can be found the most prolific liars. That's precisely what interested Lacan: the lies that give us a glimpse of truth, the lies that tell the truth.

At the beginning of his teaching the intellectual scene of his time was changing. The discontents of civilisation, and therefore of the subject, were no longer treated by theory alone. Philosophical theories of psychoanalysis, like that of Badiou, were no longer a satisfactory "treatment" of and a response to the malady of the subject. The philosopher's "love of truth" had more of a status of Platonic love that shuns the real, rather than an encounter with the real of jouissance that language impacts on the body. A shift was taking place from writing theory to a living articulation, and no one more than Lacan was contributing to this shift and to the change of scene. Lacan was interested in whisking out the minutest traces of the unconscious by means of the living signifier, which cannot be said of writing and its high priests at the time. Lacan was bringing back, following Freud's earliest work with the hysterics, the experience of the signifier in the body, moving from writing towards speech not as a commentator or spokesperson of the former but as a primary and immanent manifestation of the speaking subject. He was putting the ear of the Other to use, and through this was rendering the subject's ears the instrument of resonance and transmission of language. In a certain sense the ear replaced the pen, no longer the mightiest but precisely as might-less as speech.

For Lacan in the 1950s the legacy of philosophy was giving in to the discourse of the unconscious otherwise known as the discourse of the master. Was not Lacan picking up the debris of what after the death of God in those times appeared as what might be called the *discourse of mourning* of which Heidegger, with his nostalgia for Being and belief in the fundamental guilt, was perhaps the master proponent? Here I am limiting myself to that crucial moment in Lacan's teaching where he takes up and translates the only ever text by Heidegger, and it is not so much about *sein* as about *logos*. What then truly interested Lacan in Heidegger's work?

From the cause of truth to the truth as cause

Where does Lacan seek the truth of *logos* if not by first going to refer to Aristotle to put into a test the latter's notion of the cause? Aristotle formulated his theory of the cause by elaborating four causes: material, final, efficient, and formal, as they appear in his *Physics* (1941). This is a little ikebana of causes offered to us by Aristotle. This in effect allowed him to give an account of genesis for each thing, namely establish an aetiology with respect to what each thing comes into being. Aristotle provides four answers to the question which are the four causes. Today we would say that a car is made with a view to be driven on the road, which is its final cause. But it is also made of the material for it to be a car, which is the material cause and so on. Lacan was interested in language, in the truth in speech, and this led him to consider the question of the cause or causes of the signifier. What we find in his "Science and truth" (1966) is a consideration of the truth in relation to the cause starting with Aristotle. This consideration was therefore not without accounting for the position of the subject in relation to the lack, which is the lack in being, and to the Other which is the locus of the signifier. Lacan marks the ambiguous relation between truth and cause by passing, as it were, the truth *as* cause through the four corners of Aristotle's ikebana.

As far as truth as cause is concerned, it acquires a value of revelation. With Lacan taking on truth as having a value of a revelation, we no longer need to draw support from the metalanguage of Aristotle's logic that rests on the opposition of true and false. Truth in psychoanalysis is not opposed to falsity or lying but appears as immanent opening of the unconscious. Once it has to pass through consciousness—it lies. This truth of revelation, or truth as revelation, is the speaking truth. Truth is therefore linked to speech and the order of the signifier. As such it produces an analytical effect that is final. In other words, the final cause of revelation would be that which has an effect of a discovery and realisation: "Eureka!" Whatever the revelation and its circumstances, the final cause of truth occurs at the moment of discovery. The material cause is something else.

What Lacan accentuates in the analytic experience is truth as cause. Let's not count it as the fifth one in the Aristotelian series because it is not a category. Lacan rearranges Aristotle's ikebana of causes by marking the truth as a cause that has an effect. The truth is only a cause when it causes an effect, a speech effect. But that's not all. Lacan passes truth as cause through four contemporary discourses of magic, religion, science, and psychoanalysis, to discover in each what kind of truth orients them and causes them. Let's note that his definition of discourse at this point is a structuralist one, namely of the relation between signifiers, which presumably means that it is not to do with the evaluation of the ideal but with an encounter of language with the real. This has an effect of rendering signifiers as equal in value, all having the same dignity. Only from this perspective the definition of the work of the signifier in magic, science, and religion becomes justified with respect to the truth as cause. For Lacan the psychoanalysts become qualified to speak about magic, science, and religion not because they account for them from the analytic point of view but because each of the four is oriented by the truth effect of the signifier within. And this settles the nonexistence of metalanguage. There is no truth about truth because what speaks is the truth to the extent there is no way to say it all, as Lacan remarked a few years later. Here I will limit myself to the truth as cause in psychoanalysis.

In the psychoanalytic experience the real wrong-foots the stream of associations, causing disconnections and breaking the chain of associations. In this way the effect of wrong-footing is produced by the real impact of the signifier. The truth effect should therefore be called material because it has material consequences for the subject. And Lacan spoke of this material effect as *moterielle*, *mot* being a word, which is the material we are made of, the building block of the speaking being provided we distinguish the matter of language from meaning. That is why Lacan uses the term cause in the specific sense of *causent tout l'effect*, causing the whole effect. For Lacan, there is no truth without a relation to the real. Dogmatic as it may seem, it may need some dilution or dialecticisation. In philosophy the real has always been bumping against the wall, producing for a subject an effect of repetition that leads to more repetition. The limit of a reflection called philosophical can be found in the safety net of the imaginary as it provides the field of an unlimited *speculum*. In effect the philosophical theorisation remains linked to the formal cause Lacan found as determinant in science. The philosopher's love-of-truth affair with psychoanalysis indeed has a character of a platonic one.

When Aristotle asks *ti to on;* he does not even employ a verb "to be" lest he presupposes the answer. His question focuses on what kind of thing or thingness determines being. Is the subject a substance or an attribute? Is *being* a substance or a predicate? Lacan will take up these questions in the light of the relation between being and truth as cause. If truth is "causing the whole effect" this must have a bearing on the subject that comes to existence in the rupture of the chain. For Lacan the subject is not a cause but an effect caused by the materiality of the signifier that moves it along while representing it. Lacan finds the basis of his subversive approach in the analytic experience. While responding to Aristotle and indirectly to Parmenides' love of being, he narrows down his ontological scope to Heidegger where these ancients found a mooring. In this respect Lacan's take on truth as cause—which is not to be added to Aristotle's causes, as I proposed, but incorporated into every discourse as animated by them—subverts Heidegger's concept of Being as the cause of all causes or a ground for a cause. Lacan's position, by his own admission, as anti-philosopher, is subsequently matched by the one of anti-ontologist. There is a fundamental disparity between language and being, which Lacan already marked defining desire as a relation of being to a lack. The signifier is to be situated, and the subject with it, in the lack in being. Heidegger maintains a relation between being and truth and by this token founds Being as a ground, a *priori* to all causes whatsoever. His answer to Aristotle can be summed as follows: for things to exist with respect to their finality, materiality, efficiency, and formality there has to be that which is in the sense *that* it is, Being. Nothing could be further from the analytic experience of desire and lack Lacan was teaching us about.

The question of causality is not the only time when the Heideggerian trace runs into the Lacanian field. My second juncture concerns the encounter with which I started, and which brought Lacan to translate, in 1951, Heidegger's inquiry into *logos* (1956) as the origin of language. In his commentary on an aphorism by Heraclitus, Heidegger invites us to enter a landscape of living soil where works are carried out of ploughing, planting seeds, harvesting, and gathering the harvest. From mother-earth to the storehouse represents for Heidegger a route leading from the matrix of language to *logos* as a storage of knowledge. Heidegger constructs a lure in the form of a half mythical, half nostalgic scene of the real that consists of growth, collection, and gathering of the crops. The process perennially leads to the satisfaction of the One. And this for the Greeks came to be known as *logos*. The term preceding it, and the name of the process, the penultimate term is *legein*—to speak, state, enunciate, utter, argue, etc. But this bucolic scenery of gathering crops, turning them into flour as a material for making bread that can be shared, has farther implications.

Heidegger constructs the final effect of the process on the basis of its cyclical repetition. But the cycle would not run its course were it not for the lost origin of the seed. The gathering and bringing together the sesame of knowledge is an effect of an unceasing conversation, *legein*. At the same time the collecting, gathering, and bringing together of words is the condition of an agora where the conversation and debate take place. On the one hand, *logos* is what leads to and facilitates the conversation between subjects and their signifying representations. On the other hand, *logos* forms the final result of the signifying relations, the ultimate knowledge as a repository of the effects and remainders of the cycle of conversations.

This is how Heidegger imaginarises the formation of *logos* as a principle of language emerging against the backdrop of Being. The emergence and formation of language effects for Heidegger are no longer what I called the ikebana of Aristotle's causes. We are dealing here with a process that Lacan followed to the letter by translating Heidegger's text. The rural and idyllic scenes are not isolated in Heidegger's life and work. It is not the task of psychoanalysis to rectify the nostalgic and bucolic metaphors of philosophy. If Lacan followed their development it was to demonstrate a distinct notion of *logos* as a condition of synchronic differentiation in the play of the signifiers. Heideggerian *logos*, understood as a process and effect of gathering of the signifiers under the roof of all-is-one, runs contrary to the signifying differentiation in the life of the suffering subject ploughing his history back and forth. In the course of his discourse the speaking subject is also confronted with what is lost in the field of knowledge, which is the field of the Other, and what he seeks to refind. These were some of Lacan's concerns when he met Heidegger. They come down to a certain temptation of being as a jouissance outside phallic signification, which Lacan will later take up as a feminine jouissance. But let's take a step at a time.

Being dizzy

What emerged from Lacan's confrontation with Heidegger echoes in the term Lacan concocted in his teaching, namely *parlêtre*, a speaking being to the extent that a being is implicated in language. The verb that gives rise to *logos* (i.e., *legein*, "speaking") supports *parlêtre* by making it audible. *Legein* stands for an instance of a synchronic production of the signifying chain. In this respect it is to be distinguished from the letter and writing. The letter is what reposes, comes to a stop, a real that can be read when it is seen. The letter is what anchors it to the ground, what brings the process of articulation to a halt. The signifier, as representing the subject for another signifier, produces an effect in the real by causing other signifiers where significations are made. Having no meaning in itself, the signifier produces sense without being. An artist paints a picture not with being but by dropping it, forgetting it until the picture can hang there against being, almost like a hole in being.

Legein facilitates the position of the speaking subject who exists in the gap between signifiers as a divided subject. When the signifier passes in the chain, when it addresses the Other, the chain circumvents the gap that Lacan called *manque à être*, want to be or a lack in being. In this way the subject's existence between the signifiers gives support to a blunder and a misunderstanding, in general called parapraxes. What does it imply? It implies that the Lacanian subject is never what it wants to be or says what it wants to say. The subject for Lacan, apart from being divided along the axis of the lack that inhabits it, is also a nomadic subject. It moves from one place to another, while being discontinuous all the time, and this movement is determined by the serendipitous discovery, a stumbling, a mishit that is its motor. In this sense, the subject's desire is mobilised by a pursuit of the desire of the Other, which is the question of what the Other wants, but caused by the object called *a* in so far as it belongs neither to the subject nor to the Other. What we have come to call the Lacanian subject, both as a subject of the unconscious and as a speaking subject whose desire presents itself as a reversal of the desire of the Other around the object *a*, exists subject to a blunder. This allows me to say that the Lacanian subject comes to existence only as a mistake. In the first analysis, then, the Lacanian subject glides over the Heideggerian being. From this perspective of the gap in being it is not so much Being as a cause of all causes that we found in the work of Aristotle but the object *a* as a cause of desire. Lacan spoke of truth as cause, and now he will speak about the object *a* as a cause of desire.

For Lacan the subject is constituted in the *legein* of the discourse in which is dissolved the image of natural development. It was more or less at the same time in the early 1950s that Lacan was already working on and defining the triad of the Symbolic, Imaginary, and Real. In particular, he perceived the imaginary as a register accounting for the relation between the species of similar colours, shapes, and other external features that make birds of feather fly together. The imaginary is essentially responsible for identifications that arise from what we by and large call the "natural world". This is what Lacan extracted from the repetitive displays of plumage and movement of the members within same species. In the case of speaking beings, the imaginary is guided by the relation to the body image but supported by the symbolic in so far as it is through the Other of language and voice where this imaginary relation is cemented. To presuppose a growth and a cycle that occurs "naturally" or by inertia, cancels any dialectic of the subject within which the fundamental differentiations of positions, values, preferences, etc., are decided. It was evident that Lacan and Heidegger were not from the same flock and that they never flew together.

There was one occasion, however, when Heidegger was on his visit to France, invited by Beoufret who could at last fulfil his wish, and Lacan took him for a ride by car. Heidegger sat at the front, their wives in the rear, and off they went with a speed that made Heidegger dizzy. As Lacan stepped on it, the wives' protest grew stronger and louder. Heidegger was at this point left clinching to all he had left at this instant, to wit nothing more and nothing else but being-Heidegger. This is what we do when we have no choice and the driver steps on it. We are reduced to the last drop of our being that is left there, carried in all directions without any guarantee of a safe voyage to the point of destination. So we put the seatbelt on, crack a joke, protest—anything the subject can do. Such a voyage at speed can take us all the way to our being and back to the subject.

Heidegger's reflection on the origin of language took him all the way to the bucolic scene of country life where things by and large stand still. It was a portrait at rest, drawing which Heidegger wanted to break a new ground and capture the origin of *logos*. Inevitably, in his reading of the *logos* of Heraclitus, he was interested in the sutures of the subjective divisions that Lacan opened up before him. And one of these I found in the famous ride that gave Heidegger a headache or simply had an effect of dizziness. Being dizzy became the name of Heidegger's destination at the time. His meditation on *logos* and his search for the parentage of language come to a stop, following the cycle of nature, before the jouissance of the Other, the satisfaction the mother draws from having all her offsprings by her and with her. She has gathered them together around her, as a mother does, folding them into this moment that lasts eternity. With the imaginary fulfilment of *sein*, there was nothing left for Heidegger to say.

The invention of lies: from alienation to separation and back

At that time, Lacan was interested in the *beyond* of the imaginary idyll of nature and in the beyond of the ontological presuppositions. He found the truth in psychoanalysis by linking it to the material cause, and he started by exploring the relation between the truth and lie not as opposites but as being correlative. Lacan was not able to find any causal relations with being or consider being as cause. What Lacan found was the Other of language and its link to the lack in being. When the truth, as Lacan will say in the 1970s, passes through the traps of the imaginary relations, it lies. The truth speaks and lies—this was Lacan's discovery. Freud spoke of the first lie, *protos pseudos*, when commenting on the case of a girl, Emma, in 1895. Emma went to the shop where she was laughed at by some old men and ran away in panic. This was her second visit to the shop, which evoked, retroactively, her first visit. At that time she was pinched sexually by an old man, which emerged in her encounter with the real some years later when she returned to the same shop. She flinched. The flight from the shop was the primary defence. The signifier is first a lie that occurs at the site of the real. The first lie in this sense is a fall from being, from the primordial nature which Heidegger, for his part, kept going back to. What is this flight of Emma, this failure to stay put if not a representative of the subject's failed encounter with the real of the body, to which she is brought back nevertheless by being confronted with the master signifier, the first lie as a negation, and which Lacan situated as a condition of the mechanism of repression? What else does Emma run back to if not to a signifying inkling of her existence where there is no idyll or bucolic celebration because the encounter with sexuality intimates of a failure with language as a signifier? We can say with Lacan that at the beginning there is a lie, because the lie as a negation I have already mentioned tears the subject away from being. The same happens in torture. The aim of torture is to force the body of the Other to tell the truth. But in effect of such an assault on the subject, which is also an assault on truth as cause, what emerges is a lie, necessarily, that makes the subject. It can only be a lie, any lie really as long as it relieves the body from pain. Today some governments are so much in love with the truth about the subject that they will not stop even before torture to extract it. In the end it can amount to a dentist's operation that takes place where the subject is foreclosed. When the truth does not speak and lie, it is because the subject has been foreclosed.

Lacan startled some of us when he said in the *Television* (1990) interview that he always tells the truth because there is no way to say it all. What surprises us in this statement of Lacan is this link and shift from "I always tell the truth" to "there is no way to say it all". The truth as cause has to be approached as fragmentary, partial, incomplete, and therefore revealing and concealing. Revelation is not all there is to the truth. Apart from revealing, it also conceals, does not divulge all there is to truth. Lacan redefined the coordinates of truth in psychoanalysis by first subverting the opposition of truth and lie and turning them into an alliance of correlatives. And secondly, Lacan starts to speak of truth as fragmentary, which means immanent and discontinuous, namely the truth one cannot tell in its entirety, therefore the truth as not-all. Every reader of Lacan knows where I am going with this, in which direction I am pushed to go having said this. Around that time Lacan already started saying the same thing about the woman, the one who is not whole, *pas-tout*. I will take it up later.

Lacan's subversion of truth led him then to the truth as cause to the extent that the cause of truth in psychoanalysis is material, namely made of the signifiers and letters or simply of the unconscious as materiality. When the subject speaks in analysis to the analyst, taking him for all sorts of things and people to suppose him to have the knowledge he himself is unable to live without, a lie is told. It is a good start to analysis to begin with a lie. It was exactly the opposite in the film *The Invention of Lying* in which people live in the world where everybody tells the truth. You can imagine the amount of insults and banter that goes on there. There is certainly no shortage of the real there in the form of anger and hatred but no lies. At some point the main character, played by Ricki Gervais, becomes convinced there should be more money on his account than the bank statement indicates. He tells the cashier about it and she confirms he is right, for why would he lie, and corrects the mistake in his favour. It is at this point he realises that everybody believes literally what is said. But it is because of his mistake that he was led to the discovery that he is capable of lying and deception. Once he gains more wealth than he needs, he goes on to invent a story of God and tells it to the crowd. And everybody believes him because nobody knows he is lying. That is to say, everybody needs to believe when it comes to the matters of life, death, and pain. Descartes (1973) too believed in a God that does not deceive. But for Lacan the Other is deceitful. The Other deceives because the tools of language and knowledge we have from the Other do not suffice to tell the whole truth but are just enough to tell some part of it.

So it is good to start analysis with a lie as this gives the subject some indications about the sources of deception and confusion. To start with a lie implies that there is a mistake implicated, that what led the subject to analysis was some instant of misunderstanding, slip of a tongue or pen, being cheated on, lied to and so on. Following this opening, the subject may attempt to tell the truth about the truth. The lie at the beginning shows a fall from being. One can still fall gracefully. To tell the truth about the truth implies an articulation that opens a gap in being. That was easy. It is more difficult when the traumatic real forms the starting of analysis, where the lie is already established as the repressed, and the relation between truth and lie is much closer, more intimate. Lacan called the fall from being *désêtre*, and designated it to the analyst who takes his position and knowledge from it. For Lacan the subject cannot find any comfort in being. But it finds comfort in lies. Lacan spoke of the happiness of the subject. It is the lies, which touch on the drive jouissance, that make the subject happy. There is only misery for the subject in the yearning for imaginary identifications of being as a whole. But once the real of sexuality breaks through the idyll of nature, the subject can be happy again. At least it is busy working, ploughing through the real and rearranging the causes of alienation in his relation to the desire of the Other. That's why Lacan's direction in the analytic process was towards disidentification, which makes room for the subject to find the way out of his alienations.

The Lacanian subject, happy and busy at the time of letting its representations run their course, seeks to initiate actions without copying them. For example, the son follows his father's, or mother's, teaching career without "realising" it. The subject does not copy actions but initiates them. Only in initiating his actions the subject as speaking gets caught in alienation. The subject is happy in alienation. But he is not so happy following separation. After all, following separation the subject exists as divided, as having lost some satisfaction over the subtraction of the master signifier that was there only to represent the subject. Lacan oriented analysis between these two, alienation, where the signifier of the Other is assumed as the subject's property, and separation, where the subject's existence is assumed as a one less, namely as a division, an *unbeing*. Lacan's famous aphorism that the desire of the subject is the desire of the Other reverberates in this passage. What the subject brings to analysis, whether neurotic or psychotic or perverse, is the desire of the Other. Lacan's formulation marks the starting position for the subject and paves the way for the lie, namely for some form of negation once the manifestation of the Other's desire is brought forward. While Lacan's aphorism defines the structural and topological bond with the Other via desire, it is also a fundamental formula of alienation. Lacan illustrated it using the set theory of two partly overlapping circles. In this formulation we find the subject, or the subject's desire to be precise, on the left, and the Other's desire on the right. How does Lacan articulate the relation between them? The area where they overlap represents their relation in alienation, which Lacan marked with "is", that manifests being. It is the being of subject or the solitude of the subject. In the navel of the subject's solitude in alienation Lacan places the master signifier.

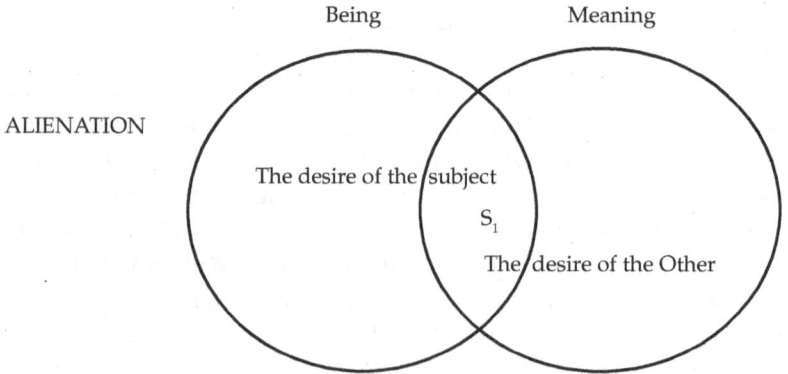

The subject is represented by the master signifier, S_1, that comes from the Other be it parents, carers, educators of all sorts. But here the Other stands for the place of language that the subject uses as the tools of representation. We could say that in alienation we are also confronted with identification with the master signifier. The subject's alienation results from its identification with the master signifier, without "realising" it, that represents the subject for another signifier. This other signifier, S_2, has often been called the master's representative, let's say its spokesperson, and it is also to be located in the Other. But before we get there, which is in fact where we started, it is worth noting that in accordance with Lacan's aphorism, the master signifier and the being of the subject are on the same side, enmeshed. We can see it in the diagram. The being of the subject as clearly unrepresented, and only showing the place in the structure, and the master signifier as coming from the Other, are in enmeshment. This being, which led philosophers like Aristotle and Heidegger by the nose, appears to belong to no one. But it does, as Lacan demonstrated, have connections with the Freudian Thing. That's why we cannot really speak of being of the subject but only of its representations that take place outside being and without being, which is the signification of the Greek *meta* provided we add "after" to it. When Lacan defined the subject's desire as that which *is* the Other's desire, he already entangled them in alienation. The French *est*, "is" and *et*, "and", are a homophony. In the definition of the subject's desire as alienation we can already hear where Lacan is taking us next—to the separation as subject's desire. From *est* to *et* shows the shortest passage Lacan takes us across from alienation to separation.

Although I started with Lacan's definition of the subject's and Other's desires, it is only in separation when we find the truth of the

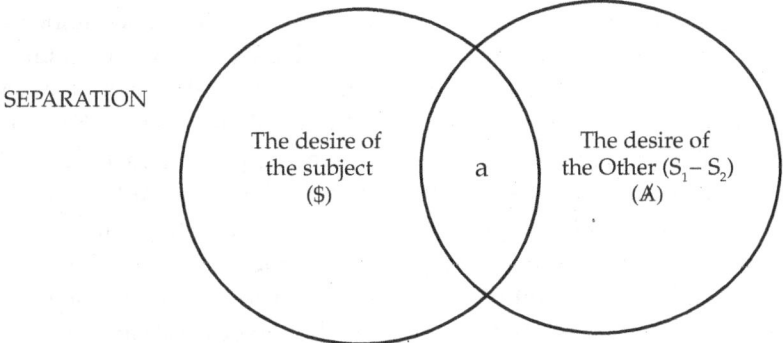

SEPARATION

The desire of the subject ($)

a

The desire of the Other ($S_1 - S_2$) (Ⱥ)

Other as desire or as desiring. On the one hand, it has to be stressed that the Other desires as it is not a place of sexual jouissance. Hence the Other's desire only confirms the lack in the Other—the Other as incomplete, not whole—which in turn takes on a function in the structure once the subject's lack takes its effect. On the other hand, the Other as a place of truth, is made of the signifiers S_1 and S_2, as two, not one, are needed for the subject to address the Other. One signifier represents the subject, which is derived from the materiality of the unconscious, and the second one is its representative in relation to the Other. With it we also stumble upon the truth of the subject. On the one hand, we have the subject as divided, which means separated from the being of the Freudian Thing that belongs to no one, and addressing the Other. On the other hand, we have the Other's desire marked by a lack in the Other. And why could we not say that Lacan's desire becomes manifest in this very equivocation of *e(s)t*? Lacan often used equivocation to respond to the Other. Here Lacan shows us that what separated the subject from its being, with the support of the primary and secondary signifiers S_1 and S_2, now appears as a product of this passage from alienation to separation, namely as the object *a*. The subject's separation is in effect a separation from the object whose loss can only be marked in addressing the Other as desiring. The separation, in which echoes the Freudian Thing, causes a dent in the subject, its division and its mourning. Whatever the lack in the Other, it cannot be patched up by the object *a* either because it does not come from the Other. But in love, as I said last time, it can serve as a gift.

If there is a lack on the side of the subject, there is a lack on the side of the Other. Topologically speaking, the subject and the Other are equivalent and have the same value. But they are not identical either historically or qualitatively and have different functions. In the diagram of separation, the place of the object *a* shows us where S_1 used to be or, as Freud said, where it was, *es war*. That's why separation, in so far as it can be presented retroactively in relation to alienation, can be marked as "one less" or minus one. From the structural perspective the correlation of alienation and separation can be found in the film *The Invention of Lying* as mentioned previously. First, we all tell the truth because we are all the same and, with the support of language believe in the Other. One by one, each subject is happy to tell the truth of his alienation. But, secondly, as a result of a mistake, a division occurs in the subject. Once the subject realises the difference between truth and lie, he can seek happiness again, but this time in the dialectic of truths and lies, by which he sustains his relation with the Other. And if he feels a bit guilty, having acquired a symbolic debt from the Other, he can give happiness to others by telling them stories of God. Following separation, then, does or does not the Other deceive us?

From the start the subject has to accept his powerlessness, his helplessness. The Other, on the other hand, may be as all-powerful as one chooses to believe in. The subject can only accept his position in relation to the object as lost, and therefore in fantasy, once the claim to the object's ownership is renounced. This leads me to say that the terms of the subject's relation to the object a in fantasy and to the desire of the Other, follow the topological terms of internal exclusion. It is not possible to "own" the object a. To be more precise, these terms are to be situated as a relation of neighbourhood as defined by Freud from his earliest work. In other words, what forms part of subjectivity is topologically excluded from the subject, and what is outside the subject belongs to it. The cause of desire, and the jouissance the subject pursues in fantasy, are not the tenants in the subject's house. They are outsiders who appear to belong to the neighbourhood. That's how one could define a foreigner as based on Freud's *Nebenmensch*. The foreigner's abode can be found as internally excluded, and that's what Lacan tells us in the diagram of alienation. The diagram of separation, as proposed by Jacques-Alain Miller, follows from that. The subject's powerlessness and lack in knowledge defines his position with respect to love. Love stems from giving what one does not have, as Lacan said. And given that the starting point is castration and the inexistence of the sexual relation, love would be one of the names of inquiry into the desire of the Other whereby the object a is an effect of castration realised in the passage from alienation to separation. Another name for love is simply this—love wants to be One with what it does not have. Will the lovers find it in the Other's desire? From alienation to separation and back.

The truth, the object in science and in psychoanalysis, and the garrulity of das Ding

In the imaginary circle of Heidegger's reflection on being we can extract a grammatical function in so far as it expresses the place of the object for the subject, namely being seen, being heard, being misunderstood or being-guilty which I will take up later. And what about *being-me* as

Lacan names it in *Seminar XX* (1998b) under the term *m'être*? And yet this extraction does not have anything to do with a symbolic representation as there is no grammar of being. Lacan stresses this point, which appears to me to be more akin to Aristotle's interrogation of being than Heidegger's. Lacan also speaks of being as the master signifier because such a function has been designated to the ontology of being in the history of the West starting with Parmenides. It is a historical fact but I could only confirm it by saying I did not find anything in the ruins of his school in Elea. Perhaps this was the spill from being, almost nothing which points in the direction of love. The same goes for the Paestum and Asclepian academy, which is the same story but in a different place.

What does Lacan bring to our attention when he evokes the mastery of being in opposition to the remainders that led him to speak of love in the same seminar? There are of course the imaginary identifications given the philosopher's concern does not cease to rely on the image. And does not being imply a self-identity in alienation? Is it not the case that being, the *Supreme Being* as cause of all causes or as God, imply that this being is identical to itself? Lacan captured this in the play of the signifiers *moi* and *être*, "me" and "being". And he came up with *m'être*, the master of being and his narcissistic jouissance of being-me. That's what we find in the first part of Shrek. Shrek, the ogre, simply loves being an ogre. But Lacan also speaks of being as real. Is being as real self-identical? He refers to being as the jouissance of the body. What body if not that of the Other, its pains, ecstasy, torture, which cannot be experienced except for delusions? What is the truth of the body of the Other? One of the references for Lacan in the seminar *Encore* is the woman's body in so far as she is "contaminated" by the mother. "Contaminated" implies that there is a trace of the maternal jouissance that the woman carries with her. Lacan does not say she is marked by the mother. Lacan followed this trace when he was led from the desire of the Other to the body of the Other. The body of the Other and the body of the mother appear to be the references that Heidegger's entire corpus revolving around *sein* flinches and never touches upon except in silence. And this silence about the woman includes his love affair, for most of his life, with Hanna. The philosophers do not speak about the body of the woman. This can no doubt become a question for Heideggerian scholars—how Heidegger lied about the woman's body?

Apart from the imaginary and real modalities of being Lacan highlights, there is no symbolic "dimension" of being. Lacan is adamant about it. There is no grammar of being. There is only grammar of the verb "to be". There is a connection between the real and being, already discovered by the ancients, but there is no connection between the grammar of the verb and being. The real, and one need not refer to it as primordial, is already there to the extent it does not support the grammar. If there is a being to which this real can be linked, and in which it is enmeshed, it is the body of the Other. These misunderstandings concerning being, or these mis-beings, converge in Heidegger's reflection on the fragment by Heraclitus. It is not without significance if of all texts Lacan chose the one on *logos*, audaciously, as he says, to translate. It is from the perspective of the audacity of the Lacanian subject, as gliding over the Heideggerian Being, that we can reread the Heracletian fragment that appears to me less obscure than in the ontological light: Listen not to me, when I attempt to touch the being of the body in the reflection that assumes its wholeness, but to the *logos* of enunciation in which speaks the touching of the form. This would be a Lacanian "translation" of the *logos* fragment as displaced from the meaning of Being to the signifier in alienation—a signifier, let's add, that is both meaningless and indeed, Lacan had a name for it, stupid. The displacement of *logos* from the presupposition of meaning to the supposed enunciation was Lacan's gift to Heidegger. We could say that Lacan delivered it in the first place during the driving lesson when the abrupt quake of the imaginary nostalgias sent the philosopher of being to the dizziness of *Dasein*. In this way Lacan introduced the real into the scene of *logos*. In effect, during his encounter with Heidegger's ontology, Lacan translates the truth of *logos* into a semblance that masks the real while at the same time reveals it. In this case the real was the ineffable jouissance of the body of the Other or the body of the Other sex.

For Aristotle, who lived as long after Heraclitus as Freud after Copernicus, being as essence was constitutive of the subject and object in the discourse of science. The supposition of being is what always allowed science to give floor to the object, so to speak. In other words, in science being makes the object speak. It speaks but also, Lacan stresses, it is spoken. The reality in science is constituted by this object, both speaking and spoken, that informs the scientist. The position and value of the object in science is crucial for the scientist's pursuit of knowledge of it, what else? This object in science, which is not the object *a* in psychoanalysis, comes to be treated as self-evident in the research, as the real that knows. Then we speak of evidence as a derivation of the presupposed self-evidence. The object is always rendered present, right there in front of us and our eyes. Here is an observer and here the observed. This is a realism of science, which Lacan translated into a naivety and a fallacy which led him to construct a discourse because there is more to it than just an object of science. What was important for Lacan to stress was that whatever the "realism" of the scientist's approach, it has a direct bearing on his responsibility. And in this case it falls on the object. It is as if the scientist was saying: the object wants to be known, which is so akin to the ethics of a journalist saying, and basing his entire work, on "the public has the right to know". Lacan did not hesitate to say that in the discourse of science the subject is foreclosed. In psychoanalysis, where the object is always lost and where the presence of its absence does not account for human sexuality except for fantasy, it is the subject, one by one, who takes responsibility for its fall. So much so that he can do without the terror of the superego. There is nothing to have to enjoy in assuming a responsibility. Responsibility in psychoanalysis brings us back to the truth of love that arises from different shades of the object's loss. As for the responsibility in the party politics, it appears as not at all remote from the journalist's ethics of a right taken as a duty, where an apology has become tantamount with truth. If in psychoanalysis we get away with impunity for saying the most outrageous things when caught in the crossfire of associations, it is because it always comes as a surprise. Thus accountability in psychoanalysis includes the lack, even two lacks of the subject, and one of the Other. That's why Lacan called the unconscious the true master, because it does not stop and never goes back on itself. If you believe in truth, you also believe in the unconscious.

There is more to be said about the difference between the discourse of the unconscious and of the analyst, but here I am stressing it with respect to the object. The object in psychoanalysis puts us in the closest proximity to the psychoanalytic cause. Lacan brings this difference to our attention in effect of his intervention in the ontology of truth. This object *a* never presents itself other than as missing, displaced, lost or absent. It may be useless for science but without considering it, science's credibility relies on the position of the scientist as a subject. Nothing is self-evident. In fact, the very notion of evidence, as coming from Latin *videre*, "to see", already gives us an indication of the optical conditions and of the drive jouissance of the object gaze at stake. What the loss of the object creates appears as a hollow in the subject's particular experience of sexuality. The discourse arises from it as an existence. Lacan borrowed the signifier from linguistics to support this hollow in the discourse, so that the subject can address the Other in alienation with regard to what the subject does not have. In love, in psychoanalysis called transference, the analyst can be in a position of any signifier as evoked by the subject. It is a perfect start to alienation in analysis because it is an accurate expression of the confusion in the realm of the foreigners which we are. Hence the analyst's position as that of semblance implies ethics and responsibility.

In "proposition of 9 October on the analyst of the school" (1995) in 1967, Lacan evokes the hollow of the object through the terms *désêtre*, *unbeing*, which I already mentioned, and links to what Thomas Aquinas called *sicut palea*, "as dross, chaff" but also "strewn, to strew". Aquinas represented in this way what remains of the object which for the scientist speaks as self-evident. He identified with what was left from the identification with the Other as God. Lacan sometimes used the device of prosopopoeia by letting the object speak. "I, truth, speak" is an example of an object that speaks as lost. Why is Lacan speaking about the dross or chaff if not to refer it to a hollow in which it emerges as a remainder supported by the signifier? As an analyst Lacan was concerned not only with the object *a* that the analyst embodies. He was also concerned with strewing its remains. To spread and to disseminate the object as always lost, and to allow it to speak in the prosopopoeia, may have the effects of causing desire. By speaking to the audience from the position of an analysand, Lacan allowed the object to cause desire, to emerge in those who heard him although often did not understand what he was saying. Sometimes to hear is just enough to awaken desire, while understanding puts it back to sleep. And by speaking of the Other sex he caused women to come in abundance and to hear what he had to say, although sometimes this awakening of desire was accompanied by an element of protest and outrage. That's what truth, when it speaks, if you believe in the unconscious, does.

And he caused most outrage when speaking of the Woman that does not exist. In Italy in the 1970s this shook the foundations of the civilised society, causing shock waves far greater than if he said that God does not exist. One got used to the nonexistence of God because everyone has a complaint about things not going well in love and in war, so it is easy to put it on God's shoulders just in case he existed. But to say the Woman does not exist was too much, and many women, especially feminists, took umbrage at his statement. But Lacan only said it after speaking about the jouissance of the body of the Other sex. And in doing so he stated that it cannot be written—despite the salient efforts of the scientists Masters and Jones—and that the Woman's jouissance cannot be experienced by man, with a few exceptions, but only inferred *a posteriori*. And this rang true, so true in fact that many did not even ponder where Lacan was coming from. But it always struck me that he would not have been able to say this had he not first worked through alienation, separation to have finally given us a formulation of the object *a*. He formulated the object *a* as causing desire and, in this sense, speaking as truth. The truth about the object *a* was the preliminary step for Lacan to take before he spoke about the Woman. The object *a*, being a precondition of the subject's division, paved the way for the reception of Lacan's pronouncement "*La Donna non existe*". That's what the object does, it can cause some outrage and it can awaken desire. In "Science and truth" (2006g), Lacan spoke of the object *a* with the view of it not turning psychoanalysis into science. It didn't. Scientists did not prove as eagerly listened to on the subject of the woman as psychoanalysts, and for a reason. So it was left for the discourse of psychoanalysis to strew the remains of the object *a* in order to cause desire. This object *a* disturbs us, so Lacan spoke from there.

It follows that in analysis, the truth has nothing to say about the truth. The truth only speaks about what causes it, from the lack, namely between the lines, in hints and allusions, as untold on the whole. Over and over again, the famous statement of Lacan that there is no truth about the truth allows us to grasp the disparity between the symbolic and the real of the body. The truth, when speaking, says what she is not. I say "she" because it is feminine, *aletheia* or *la verité*. In English the feminine gender is attributed to women, boats, ships, and cars, to what is mobile, comes and goes. Here is my little fantasy, I propose that in the English language we refer to the truth in the feminine, given she is the vehicle of movement, of coming and going. Is being not-whole, and speaking in fragments and in allusions, the only thing that can be said about the truth?

For Freud the encounter with the real of sexuality led Emma in the direction of *protos pseudos*. It was her first lie, almost as a negation, in the face of jouissance, and one of many examples of the Freudian truth. Truth is authorised to speak by a lie, not just any lie but a lie in the face of the disturbing real. After all the truth is ephemeral, or *e-femereal* which signifies a connection between a woman and the real. The object *a*, being in the place of truth in the hysteric's discourse, has a capacity, and a skill, to divide the subject. At the same time she remains elusive. Is it not the case, as Lacan said, that goddess Artemis, chased by the hounds of Aries, is never to be caught up with? She is never to be found because the truth of man's desire will never lead him to catch the woman as a cause. Which is why he is on the right track. She cannot be caught as the truth of man's desire for a woman fails to lead him to the truth of the love object as it was lost from the start, the flower being a beautiful reminder of the seed. Or is it the goddess of forgetfulness, *Lethe*, who dwells in *aletheia*, truth as veiled in unconcealment? Does such an opposition make the truth unforgettable? In his wonderful book *The Masters of Truth in Archaic Greece* (1996), Detienne even went so far as to speak of *lethe* and *aletheia* as inseparable, making both an integral part of the political system, justice, religious liturgy, and recitation.

For Lacan of the 1960s and 1970s, the analytic truth has the same function as the cause, the object that awakens desire. Truth as cause implicates the object *a*. To follow Lacan further in *Science and Truth*, we stumble upon the Freudian *Wo es war, soll Ich werden*. In the schema of separation we discovered that the place of the object *a* is where the master signifier, S_1, used to be. If you like, the flower is where the seed used to be. If Lacan retranslates Freud's statement, it is on the basis of the relation between the object *a* in separation and the master signifier in alienation: where it was, where the primary signifier was, there I as subject must return. In analysis the subject always returns where it used to be, which is where his future lies. For he never returns to the past. But when I do return, I find there what is lost because the master signifier failed to hold the whole of the subject, and what is internally excluded from it remains unrepresented. This is where Lacan sought jouissance in speech and where he found jouissance as speaking. What is found there, outside the primary signifier and as speaking, unrepresented, belongs to serendipity, a lucky find. This lucky find, Lacan says, belongs to the subject. The subject is constituted through the lucky finds and if one does not find there what one expects, as Schliemann did not at first, one comes back for more. The experience shows that the same happens in the relations between sexes, when what is sought for cannot be found, one comes for more. There is more to the Lacanian subject than the primary signifier that represents it. Jouissance for one as speaking remains unrepresented. The laws of representation are insufficient to isolate jouissance as speaking. Going back, then, always back with the view to progressing, we return to alienation where we find the primary signifier in the place where it always was. It is there from the beginning as the first gift of the Other, the gift of love as speech. This signifier one that has always been there from the start has for its neighbour *das Ding*. This is where Freud situated it and where Lacan takes us. Freud placed it there as mute and dumb. But for Lacan "mute and dumb" did not imply that it does not speak. Lacan had made it speak already in the mid-1950s, and already established a relation between the "mute and dumb", between *das Ding* and truth. Before saying in the 1970s "I always tell the truth because there is no way to say it all", Lacan, already in the 1950s states "I, truth, speak". He had different reasons for making each statement but they are related. For Freud *das Ding* was a mute and a constant part of what he called the "neighbour's complex". He also called it the "perception complex" because we are at the level of perception. The "Thing" is that part of the complex that is always the same, never changes place. The other part was a predicate and Lacan designated it as a signifier because it is a part of the subject's body as marked by the Other. Not all of the subject's body is marked by the representation of language as coming from the Other. For example what Freud called *das Ding* is left unmarked. This mute part Freud isolated in the perception complex in his "Project for a scientific psychology" (1950a [1895]) became the one that Lacan made speak. He made it blabber away as some of Freud's hysterics did, whether under hypnosis or not. No doubt we find in this place the sediments of being of the ancients, and the remains of Schliemann's Troy. But for Lacan it was the real he found, the real that speaks, the delusional jouissance. He later built up on this real by calling this blabber *lalangue*, the presyntactical speech that in alienation becomes subjected to the primary signifier of the Other. The garrulity of the Thing ventriloquizes the subject, making it blabber away without knowing what or who and where. In speech there is for the subject that which does not make sense, what speaks without knowing where it goes, what it says. And if it is left without being returned to, alone, that is to say as "unsymbolised", it returns to the subject, as Lacan said from the start. This was the real Lacan discovered as unsymbolised, namely as that which makes no sense, yet plays a part in the subject. This both mute and blabbing real returns to the subject whenever it is left unmarked. It happens all the time, in neurosis and in psychosis, although with different implication as the belief, or its exclusion, is implicated.

The origin of language and semblance

Lacan made the Thing speak. We can read it in his text "The Freudian thing" (2006c) from 1955. There is also *L'Etourdit* (2001), written in 1973, a text where the garrulity of the Freudian thing is to be read. Is it Lacan who speaks in those texts or is it the Thing speaking? It speaks as truth to which I return as subject, and for which I take responsibility. The subject is expansionist. It expands by saying more what it does not know it is talking about, and then takes responsibility for the remainder and its causal effects, whether represented or not. It is an unusual type of responsibility, and not the one you find in the speeches of politicians when they don't know what they are talking about while insisting they do. The superego insists. But the object *a* does not insist, it disturbs and wrong-foots. The subject takes his responsibility for his symptom because its insistence derives from the insistence of the garrulous real as unknown in the subject's speech, as the blabber of the Thing.

We can now say that the object *a* that appears in the place where the S_1 used to be, only emerges as an effect of some part of the subject being left unsymbolised. This object *a* is in a sense a refined remainder and reminder of *das Ding*. Lacan made the Thing speak but he also allowed the object to speak to awaken desire. *Das Ding*, with its overtones to subject's prehistory and to maternal jouissance that contaminates women, is not the same as the object *a*. We can also say that the unforgetfulness in truth, or the *lethe* in *aletheia* that in revelation conceals, can only be found on the way back to *das Ding*, which is beyond alienation. I am trying to approach the elusive and allusive object *a* from the perspective of the Freudian *das Ding*. Perhaps it is not possible to have a grasp of the object *a* without the blabber of *das Ding*. What Lacan highlighted in relation to object *a* he nevertheless invented, is that the connection between truth and being arises solely in the passage from *das Ding* to the object, that causes the subject's desire, and back. The status of the object presented in this way decides the status of psychoanalysis in relation to science.

And this leaves me with the question of the origin of language. Is it a question? It is certainly not on the cards for Lacan. But he does confront those for whom it is. When Heidegger asks about the meaning of being and about the ontological origin of *logos*, is he asking about language? Has this question not been already posed by the science of linguistics? If psychoanalysis was a science what would it be a science of? Despite his unquestionable adherence to the laws of science of his time, it was Freud himself who put the fundamental premises of science into question. And we recall his assertion, which everyday practice confirms, that the unconscious knows no contradictions, no linearity of time. Lacan turned our attention to the real, and to the object *a* as its remainder, saying there is no science of the real which can only be said in relation to the unconscious. From it, like from the object (oral, anal, gaze, and voice) that chooses its subject, arises the position of the subject as included in the supposition of the signifier. Responsibility results from this. In other words, the subject, and the symptom with it, remain implicated in the pursuits and discoveries. In psychoanalysis the question of genesis of language does not arise because the position from which it would arise is already supposed by the signifier connected to the desire of the Other. To want to know, is already a response to that desire. The question of origin as relative to the psychoanalytical knowledge or of what I can know, want to know, do not want to know, as Lacan remarked in *Television* (1990), interweaves the signifier as material cause and the supposition of this signifier. Hence the aim of the pursuit of knowledge can already be found at the start under such confusing and metaphorical terms as, say the *Selfish Gene*, which is the title of a Dawkins' book.

What does Lacan say when he states at the beginning of his interview with Miller that "I always tell the truth, there is no way to say it all"? He says the same thing he said to Beoufret: tell me the truth of what Heidegger said to you. Because what he said to you is for your ears alone. This is where desire is passed, where it crosses between the subject and the one who is in the position of the Other. So what is said in this passage? This indeed appears to us to be the crux of the matter. In what is said there is the unsaid, the impossible to say. Which is why Lacan chose the story of Artemis to illustrate the pursuit of truth. There is no way for Artemis to be caught naked by the hounds of the science before she turns into a tree. And this is also how the genius of Magritte allowed us to see what he perceived as the woman's place in man's eyes, namely between his legs. "There is no way to say it all", Lacan concludes. Say only what is always left to be said. If there ever was a project of a logic of completeness, to which Heidegger would doubtless bear witness, it would turn into a "logic of incompleteness" because it revolves around the Other's desire. What Lacan is saying to us when he constructs his discourse is that in analysis the subject can be expected to vacate the place of truth to allow the object *a* to occupy it. By that time the divided subject has moved to the place of the Other, just vacated by the master signifier, which accounts for the analyst's discourse I will take up later. Only in the analyst's discourse does the object become dominant while the place of truth is occupied by knowledge.

From the psychoanalytical point of view the project of the "human sciences" is therefore as good as collapsed from the start as it excludes any signs of the sexual real that trips the subject into believing that the semblance and the real are one and the same. What Lacan called the foreclosure of the subject in the discourse of science remains on a par with the foreclosure of the object *a* as the cause of its division and desire. Lacan doubtless read and translated, which is where I started, Heidegger's text as a "thing" speaking, blabbing away. And in reading what he has to say Lacan sieved the chaff from the grain, the said from the unsaid. This is not how Heidegger would have wanted to read Heraclitus whom Lacan brought out from the ontological obscurity to the light of language. In effect, Lacan's reading pierced the bubble of infatuation with the being of *logos*. In this sense, his "Science and truth" (2006g) should be read not only as a supplement to any metaphysics but as a thorn to any theo-ontological project whatsoever. If psychoanalysis has any value it is because it is not concerned with the magnitude of the claims of an author, and only offers a response and an account, however ephemeral its truth, of the impact of language on the body. And it can only attempt to do so by going back to where it occurred, to read it literally. Lacan was very precise about it. Psychoanalysis is unable to correct the mistake or to find the origin of origins, but only to make the untouched, be it chaff or else, resonate for the subject. There would be no effect for the subject emerging from this reprogressive experience at the gist of which lies the failed encounter between language and body, if it was not for the truth speaking. But truth speaks and speaking lies. For this reason Lacan invented *parlêtre*, the "speakingbeing", as he was concerned with the real sediments of the said, of what in analysis remains of the said, what does not deceive.

CHAPTER FOUR

The signifier, the letter, the voice, and the subject of certainty

The letter and the experience of satisfaction

There is a signifier and there is a letter. Lacan kept them close. But as he advanced his teaching, with a growing interest in writing, they grew more apart. Early on, the signifier and the letter were close allies. If the signifier is a building block of the unconscious and constitutes the principle of difference in it, the letter is what offers a material support. The letter is the materiality of language, its reality if this term denotes things that exist. Things exist because symbols exist representing the subject as existing for another symbol. In the course of symbolisation the subject follows the truth effects of his speech. Following from this Lacan linked the truth as speaking to the material cause. But what does materiality signify here? It implies that we do things with language, make anagrams, metaphors, metonymies, synecdoches, and so on. They all have a particular place for Lacan in his teaching. If the unconscious is structured like a language, as Lacan teaches us, the formations of the unconscious are essentially formations of language. One can do things with the signifiers by producing meaning effects and by making words from words because each act of this kind draws on the materiality of the letter. Apart from the material support given to the production of signifiers, Lacan also speaks of the materiality of discourse in a given community of speaking subjects. For Lacan the discourse is the materiality of the social bond, as it provides points of reference and meanings that operate within a group of language users.

From the start Lacan insists that desire must be read to the letter. What does this mean? It means that the subject's reading of desire reaches to aim at the point of unequivocality. When the desire is read, when the unconscious interprets it, because it is not the analyst or analysand who interprets, as Jacques-Alain Miller reminded us, but the unconscious, then this reading occurs within the framework of equivocation and disparity between saying and meaning, the signifier and the signified effects of meaning. The signifier produces meaning effects because structurally the context and neighbourhood of the signifiers produces distinct meaning effects. And this is what Lacan says from the start. But to read desire literally, on which Lacan insists, suggests that we engage in a reading aiming at the letter of desire, its unequivocality. This would be the point where there is no longer disparity between the signifier and the signified but where the symbolic and the real at stake come into some form of entanglement, like a knot, which is the letter, the knotting of the real and the symbolic. Early on in his teaching Lacan speaks about the "letter of law". A letter signifies unequivocality, that there is an agreement between what is said and meant. Early on Lacan considered desire as depending on the law of the signifier. In fact he spoke about the law of desire. When Lacan speaks about desire (e.g., desire of the mother) its existence depends on it being passed through the Name-of-the-Father, which is the signifier of law. It is almost like a stamp, a symbolic validation of what otherwise pertains to the real without law. Hence in that period of Lacan's teaching, the "letter of law" is supposed to capture the law in an unequivocal way so that there is no room for interpretation or ambiguity. What the lawyers work so hard on is how to eliminate any margin, however small, for interpretation. They themselves do this believing in the law of unequivocality with no room for the subtlest innuendos of language. It is the other way round in psychoanalysis. The psychoanalytic clinic is the space for an experience of speech where the saying and meaning are in a constant play of oppositions and dissymmetry, which is contrary to the theories of communication Lacan took up early on. This creative play of difference between saying and meaning drives the subject's associations at least up to the point when, as Lacan says, we should aim at the literality of desire.

Despite the fact that in the analytic practice there is always room for the interpretation of the unconscious, in both senses of the genitive, and for ambiguity and equivocation, we nevertheless aim at the real of discourse. So unlike in the courtroom, the analytic experience consists in the subject being displaced by signifying equivocations while following desire to the letter. This aim primarily emerges from the analytic experience where the subject aims at the real embedded in the materiality of the unconscious and in the unequivocality of the symbolic. The letter of desire thus combines the real and the symbolic.

But Lacan does not aim at one meaning of desire, or at one meaning at all, when he speaks of taking desire to the letter. What is the One Lacan aims at, and of which he says in his later teaching that it exists, that there such a thing as, or something of, the One?

This insistence of Lacan on the literality of desire, and on the relation between the real and the symbolic, led Lacan to different formulations of the letter. In his later teaching Lacan was increasingly preoccupied with the letter in writing. In this way, he opposed the signifier as the motor of equivocation in relation to the desire of the Other, to the letter as self-referential. Whereas the signifier derives its support from the Other as a place of signification, the letter can be written without reference to the Other and to the logic of the signifier. The letter is self-referential and self-identical reducing the meaning effects to an inscription. In writing the utterance is reduced to univocality. As such the letter is meaningless. The letters a, A, S are of course meaningful to students of Lacan but other than that they are meaningless.

Lacan also spoke of the love letter that can be sent or received or lost. This shows, among other things, that the letter can have several meanings and that when we speak of the letter of love there is some uncertainty whether this refers to the law or to love, or to the law of love and what this means, or to love poetry. In the end it was Lacan's poem on love where he read love to the letter. In this sense he produced a new twist to love—reading love to the letter, which he pursued in the seminar *Encore* (1998b). Lacan also makes a reference to the letter as "litter" or as that which is ultimately discarded as superfluous because it does not have the same impact on the body as the signifier, closing rather than opening it. I do not propose to exhaust the ways in which Lacan referred to the letter in his later teaching but want now to move on to the letter of Freud, more precisely to some fragments of his "Project for a scientific psychology" (1950a [1895]).

In it Freud advances a view concerning the primary satisfaction in relation to the object. His starting point is the mental apparatus that, let's remind ourselves was constructed around the fundamental fault, which therefore does not work, and in contrast to which every diagram and schema of the mind is merely a *model*. Freud tells us in it that the subject's primary experience of satisfaction is essentially a hallucinatory experience. It tries to recapture the original object that is always lost. In my reading of the "Project for a scientific psychology", I was led to a conclusion that for Freud the primary experience of satisfaction, which is real in the sense that it is a failed attempt to capture what is lost, is an experience of the letter. The "experience of satisfaction", *Befriedigungserlebnis*, as hallucinatory is evoked in the subject's experience of speech where the signifier resonates as a representation of the lost object. In the face of it, which discerns the being of need, the demand from the Other facilitates for the subject to enter the field of language which is material in so far as it precedes subject's entry to it. It is how Lacan approached it. In accordance with Freud, the satisfaction of need will therefore be always a hallucinatory satisfaction, as the subject's entry to language through demand, will always hallucinate over the lost object. Entry to desire, in turn, which is reading the Other's desire to the letter, occurs with some satisfaction, in psychoanalysis called jouissance, as subtracted. To access the Other's desire is only possible when jouissance of need has been subtracted, which is why Lacan said that jouissance does not signify love, to which I will come back later. It does not signify desire either. Reading desire to the letter carries with it what Lacan was interested in, namely the hallucination in speech, jouissance as speaking. In this sense the letter remains the shadow of the signifier. In his text on "Mourning and melancholia" (1917e [1915]). Freud spoke of the shadow of the object. But here we can speak of the letter as the shadow of the signifier in the sense in which Lacan says that the materiality of the letter pre-exists the subject's entry to the field of the signifier and speech.

In view of this, Lacan's effort to read desire literally brings us closer to the entanglement of the real and the symbolic I have just spoken about. The interpretative equivocation of desire leads in the direction of the signifier of the lack in the Other. Desire, according to Freud, is an experience of the symbol, namely a representation. The other direction for reading desire, not opposite but I would say parallel and correlative, namely reading it to the letter, implies that the real aimed at is entangled with the symbolic in the sense of the materiality of language. Both directions, the one concerning the lack and the inconsistency of the Other, and the one aiming at the reading desire to the letter, lead us to say that, the letter involves what in the unconscious knowledge is irretrievable, and what, at the same time, contributes to the formation of the subject's symptom as primary defence. And this point of intersection forms a point of support for Lacan's later teaching.

What is not the signifier?

When speaking in the 1970s about the letter in writing, and especially in Joyce, Lacan will refer to an operation whereby jouissance is fixed by the letter. This compound of the symbolic and jouissance allowed Lacan to speak about the *sinthome* as a writing that stabilises the real of the subject. In a sense we encounter the letter, it is flanked by two phases of Lacan's teaching. First, it is what takes him back to Freud, and in particular to the *Entwurf*, and second, his later formulation of the letter in writing. Freud situated representations at the level of primary processes, responsible for a formation and reproduction of *memoria*. This would be the signifier in its raw, namely nonsensical primacy, a signifier without quality or, as Lacan will say, a signifier without a signified. The qualification or *quality* emerges as an effect not as a cause. And it is in this that Lacan radically differs from the theories of communication and semantics, where sign and meaning are always in a fruitful correspondence to each other. To follow through Freud's findings in the "Project for a scientific psychology" (1950a [1895]), quality, which is a separate category to quantity, is determined following an encounter with the real, which for Freud is an experience of the *Nebenmensch*, the neighbour. This translation does not reflect adequately the overwhelming character of the presence of the Other (A). It is the case of "lost in translation". In the encounter with the *Nebenmensch*, the subject is pushed out from the paths of the pleasure principle. There is a split there and as a result, Freud tells us at the end, there emerges a predicate or a variable, on the one hand, and the permanent component Freud designated as *das Ding*, on the other. The Thing, were it only some raw libido, a pure jouissance of the living organism as such, but Lacan made it speak, and I have already touched upon the garrulity of *das Ding* previously. This invariable has no quality as such because it has no meaning as such. It is made of the unqualified real that does not change place and forms according to Lacan the kernel of the experience of speech of the subject without being accessible to him. The experience of the real as "lost in translation" appears therefore as having the characteristics of Freud's *Befriedigungserlebnis*. The quality of this experience is yet to be determined. It has to do with the category of judgement that enables the neurotic subject to qualify or predicate his experience of the other component, the mute *das Ding*. This was sufficient for Lacan to subsequently speak of the quality of neurosis on the basis of the relation to *das Ding*.

These two slopes of the analytic experience correspond to what we customarily call the clinic of the signifier as the law of desire in the early Lacan, and the clinic of the real called jouissance in the later Lacan. He will then develop, starting with the mirror stage, the dimension of the imaginary as based on the aggressive rivalry with the other who always occupies my place and is always happier, more successful, richer, more handsome, more beautiful, and so on. This imaginary, which Freud linked to the death drive in his introduction to narcissism, will be linked for Lacan not only to the symbolic but, more importantly, to the real. At this point, which is around his *Seminar VII The Ethics of Psychoanalysis* (1992), Lacan is now endowed with the necessary terms and registers to take up Freud's mental apparatus. These terms, as forming a tripartite structure and the basis of his topology, are the symbolic, the real and the imaginary. These terms form the coordinates that allow us to find the connection between Freud and Lacan's later teaching. As we know, in the beginning Lacan favoured the symbolic and often reproached the post-Freudians for confusing the symbolic with the imaginary in their formulations concerning the ego. This was no surprise as for Lacan the ego forms the pivotal part of the imaginary. What Lacan stressed with regard to the pleasure principle, responsible for the passage between the signifiers is the fundamental disjunction between the signifier and jouissance. For Freud this disjunction formed his Oedipus complex as "complex" could be regarded as a predecessor of structure. This disjunction thus allows us to speak with Lacan of a structure of the signifier as that in which not everything is a signifier. Jacques-Alain Miller has been stressing this disjunction for a long time now. A signifier, any signifier, is structured in such a way that not everything in it is signifier. To redefine the letter, the Lacanian letter in this way, would be to say that not everything entangled with it has a value of the symbolic. And it is with this "not everything in the structure is signifier" that

Lacan insists, especially that it concerns the clinic, on the primacy of the signifier as animating the function of speech. On the one hand, we have the primacy of the signifier as designating not everything in it has the value of the signifier and, on the other hand, we have a detotalisation of the signifier, in the sense Jacques-Alain Miller gives to it, namely by subtracting a pound of flesh from what in the structure is not signifier. And this allows us to say that primacy and totality are not one and the same thing.

This, in short, is a recapitulation of Freud's early experience formulated in the "Project for a scientific psychology" (1950a [1895]), where the signifier, albeit he says neurone, is without quality precisely because its structure, and its function, is entangled in the network of tracks and passages or places. These do not have as a whole the structure of the signifier but include breaking through, getting across or around the empty place of the lost object, and the libidinal *quantum*, in the course of which quality is given at another level. As we know, Freud's view is dynamic and libidinal rather than mechanist's as was common among scientists of his time. Secondly, the statement "not everything in the structure of the signifier is signifier" highlights the opposition of the signifier/signified that Lacan formulated on the basis of Freud's difference between quantity and quality, and Saussure's sign. Again, another form of recapitulation of the Freudian experience finds its expression in the algorithm as a primacy of the bar. Based on this, Lacan will emphasise that the ciphering/deciphering of the unconscious, in accordance with the pleasure principle, is based on the mechanism of negation. The subject's "no" in the statement "this is not my mother" is in this sense what gives rise to meaning ("this is not A" as distinct to "I don't want to speak about A"). The subject says "no" at the very moment when faced with the meaning effect or a particular quality. Through this qualification as judgement, negation is implemented.

Negation is implemented through qualification, that is to say it is qualified through judgement. This is Freud's founding step of the clinic of neurosis. When a session ends on a cut, this has to do with quality, that is to say, the cut punctuates the disjunction between the signifier and the judgement of quality. What is left is what in its structure of the signifier is not signifier. A different quality is called for, and the repetitive action that forms part of the symptom can be requalified, given a new meaning. And this would allow us to say that a qualification of the analyst—if there is such a thing as a qualified analyst—has to do with the maintenance of the disjunction between the signifier and jouissance, which he supports. This brings me to Freud's representation, *Vorstellung*, that Lacan highlighted in every way he could because this allowed him to demonstrate what he meant by the symbolic register, namely the dyad of the signifiers $S_1 - S_2$. Lacan's emphasis is on the fact that for Freud *Vorstellung* remains detached from the philosophical tradition and appears as without meaning. It is therefore close to the signifier. But the signifier is not all there is to the symbolic. Reading desire to the letter takes us to the neighbourhood of the primary signifier(s) S_1, the *Es* One, and directs us to the one that represents it. Lacan called it the representational representative, *Vorstellung representäntz*, pointing to the second level in the unconscious structured like a language. You could say that the *representäntz* acts as an ambassador, representing the original repressed representation in the unconscious. Or that it stands for a solicitor representing the client. To whom if not to another symbolic agent, namely the barrister. In his definition of the signifier as representing the signifier for another signifier Lacan stresses that secondary level of representation. The dialectic between them determines the quality of subject's identifications.

The Pope, the letter, and the birth of interpretation

And yet it has to be said that at the time of "The instance of the letter in the unconscious" (2006e), Lacan does not speak of the subject's division in terms of disjunction between the signifier and the signified. The signified, as that which operates in the formulae of metaphor and metonymy, is a form of qualification. A qualification of what? Of that which is essentially unqualifiable but which is supposed in the message, namely knowledge. Quality or judgement, constituting what in the cut is unqualifiable, leads to a supposition of what in the unqualifiable *via* the analyst is nevertheless supposable as unconscious knowledge. We are here in the framework of Lacan's formula of transference that is of double use to me here. Firstly, because the formula indicates that the subject's supposition includes the "x", the unqualifiable signified, although represented by the signifier. In the subject's relation to the analyst, the unknown meaning of the Other's desire is brought into the love relation. It is that element Lacan designates on his graph of desire as s (A), the signified of the Other. What is the signified of the Other if not what is represented but without quality as the unknown in the message passed to the subject from the Other? Lacan says that it is what *he does not know*. The Other does not know which does not prevent the subject, on the contrary, from supposing a subject that has the knowledge *as unknown* that comes from the Other and which Lacan called s (A). By what is the subject supposed if not by another one? The structure of transference as supposition of knowledge can be found by and large in the lower part of the graph of desire. The s (A) carries what the Other does not know but what nevertheless forms the signification of the message that gives the subject its place. This signified should thus be linked to the Freudian experience of *Nebenmensch*. It is love at first sight, albeit of unknown quality. Lacan provided us with the formulation of transference, first combining then isolating in it, love and knowledge. The supposition of knowledge as an articulation of love evokes the Lacanian letter, the love letter, to be precise. But in the second instance, the formula of transference appears of use to us at this juncture because it is crucial in situating the difference between psychoanalysis and science with regard to knowledge, which is where I am going. Both have a relation to knowledge but only in analysis can its supposition be directed, let's say addressed, to the subject. I have already mentioned the reason for this. It comes from the paradox that although the Other does not know it is not without the Other that this knowledge is supposed. Whom does a scientist address then?

As we know, in his elaborations of language Lacan borrowed some material from modern linguistics, chiefly from Saussure (1983) and Jacobson (1987). There are other, less known references in this respect, too. As a representative of science, linguistics, as well as philosophy of language, has a particular aim. This aim of the science of language, generally speaking, appears to be the knowledge of language. If it was the knowledge of the subject, then it would be a different matter. When a plane malfunctions while airborne, the knowledge of the mechanics of the plane is not of as much use as on the ground. But the knowledge of language aimed at by science makes as much room for its articulation as when it is stationary and not in use. In short, what language is to science, falling is to psychoanalysis. It is the different modes of subject's fall that make supposition of knowledge possible. And this allows us to distinguish the experience of language as a knowledge of the symptom from the meaning as operating in science.

The connection with modern linguistics was not the only one for Lacan to consider and borrow from in his theory of the letter. Lacan was aware of the medieval and pre-Cartesian tradition that till today remains paradigmatic of making a decisive distinction between modalities of literary expression and vocal articulation. And this took me well beyond the courtly poetry in which these distinctions culminate. When the grammarians and poets of the Middle Ages begin to speak of interpretation, this marks a separation between the written and the spoken. Augustine stands out as the one who isolates the inner *vox* as it emerges from the backdrop of textuality of the scriptures (Leff, 1959). This process already starts to take its weight around the fourth century and runs all the way to the tenth and eleventh centuries with the culmination on the troubadour songs. An important event takes place in the eleventh century in Germany that will serve well to illustrate the separation of the written and the spoken. At that time, King Henry IV had a long standing issue with the Pope about episcopal investiture. The Pope had eventually come to the decision of banning the king while relying partly on the hostilities of the Saxon magnates towards Henry. The king managed to redeem himself through a show of remorse which led to the lifting of the ban but the new king was elected by his Saxon enemies. Then the ban was renewed and the hostilities and conflicts escalated. Up to this point the Pope made his power felt through written edicts coming either directly from his holiness or from his legate, today we would say ambassador, called Odo of Ostia. Since the written edicts did not produce the expected effect of putting the end to the conflict both internally and with papacy, it was decided that the matter would be solved not by force of the written law but by debate. A medieval agora took place involving officials, bishops, royals, including Odo himself. The literality, and ineffectiveness, of the edict opened the way for a different end, *terminaretur libris*, and interpretation was born. More precisely a conversation was born. Both sides of the debate were represented by the scholars, *literati*. All this was of course to contest the written law and do justice. The conversation was not without precedence as it was around that time when public debates between Catholics and Cathars were taking place in Languedoc. After the debate, Odo wrote a report to quell the view that the royals gained the upper hand. The debate continued about the interpretation of the law (e.g., whether anyone banned or charged with a crime should or not have his or her *status quo ante* restored before answering to the charges). Odo was at pains to provide arguments that would bend interpretation to the meaning of the original edicts.

From the start interpretation is established in relation to the letter of the law and works in the opposite direction to the unequivocality. In fact, the arrival of interpretation facilitates the conditions for an emergence of speech and equivocation. Whether written by Odo in his report or not, interpretation supports the disjunction between the law of *gramma* and the signifier. In this sense interpretation supports the production of sense that already has as its basis the unconscious structured like a language.

This is what happens in analysis. The subject goes to analysis with a letter he presents to the analyst and states that it defines his being, his love life, his work, his entire world. And the analyst says: "Tell me what's in it …". What follows is the interpretation of the letter of the unconscious. In the course of the subject's articulations supported by the analyst's interventions, silent or not, another sense emerges. This shift is crucial in the work of and with the symptom, as the disjunction between the signifier and the jouissance knotted in the letter is punctuated.

It is in opposition to the written law of the Pope's letter, that the production of meaning led to the emergence of another quality in the passionate exchanges of the participants, namely the voice, and the disputes of the *literati*, the scholars and men of letters alike, were heard at that level. It was already the case for Augustine centuries earlier that the truth appeared as a spoken one. For Augustine the truth is neither in Hebrew nor in Latin nor in Greek, but rather assumes a value of an intimation, that is to say opens a *dit-mension* of vocal articulation (Leff, 1959). The experience of truth is on the side of love where the search for certainty comes over and above the search for reality. And this is where Lacan was aiming at, namely certainty. What the already pre-Cartesian passions show us is that truth can only be guaranteed as heard and as pertaining to a love of knowledge.

Augustine's voice and Lacan's desire

It does not go without saying that for Lacan speech is not only a passion that comes to challenge the unbearable prejudice and injustice of the letter. It is above all the sole medium and instrument of analysis. The speech and the signifier, not without jouissance, make the air and the substance of the analytic process. Lacan had to state the obvious nevertheless, and he did so especially at the time when he had to continue to challenge the easy reliance on the power of writing as well as the establishment of the post-Freudians. It was his passion to speak the truth as not whole, as not wholly, as not all ideal and as real, to the other, that led him back to Freud and then to new formulations in the field of psychoanalysis.

Augustine had a term for love of knowledge, *amor studentium*, and it concerned the object of love in that which the subject wants to know. This transference to the subject of knowledge was not then without the object of love. We can find in it an expression of desire to know, which Freud was so keen to evoke in a generalised way in the era of science. He thus echoed in this desire to know Aristotle's assumption about the drive to know. Augustine takes it up after Aristotle in his exceptional piece of work *The Trinity* (1991) where he lays foundations to any science of language. Augustine ponders about love of knowledge by taking up a random signifier, say *temetum*, and asks: how does one come to love knowledge if it has no meaning? How to love a signifier *temetum* if it does not mean anything? And he concludes that one cannot love what is unknown. But, he adds, that if one were to love such a name after all, would it not imply that we also love any meaning it may carry with it? What does this love of knowledge consist in? It consists in, it seems to me, the subject supposed to know as Lacan's formula of love in psychoanalysis. It therefore involves not only love as a love of an object, but also a desire to know and therefore the subject of knowledge. Is not love of a signifier also a love of the one whose desire, whatever its particular meaning, is implied? And could we not approach this question by opposing love of knowledge to another tradition that developed in more recent centuries? We could oppose love of knowledge to the tradition that seems nearest, most *Nebenmenschly*, to Lacan's early pursuits, namely that of psychiatry and linguistics. Both psychiatry and linguistics as discourses of science, separated and joined by the genitive *of*, deserve to be uttered in one breath here as they focus on the certainties and prescriptions of knowledge of love and of language respectively. The question is whether their value is the same on the ground as in the sky.

Augustine was one of the first ones who pointed to the difference between the written, associated with knowledge, and the spoken as an indication of the unknown. He did this by isolating the voice as representing the real of the body and, on the other, as *memoria* of a particular image of the body, image in the Freudian sense of *Bildung*.

<u>vox</u>
verbum

If Lacan insists on the primacy of the signifier in his teaching, it is because he insists on the primacy of articulation supported by the materiality of language but opposed to the letter as Augustinian *verbum*. Articulation touches on the body, and it is in this way that Freud articulated his earliest work on hysteria when he spoke about fantasies made up of things which are heard. I am referring to his Draft L of 2nd May 1897 (1950a [1887–1902]). Freud speaks there of the servant girls who are always left outside the main events of the house and like to eavesdrop and overhear what is being said inside the room. What is heard is the signifier in so far as it touches on the body of *memoria* which is simply the unconscious. Freud points out in this way to the topology of outside/inside, which is also how we find inscribed the social dimension, for example in Chinese paintings. We can see there that the depiction of erotic scenes at the front of the painting is accompanied by the presence of others lurking behind the screens. This dimension of the *Nebenmensch* appears as already present in the thought of Augustine when he speaks of the relation between the voice and the Word. According to Augustine's initial observation (*The Trinity*, 1991) the voice touches on the *verbum*, and these correspond to two modes of temporality, namely *attentio* and *memoria*. To these he adds *anticipatio*. Those three, *attentio, memoria* and *anticipatio* constitute a tripartite structure of the Augustinian subject. And what he brings to our attention is what Freud formulates in his *Entwurf* as the libidinal investment of the memory of an object. This investment, more commonly known as cathexis, which at all times seems to be sustained equally and at a certain minimum—and which Freud calls "attention"—produces a satisfaction in relation to the object that is not real but imaginary. The anticipation of pleasure directly depends on the degree of suspension of satisfaction, which is how the pleasure principle and the reality principle intersect according to Freud. The object may be imaginary but the satisfaction, the jouissance in the failure to reclaim it, is real. It is real because fantasy always fails in the real although not as fantasy. The real makes its presence as a result of this failure. Language plays tricks on us, revealing between the lines that it is not only made of the symbolic terms or that not everything in the structure of the signifier is signifier.

This tripartite structure of the subject will subsequently lead us to Lacan's logical time, and to making a step that breaks the limit imposed by the meaning and by the law of grammar. Any *parapraxis* serves as an example of law breaking, albeit the reverse is not the case. What kind of satisfaction is produced in relation to the imaginary object? It is a satisfaction of understanding. Understanding always concerns meaning and the fixation of meaning that in analysis has adverse effects, bringing the subject back to the letter with which he started. To address the repetition outside meaning and to move beyond the patterns of love relationships, the question "What does it mean?" has been suspended. Understanding only sets the imaginary in place and no more than that. Of course it is important we do not try to eliminate the imaginary from analysis but in the analytic process the imaginary is not the aim and not even a means. It produces a meaning delusion that is akin to Freud's hallucinatory satisfaction in the face of the lost object.

The passion of speech

The Augustinian algorithm *vox/verbum* gives us an inkling of a relation between the signifier and the letter, and of the value of this relation (Vollrath, 1991). It is a predecessor of the Saussurean algorithm that was for Lacan the point of departure. For Augustine this relation between the voice and the *verbum* is not without links to the name of God that was supposed to serve as a universal paradigm of the relation with the other. Lacan's term the Name-of-the-Father has a more specific place in the structure. The Name-of-the-Father is an operator, a special signifying operator regulating jouissance by enabling the signifying chain to unfold and its elements to form associative connections with one another which can produce new and surprising meanings in accordance with the pleasure principle. The Name-of-the-Father is therefore a structural element, a guarantor of neurosis and perversion but foreclosed in psychosis. In the Augustinian sense, a name is an articulated signifier. That is to say, the name is linked to an auditory impression of the voice. In this sense the name of God has to be pronounced, uttered by way of calling which involves saying and singing. The repetitive character of the vocal calling and naming, which supports prayer, can produce a hallucinatory effect that interested Lacan in the discourse. In the Augustinian sense the voice has a value of the signifier, as in praising and calling the name of God, the voice is the medium, just as speech is the medium in analysis. In effect, the voice carries the Augustinian subject as the one that addresses the other that does not speak back. That's the connection and disconnection between Augustine and Lacan.

In psychoanalysis the voice has a different value than it had for Augustine. Lacan does not tell us much about the voice. He mentions it twice or thrice in *Seminar XI* (1977) but we do not hear of it more than that. For Lacan the voice is an object in the economy of desire. He marked it with the letter "*a*", the object *a*, to designate its separateness and antinomy from other elements like the signifier and the signified. This is the novelty. Lacan's voice is not a substance or a materiality in the sense in which language and the unconscious are. The voice is aphonic and does not belong to the order of material sonority. Voice as object is both lost and imaginarised as refound as silence, hence the italicisation of the letter *a*. It is therefore separated from the Other which is where it comes from. The voice as object lost can nevertheless be an indication of a prohibition or of an order, and in this sense can support the fantasy of being instructed and told what to do. From the Lacanian perspective the voice as object lost can be found in the Gregorian chants where what is heard is a modulation of silence with the voice lost in the midst and in the loop that this singing circumscribes. In psychosis the voice can be invasive and persecutory as it does not support the belief of serving as a message to/from the Other but presents itself *as* the Other. Lacanian voice in the strict sense of the voice object is therefore not the voice in speech and does not belong to speaking.

For Augustine the voice is not anybody's voice or a universal voice like for Kant (Leff, 1959). At the beginning it is rather the voice of the Other, which comes from God and which Augustine marks as written down in the laws of Moses. Throughout his *Confessions* (1961), but more specifically in *Book XI*, he expresses a desire to hear and to listen to the voice of the Other, which in Lacanian terms, is constitutive of the fantasy and has to do with the desire to know, to hear the Other speak and, therefore, love. Love of knowledge is one of the modalities of love. Lacan read *The Trinity* around 1953, four years before writing "The instance of the letter in the unconscious".

In the voice of the other we have an articulation and what is not articulated, what remains silent in the body. Then there is the name. To pronounce it implies making it resonate, inscribing it in the body as a letter. The name, as Lacan will say in 1963 in the seminar *The Names-of-the-Father* (2013a), is subject to reading and this reading does not go without saying, namely it is read neither in Hebrew nor in Greek nor in Latin. In short, the name is inscribed in accordance with the signifying logic that is not the same as meaning and grammar. Meaning and grammar are what linguists and philosophers of language refer to when they put desire in conformity with the law. This is precisely what we come to learn from modern theoreticians of language like Austin, Searle, Henson or Cavell. It is meaning as an effect of the signifier that becomes the starting point of orientation in their research into the knowledge of language. Lacan proposed an inquiry into the language of knowledge or language of the symptom formed between the lines of the unconscious logic in effect of anxiety and of the subject falling from the sky whether it is that of the early Church fathers or of the airplane. I will come back to this.

But where does the Augustine's passion for the voice come from if not from the dialectic of the written that conceals the prohibition to speak, to utter? How many times do the neurotic subjects in analysis come to the point of saying what they were not allowed to say, indeed were forbidden to speak about, the family romance, the taboos, the secrets no one must know about? The prohibition to pronounce the name of God was marked by the use of consonants, JHV, that are unpronounceable without vowels. Augustine makes the voice into an agent of articulation that is detached from the written. Writing cannot be said without introducing us to the order of the signifier. In this way we can read it, which is what Freud pointed out already in his text on *Aphasia*. So, when the voice becomes detached from the letter, when you subtract *vox* from *verbum*, you have a pure sign, something which is essentially unqualifiable and unsayable. This is what Plato says in *Phaedrus* (1973), through Socrates who never writes, that the written word says the same thing forever. That's why in the early days of Christianity it was important to write it. Writing was an assurance of eternity because the letter was tantamount with unequivocality. Plato, or Socrates in *Phaedrus* (1973), accuses Phaedrus of promoting writing as a way of promoting forgetfulness through deletion of memory. It is a powerful accusation. But Socrates gives the signifier to Lacan, starting the analytic process and paving the way for the blabbing of the unconscious. It is back from *logos* to *legein* where the realm of the signifier as acoustic image reigns. Of course the Socratic method of inquiry is not a blabber in analysis, but Socrates does aim to wrong-foot his interlocutor to bring out contradictions, and that was a good start. When in the beginning of analysis the analysand brings a letter to his analyst asking him tell me what it means, it is not for the latter to inquire about the contents of the envelope. It will soon transpire that the envelope in question merely represents what Lacan called "the formal envelope of the symptom", a symbolic dimension of the symptom, which is yet to show us what material, in his deciphering and reading of it, the subject is made of. Unlike for Plato who was not just a writer but a reporter and a secretary of what Socrates says, the experience of psychoanalysis consists in the experience of the signifying effects of speech. These effects are subtracted from writing in the way that is particular to each subject. Of course, in the analytic session the subject maintains some relation to writing and writes his analysis and of his patients but the analytic experience relies on the experience of the signifier and on what is lacking in the signifier. That's why Lacan's subject remains divided and finds the support for his discourse in the materiality of the letter. Sometimes it is the analyst who occupies that position, the one of the letter.

For Augustine and for the grammarians of the Middle Ages, the assumption of the voice starts with an articulation of a sound, which is an articulation of a name. For him it is about the name of God, called to in prayers and in mass. If initially it was prohibited to pronounce God's name, it was because the articulation of the name can bring to light some imaginary effects of the ego. Lacan notes that this prohibition refers to one of the commandments that forbids the use of the imaginary. The name of God is not to be pronounced because to pronounce it implies to represent it, to corrupt it with the division between speech and writing, which in turn would involve artistic expression, the *techne*, the duality between appearance and essence, and so on. To pronounce the name of God is to present it by the medium of speech, introducing vowels—the agony of vowels—and raising the name through speech and singing to a song. It appears that the prohibition to pronounce the name of God amounts to an exclusion of the signifier that was later added in the form of vowels to enable communication between people. Without vowels there would not be room even for misunderstanding. It seems that in the end only one name remained forbidden to speech. Does it mean that nothing is forbidden in analysis? In Lacanian terms, then, the prohibition to pronounce the name of the One has the same logic as the prohibition of representation that carries imaginary effects of the ego. It is this imaginary import Lacan elaborated so meticulously in the mirror stage that constitutes the logic of the difficulty to say what is impossible to say. In analysis we say "say it", say what it is impossible to say. As for the written letter it is unsayable and appears as essentially and radically exterior to the representation of the signifier or, we could say, the letter belongs to the order of self-identity and self-referentiality.

The letter always says the same thing, because it symbolises the same thing—it is a seal like the purloined letter in Poe's story, sought and found by the detective Dupin (2006d). This is what Lacan tells us and it has a bearing on the clinic. In analysis a letter, any letter says the same thing until it is opened and read out, which implies articulation. Then the letter is lost. The subject in analysis starts reading a dream letter only to drop it and to continue to speak. Reading the letter is first of all reading what does not speak back. When the letter is dropped, the subject's speech addresses someone else. It is always addressed to the other, present as absent, in transference. In the analytic experience the subject speaks because speech is the material medium with which the subject seeks to ascertain his existence as subject, namely the cause of being supposed as subject, which is not self-evident. In doing that, in addressing the other when speaking to the analyst, demand and desire change places and the supposed subject becomes the supposing subject. In seeking the other of which the subject is supposed the latter discovers the hallucinatory effects in the satisfaction of speaking. It is not a straight forward process but it can be deducted. In being supposed the subject is speechless, reduced to an object in and of fantasy. Then, in speaking, the subject comes to live, becomes enlivened by being brought forward by the signifier that calls him, like Lazarus, to articulation, saying what is possible and saying what is not possible, what in speech can and cannot be said. For Lacan it is the Other where this signifier can be located, but it is for the subject to suppose it as knowledge, which is where the analyst can be found. In the place of the Other can already be found the material cornucopia of language from which knowledge is made. Lacan wrote this Other, *l'Autre*, as A. The subject's desire is thus animated by the signifier of the lack in the Other, the unsaid mystery, which is connected to the object *a* in the way that only every subject, one by one, by speaking back to the one who functions in that place, an analyst, discovers for himself. In Lacan's algebra we write the signifier of the lack in the Other as S ($\cancel{A}$).

Between the "speech acts" and linguistics

However we approach the process, it is based on the disjunction. In this particular case, I have been highlighting two disjunctions, one of the signifier and the letter, and the other of the Augustinian voice and

Lacan's desire of the Other. This disjunction, in its bare form, is at stake for John Searle, an American philosopher of language, who developed a theory of "speech acts" (1971). What is at stake for Searle is, on the one hand, what Jacques-Alain Miller called an "ontology of reality" and, on the other hand, the Other's desire that for Searle represents a mythical "intention". What is at stake for him then is a question of meaning of what is said as external to and separate from the real. To be more precise, it is a question of how the signifier can generate meaning representing the subject to another signifier, while naming the lack in the Other that he takes for "reality". The Other then is "reality", and the question arises how is it possible that the subject can produce meanings without the guarantee of the Other as "reality". For Searle this Other is the Other of tradition and convention. At the same time he tells us, by way of producing a list of aphorisms, that the meaning of the sentence is entirely a matter of the conventions of the language. What then are the conventions of the language?

In the first instance, these "conventions of the language", either Hebrew, Greek or Latin, are enacted in a "speech act" in which the subject imposes his intentionality on the symbols or words. In the second instance, although these are not temporally separate instances, the imposition of intentionality on the symbol appears as a condition of satisfaction. So, you have an intention of the speaker, which is on the side of meaning, meaning to say this or that, and you have a satisfaction as a kind of successful imposition of this meaning on the sound. These two, desire as "intention" and satisfaction as a success of imposition of meaning outside its tradition, are in Searle's speech acts integrally intertwined. And the place in which they intertwine or intersect is, of course, the good old ego. Does not this little theory sound like a true ally of another ego tradition that flourished in the United States?

Once you situate meaning as a fixed derivative of the Other's desire, you have doubtless failed to establish the conditions of the subject's existence in language as well as those of the experience of satisfaction. That is to say, to situate meaning as a fixed derivative of the Other as tradition and convention is relative to what Lacan called alienation, namely taking the master signifier from the Other via which the subject was initially supposed as the subject's own. In alienation the subject speaks in the name of the master signifier of the Other. When it comes to producing his own speech act, Searle seems to take the Other's word for everything. What we find in his theory could be traced back to Plato's *Cratylus* and works in support of the semantic treatment of language. It is a successful alienation whose logic I tried to show in the previous chapter as one of our crucial points of orientation. Searle is the Antaios who walks the earth, invincible as a wrestler, because he draws his strength from the ground. But Heracles knows that the source of Antaios power is his mother Gaia, so he lifts him above the ground and, not being invincible himself, thus defeats the undefeated fighter. Searle seems to overlook the fact that the real cannot be mastered by meaning that the Other of tradition has laid down for him.

But let's take it a step further which is where I found it interesting. Searle goes on to distinguish an intention to say something from an intention to mean it. First you have a kind of wanting-to-say, and then you have wanting-to-mean. They are not the same. To put Searle's claim up to the test, we could refer to the language of lovers, which I will do later. Suppose a woman says to a man "tell me that you love me even if you don't mean it". And if he gladly obliges she immediately asks: "do you really mean it?" Saying and meaning or, more precisely, saying and enjoying the meaning of what is said, the *enjoy-meant*, as one attempts to translate *joui-sens*, are two different things for Searle. We would go along with this claim if it allowed for the move from alienation to separation. But it does not. Speaking and meaning, especially in love relationships, which psychoanalysis as practice works with, remain alienated. Lacan pointed to the difference between them by showing that the signifier only produces meaning effects, provided there is a subject to do so, which Searle neglects stressing the acts of speech and not of the subject. There is a difference between just saying "I love you" without nothing real touched by it, and saying it and meaning it, which implicates the subject and the truth as real at stake. If this results in separation, it is because the master signifier that contributes to confusion as to who speaks to whom.

In Searle's terms, the difference between intention to say and the actual meaning falls outside the field of the subject as telling the truth. After all when saying something I can actually lie. Searle has no answer to that taking the lie at the level of conscious distortion of what *I know* to be the truth. Searle would not be favourable to the Freudian idea of *protos pseudos*, the lie as a defence against the real of suffering or as an attempt to protect the Other from being hurt, without really meaning what one says. For Searle the truth conditions are very simple—that we do not tell lies. So for him truth is related to meaning and not to the real. Telling the truth as not telling lies would therefore presuppose a world without pain, suffering, discomfort or guilt, because it is these conditions of the real where truth lies. Searle wants to have a purely symbolic and disembodied dimension of language without any collusion from the real, and that's precisely alienation. The theory of language Searle espouses is the theory of the symbolic without the real, a kind of symbolic delusion. That's why there is nothing to say in it except for exchanging items of information that are self-identical and self-referential, which is the letter. For Searle, therefore, when a man satisfies a woman's demand to tell her he loves her even if he does not mean it, he does not lie. And because he does not lie he also satisfies the conditions of truth. Thus truth is equivalent to meaning and meaning to truth.

Psychoanalysis derives its orientation from an encounter with the real. Lacan's symbolic, perhaps not as strikingly in his earlier teaching as in the later one, arises at the site of the real either as a formal envelope of the symptom or as a crypt that conceals the loss. And the speech act, in the psychoanalytical sense, implies the real as subtracted from the speaking subject, as a (-), in the discourse that addresses the Other. In short, the real of love, hate, shame, anxiety, frustration, dominate the scene of analytic discourse as embedded in it.

Is the unconscious written?

The ancients like Aristotle conceived of speech as a meaning of the mnemic inscription. To make sense of the mnemic trace, to make sense of the unconscious *memoria*, implied for Aristotle the use of voice. This would allow us to say that in the theory of semantics starting with Plato and Aristotle the meaning is already present when a communication takes place, and speech serves to convey it. And what does not make sense remains written.

Is the unconscious written then? The unconscious does not make sense. Only the subject can make sense when the signifier and the signified are quilted. The unconscious does not make sense because it is made up of the signifiers that are purely nonsensical. For Lacan the truth of the unconscious is on the side of the signifier as nonsensical. When things do not make sense, it is because the unconscious does not make sense and the consolations of the ego are called for to give a neurotic subject something friendly and meaningful that can be understood—a consolation of meaning. But the unconscious is not friendly and without meaning. In his "Introduction to the English edition" of *Seminar XI*, added in 1976, Lacan says that only when we no longer call for the friendly and meaningful consolation to what does not make sense, only then we are *in* the unconscious. Only when a lapsus or any associative link does not carry any meaning, one *knows*, one is in the unconscious. It is a beautiful statement in which Lacan separates the imaginary of friendship from the real of solitude.

Lacan captured here the unconscious as without meaning, as written, to be precise, as written before the subject utters and articulates it. On the other hand, writing can imply a record and an inscription of what is said. And this is crucial for Lacan, namely that the unconscious as written before it is said, is first of all an effect of the desire of the Other, left in the body as an essentially meaningless trace, as what the Other does not know, the s (A). The hysterics Freud was working with were trying to work out what they were saying because speaking is essentially linked to desire and desire to language. Lacan established this link in metonymy which consists in the concatenation of substitutes relative to the object of desire. Having connected desire and language, Lacan was able to say that the unconscious is structured *like* a language, *any* language, in fact, because any speech act, any subject speaking, is caught in the relation between desire in speaking, and language as the condition of the unconscious. Searle fails to recognise this. He does not acknowledge that meaning—uncomfortable, anguished, embarrassing, unknown—can be inscribed as the effect of the conditions of speaking. Under these conditions the subject may try to convey, in a more or less satisfactory way depending on how well it is put, the desire that in this act fails to say what I want to say. The truth, speaking, passing through awareness, lies. The disjunction between saying and meaning does not allow for establishing a once and for all link between the former, once I say something, and the latter. What the subject says, can be partly satisfying, or not, but the meaning this saying produces is something else.

Starting with what Lacan says about the passage of speaking without meaning through the unconscious, that which does not follow meaning, and which finds satisfaction without meaning, can be found not only as written but as spoken. The dimension of the nonsensical opens not only to the written as unsaid. It also opens to saying that does not seek to produce meaning. That's what a lapsus is. A lapsus is not so much about nonsense as about a surprise that may lead somewhere, to another meaning, if analysis continues to decipher it by producing more and more meaning. But it may also lead to another lapsus where a production of meaning is no longer enjoyed because it does not have to depend on a generation of jouissance. Then an analysis comes to an end. It is when you have another meaning that the unconscious as written somehow shows itself in the gap, as Lacan said. And it shows itself in what we say.

This, incidentally, is the title of an article by Richard Henson, "What we say". In it, Henson states that in order to understand a speaker, we need to rely on our knowledge of language. What concerns him more generally is the nature of a mistake. As a semantician he presents the dimension of understanding as a correspondence between a sign and a meaning. This is a repetition of Saussure, you might say, but not exactly. Suppose, when uttering a statement k1, one is mistaken. Does it imply that one is mistaken when uttering any statement which also belongs to the set K of which k1 is a member? Henson's answer is no for the following reason: k2 or k3, which belong to class K, may also belong to another class of statements, say the set P concerning which one is never mistaken. And in supporting this Henson says that in delirium or amnesia, perhaps he *would* be mistaken about or ignorant of his daughter's name.

He thus distinguishes two classes of statements, one in which one is always mistaken, like in the case of delusional subjects who forget their children's name, and another in which one is never mistaken. Two things follow from this: firstly, the division of statements into these two classes is based upon the knowledge of language just like the knowledge of hydraulics of the airplane on the ground. In this definition of language its knowledge boils down to a correspondence between meanings and words, remaining subservient, like for Searle, to the Other of tradition and convention. In other words, the reference here is an index of statements in which an order of symmetry is maintained. Secondly, the class of statements in which one is mistaken makes up a set which appears as a dump area. If you are mistaken about saying something, this is the set where your statement belongs. It goes to the bin. But then it turns out, as Henson tells us, that whatever can be thrown into the dustbin of error—"it is nonsense", as the politicians say—in fact belongs to another set where the mistaken statement can assume a different meaning, like a lapsus that Henson does not even consider.

In the example given by Henson there is a set of true statements and a set of mistakes. A definition of a word is a description of its meaning.

And when you make a mistake it is because you did not know the correct definition of the word. This is more or less consistent with Plato's definition of doing evil things. According to Plato you do evil when you do not know what the good is. So it is a question of ignorance in the classical sense of the term *ignorantia*. But what is the correct definition of the meaning of love? Who is the subject of love? In psychoanalysis we never know the correct meaning of a word because it is up to the subject to provide it and the subject always errs. He errs and is happily duped by the semblance of meaning having failed to come up with the correct definition of love which is what brings many to analysis. But this failure does not prevent him from shedding some old and new light on the experience of love, which happens in speech and in an encounter with an analyst. Why the failure? Because the signifier Lacan speaks about does not know. The unconscious is written as that which opens up but it does not know about the unconscious. One only knows when the meaning and understanding have been left outside. Other than that the unconscious does not know how to write the sexual relation or what the Woman is. Or love. Or death. And because the unconscious does not know these things, the signifier of the unconscious knowledge comes to represent it.

Without question the subject lies when attempting to articulate the unconscious knowledge that does not know. I have already mentioned the Freudian *protos pseudos* of Emma. In this sense truth is not the condition of speaking, believing that what you say is true. This belief may be more a condition of love effects. Speaking, on the other hand, is the condition of lying about truth. Truth is only the condition of acceding the unconscious that closes when acceded. In the course of lies, there is a flash of truth, bingo! Perhaps Richard Henson did not tell us the truth about his knowledge of language, perhaps I did not tell you the truth about him. Perhaps Beoufret did not tell Lacan the truth about what Heidegger said to him. What the analytic experience shows is that what passes through intention pertains to the order of lying in the face of a trauma, a hole in the body or a gap in language. And, in effect, what passes through awareness, preserves some anonymous *status quo* of I don't know what. The subject lies when, confronted with the real of the body, while trying to satisfy the conditions of truth which are the conditions of semblance. Hence Lacan proposed the term semblance because semblance is not an illusion but a truth speaking about the real in the sense that the real is not excluded from the symbolic. Semblance is a fiction in which truth reveals its structure as implicating the real. In short, semblance is an existence of what is not there. Is it not precisely what we have just said about the Freudian *das Ding*?

We can say that in articulating the letter of the unconscious the subject lies. In articulating what the unconscious does not know, the subject invents fictions. An example of such a fiction is a theory of language understood as a knowledge of language. In this respect we could say that the Augustinian *vox* lies when touching on the *verbum* of the real. And when the subject is represented and supposed by the signifier from the unconscious, he lies. This was for Lacan an effect of joining desire with law, of making desire, Searle's "intention" subservient to the law (e.g., of grammar, convention, etc.). If anything, the Lacanian desire has always been entangled with *das Ding*, which continues to be the case in our daily relations with the *Nebenmensch*. This real of the jouissance that precedes the subject as speaking has for Lacan always been associated with the letter and reading literally. The Freudian Thing and the Lacanian letter have always been neighbours. And this tells us something about the difference between desire and jouissance in speech. When the desire of the Other is mistaken for the Other's jouissance, then the maintenance of jouissance makes perversion the way of keeping the Other satisfied, namely consistent, which is one of the names for tradition.

What we say

The letter, then, is how the experience that bears the name of a trauma becomes inscribed in the body by the unconscious. The material support Lacan speaks about is already premoulded and affected for a particular subject before he enters the pathway of speech. Lacan gave us a definition of the unconscious that is striking in its simplicity. I am referring to his article of 1966, "The position of the unconscious" (2006b), where he states that the unconscious is what we say. Both simple and beautiful, it is also a truly topological formulation that transcends the boundaries of understanding. It can be read but it does not have to be understood. The unconscious defined as what we say it is provides a different perspective on the older sister formula of the unconscious being structured like a language. The latter, coming from 1953, concerns Lacan's work in the field of the symbolic and imaginary. It is also from this period of his work that we can extract his attempt to define science by means of a particular relation between the imaginary and symbolic. This can be found in the early seminars and in Lacan's passionate dialecticisation of the work of the post-Freudians. In effect, his critique allows him later on to define science as the imaginarisation of the symbolic of the real. First you have to define the symbolic of the real in science (e.g., the gene that knows) and then to imaginaries it would imply to make it understandable, namely appealable to the ego. And it works. Why not? If you look at the results of the so called genome project, Lacan's definition works perfectly well. In genetics you have a kind of literal interpretation of the letter, so you have a set of letters whose combination corresponds to a particular gene responsible for a particular bodily feature. It would be impossible to embark on any application of this scientific research without the imaginary register, namely without taking a defect or fault in the body image that requires a correction or a modification, and which does not involve the subject. This appears to be the position of medicine and psychiatry. Thus, the imaginary provides the basis for the production of designer babies who have their bodily features and immunity system adjusted to order. And until some major disaster takes place, the question of ethics, that is to say of the subject, will not arise.

The imaginarisation of the real by means of the self-referential letter that stands for the gene as real, allows us to define science as the imaginarisation of the symbolic of the real. What about the science of language, then, and the knowledge of language I tried to encapsulate by referring to the philosophers of language? What about an attempt to compile and exhaust a referential system of definitions of meanings that which supposedly give us a symbolic compendium of the real as such? Of course, unlike in the applied genetics, the philosophers of language do not seem to rely on the imaginary register that would motivate their research into the meaning of words and what the other is actually saying. Here the focus is on the "intention" as such, the name of the real as such without any attention paid to the reality as dividing and setting apart what we say and what we mean to say, the two reaching an eternal fusion in the writing of James Joyce. It is a completely different matter when, like in psychoanalysis, one has to take into account the real as dividing, as impossible to symbolise as such but as imaginarised by means of the symbolic. This real can only be of highly particular and singular nature separating one subject from another and one experience of language as speech and as writing from another. And until the signifier is perceived, and the meaning taken as its effect and not a cause, and until the letter read, before any leap into meaning and understanding, it is back to the imaginary although under the aegis of the symbolic order. The philosophers of language, like Searle and Henson, the children of Aristotle, like the semantic order where words correspond to meanings and the truth conditions of such a relation are assured. Then a mistake occurs and it is all panic and anxiety, defence and repression. One way or the other, the mistakes, the slips, the delirious and blissful forgetfulness—all point to the unconscious as a structure of a language.

In opposition to the imaginary of the mirror stage, and in reference to Freud's work, come Lacan's definition of the unconscious as structured *like* a language with the primacy of the signifier as its building block. Further to that comes the shortest and most elegant definition of the unconscious I have found in Lacan's teaching. It is what we say, namely it is what I *say* it is. In the end the Lacanian unconscious is topological, which is his new and last name for the structure. "The unconscious is what we say" isolates the nonsensical element of language as structuring the unconscious. If the letter leads to reading, the signifier leads to saying. But none of this happens without the real. In his definition Lacan tries to grasp what an act of speech consists in, and how its work, its impact has an effect of a cut. "The unconscious is what we say" tries to grasp an act of speech by separating what in saying gives a satisfaction as unsaid from the pleasure of saying it well. Lacan's definition of the unconscious incorporates the division between what in the topology of "what we say" is not signifier. In other words, "the unconscious is what we say" includes and excludes at the same time the little real Lacan called object *a*, the little extimate real as unsaid yet bound up in speaking about love.

This of course would not prevent a philosopher of language from asking: What do you mean "the unconscious is what we say"? The question leads the interlocutor to represent the original statement, and then again and again until the question vanishes, lost in the proliferation of quotation marks and in the discourse of the subject which is where it started in the first place. The unconscious is what I *say* it is. Lacan does not say that what we say makes up the unconscious. He does not say that the statements produced by the subject make up a reservoir called the unconscious, as Freud at some point did, or a compendium of meanings, for example of love, one can refer to at will. The unconscious structured like a language is not made up of meanings, and not even of statements. The unconscious is what I *say*, what in saying what I say,

I say without knowing and what touches the body as unsaid. Hence the inevitability of a lie in the passage between these little truths, fragments, and hence the inaccessibility of the unconscious knowledge as such. Nevertheless, in topology this disjunction allows for a connection between the disjointed points, and this renders Lacanian unconscious topological, namely transformable. The definition of the unconscious as what we say may be the most meaningless definition of the unconscious ever, but its value is elsewhere. It has a value of an act that divides the subject, making him ask "what do you mean?" Lacan's saying follows equivocation and is not in this sense without meaning effects. What Lacan does not do is to throw at us any meaning or invite us to understand it. His saying therefore has a *direction*. We can only say what we mean by saying it well, at least well enough to give direction to what we say without understanding taking over. This or other direction is an effect of how the signifiers resonate. So we can isolate these two new points of orientation for the unconscious in analysis: its resonance and its direction. How then do we say what the unconscious is?

The meaning of certainty—I love you therefore I am

If the discourse of science consists in an unconditional search for the real as such, this implies that the real is to be situated and expected to be found outside the symbolic. Secondly, a search for the real as such obliges scientists to put forward the conditions of knowledge within which the real is to be sought. Hence Lacan's formulation about the imaginarisation of the symbolic of the real as capturing the process. But the symbolic in science, say a mathematical symbol or a letter, is not the same as in psychoanalysis. Lacan invented a matheme that captures some real by way of subtracting it which concerns the subject. The same cannot be said of science where the value of the mathematical symbol is always the same and does not involve the subject. This makes the relation between the mathematical symbol and the real very specific. If in the psychoanalytic clinic we were to approach the subject's symptom from this perspective of the symbolic and the real being extraneous to each other, it would amount to qualifying psychoanalysis, as Jacques-Alain Miller remarks somewhere, as a kind of fraud. In this sense, science deserves to be called a false psychoanalysis as it leaves the subject untouched, Lacan even says foreclosed. What I am trying to say is that if the real and the symbolic were extraneous to each other, then the knowledge of language would be external to language. In which case science and psychoanalysis would have nothing to do with each other. But they do because they are both concerned with the real.

This is my second distinction. The first distinction concerned what Lacan says from the start about language being the condition of the unconscious. Which I take it to mean that the language referred to is the signifier as meaningless. In other words, the making of sense of the letter of the unconscious implies the division of the subject. What my second distinction proposes is that the knowledge of language as professed by the scientists and philosophers of language is not outside language of knowledge. This language of knowledge implicates the subject in the Lacanian sense, namely the divided subject, defining the psychoanalytical field in accordance with Lacan's formulation, namely that, in distinction to science, psychoanalysis symbolises or subjectivises the imaginary of the real because the real cannot be captured as such. The real, the real of the body, Lacan says, captured as real albeit the image, the narcissistic image of the other, is not without jouissance and therefore has a relation to the real. The real cannot be said or named as such because it remains entangled with the symbolic, and this is the direction Lacan took when he was formalising it in his work on the *sinthome*. The real enters the subject as imaginarised in so far as the real, the incomprehensible jouissance of the Other slips in between the lines and what in the Other is not signifier. And it is precisely in the *extimate* relations with the Other as maternal *Nebenmensch* that Freud placed the real as internally excluded in the subject's desire. What is subjectivised of the real is first imaginarised in the relation to the specular other, along the lines of narcissism, the death drive, and aggressivity. But the mirror image can only be formed with the support of the Other whose yes, or no, marks the entrance to the symbolic. Where does it all leave science?

Everything we read from *Cratylus* and *Pheadrus* (1973) of Plato, through *De interpretationes* of Aristotle, to the theories of grammar of the Middle Ages and the modern theories of philosophy of language revolves around language as meaning, "what do you mean?" being the master question. What the question supposes, though, is the subject—the subject of meaning. So we refine the statement to please the master in waiting but once it is understood, there is nothing else to say. The axis of breaking this *perpetuum mobile* of meaning comes from Lacan gravitating towards the Cartesian subject, to be more precise towards the subject of doubt. With Descartes we have a new modality of the subject. For Augustine, the subject is that which follows the object of love in what he wants to know. Here the principle is the connection between love and knowledge. The Augustinian subject cannot love what is not known. Can the Lacanian subject love what does not make sense?

With Descartes the subject of knowledge establishes itself as a subject of certainty. Here knowledge is a matter of certainty. It is certain that one knows. But is it also certain what it is that one knows? My logic professor, whom I mentioned earlier, was certain the unicorns did not exist but he did not know the nature of that which did not exist. In other words, the certainty for him related to the subject of *perceptum*. Lacan took up the Cartesian subject of certainty to explore the ubiquitous relation of the love of knowledge. If the Augustinian subject is concerned with reality, with what is and is not known about the reality which, let's recall is a point of departure for Freud, for Descartes the aim is not reality but certainty. This is of course confirmed by the lovers who could not care less about reality, including convention and tradition. All they are concerned about is certainty. I don't know if it was love that inspired Descartes to his search for certainty but he certainly contributed to the close relation between love and certainty.

From his earliest seminars Lacan insisted that what the subject aims at is not a reality but certainty. In transference, which is the position from which the subject speaks addressing the other, the subject demands certainty of a reply, and more generally of love. Through love the subject supposes another to be able to make love present and certain. Only then would knowledge come from it. The patient wants to assure that in analysis love is in the air which would subsequently lead him to ask about knowledge. Love is inscribed in the question of knowledge. The idea of knowledge without the subject's suppositions, which entails it having been supposed first, reminds us of the subject as foreclosed. Is certainty then what the subject aims at when asking about meaning, the meaning of desire? Is certainty of the Cartesian subject the ultimate goal in the preoccupations of the philosophers of language like Searle, Henson, and others?

And when I say "meaning", I do not mean the meaning *of* something, the meaning *of* the word "love", for example. The meaning of love is always secondary to my certainty *that* it means something to me. What the subject in love demands and expects is not what is meant by love, not whether love means this or that. Love can mean different things to different people, but that's not what it's all about. What the true love implies when the subject's certainty is at stake, is *that* it means something to me, in other words, that saying it does not go without meaning it, meaning it when saying it, because meaning it in some way gives saying a quality—a quality of saying. Meaning what the subject says allows saying to acquire a quality of truth as real.

What Lacan was at pains to stress time and again was that Descartes' *cogito ergo sum* follows the direction of certainty, namely that something else be acknowledged, confirmed, indeed, guaranteed, when the subject thinks. Such would be the principle of certainty according to the Cartesian formula. Thought guarantees existence. Does love guarantee existence? According to Lacan love is reciprocal and guarantees being loved. I will come back to it later. For the moment let's deal briefly with the Cartesian *cogito*. If I think, my existence is supposed to be guaranteed. That's what Descartes claims. But is it? If we approach the problem by situating *ergo* in relation to love can we say that "I love you" guarantees anything, let alone my being? Or does speaking of love guarantee its true meaning, namely that I *also* mean it, not just say it, or, because this is where the question of meaning takes me, that there is a thought, an unconscious thought that precedes my saying "I love you"? In short, does a subjective act guarantee subject's existence?

The logic of certainty is, of course, not whether my search for existence can be sealed at the level of what I do, think, doubt, love, dream, someone even said "I stink therefore I am". The logic of certainty follows the logicisation of the real where it appears as most compelling, insistent. Lacan brings the Cartesian *cogito* to a new level by highlighting both the implication through which thinking should assure my existence and thought at the level of cause. A doubt, which is of vital importance in the psychoanalytic clinic, lingers on. It is connected to thought. What Lacan undertook in his teaching to emphasise was, first, that the Freudian method is Cartesian to the extent that he, Freud, doubts. He doubts not only as a scientist but as a subject. Does the blabber of the hysterics guarantee their existence? There is more to it than that. Freud doubts because he is increasingly aware that this "I think", which has the same linguistic function as "I mean", and which is what brings him to doubt—not the other way round—is not the cause of his thought. "I think" is not the cause of thinking. Before I think, before I address the Other what in saying what I mean I miss out, there is something else that comes to view, that makes us doubt, that interferes with what I say. And we can see this interference clearly in Descartes whose primary concern is certainty. What is the cause of thought? What causes thinking, Freud tells us in *Entwurf*, is an attempt to close the gap between the primary object of love as lost and wished for, and the experience of perceptual reality where the object, too, is missing. Freud speaks of thinking as a process whose aim is to bridge this distance, to patch up the gap arising from the fundamental fault in the subject, namely that its object is lost. Thinking therefore is a mode of hallucination that brings out the *attention*, the vigilance in every one of us, but remains opposed to perception. In effect of this loss of the real object thinking as an unconscious process, as Lacan stresses, follows the pleasure principle and presents itself as a hallucinated satisfaction which has a bearing on doubting. In this way, Lacan adds, thinking as a process is always on the lookout for a new reality because it is determined to refind the object.

If the subject expects through his thinking a guarantee that would be sealed and confirmed by the Other, it is because Descartes supposes the subject of certainty to be located in the Other. If he doubts, it is because it is the Other that is uncertain from the start. As real and consistent, the Other, as Lacan said, and Jacques-Alain Miller and Eric Laurent elaborated, does not exist. And this leaves the subject's certainty in the domain of desire. The Other does not exist because there is no Other of the Other as truth telling us about the truth. It is not only the mental apparatus that works around the fault. Here we are also confronted with a lack in the Other, with an insufficiency in tradition and gaps in referential knowledge to account for the real of the subject. Descartes supposed that his God would assure his truth and would not deceive him. This uncertainty about the Other haunted Descartes at the level of desire. Before he became the man of science, he was a man of dreams. His strong willed father expected René to settle down and establish himself, all the usual trappings of *bourgeoisie*. He wants to be worthy of his father's wishes but in fact does not live up to his father's expectations of following the commercial career. In his dreams he struggles, there is a sense of impediment, he cannot get up, straighten up, feels unsteady on his feet, cannot move forward, walks against the wind. He is stuck and seeks refuge at school, preys in the church. This confusion, one wonders, drives him on nevertheless, his search for certainty imposing. And when he becomes the only one in the family to have disappointed his father, René rebels and embarks on the search for truth.

His pursuit of certainty in the face of the Other as deceiving, playing tricks with his *perceptum*, the piece of wax changing shape, makes him hungry for truth. We only need to ask whether the truth of God or the truth of the subject? Lacan remarks that if the truth remained in the hands of the Other, say God, then every statement would have a seal of guarantee. What we say would be what we mean and the other way round. The meaning of the subject's statement would be assured beyond doubt. As we know, the search for guarantee can have a similar effect in the case of love. The church has always left love in the hands of God so that his children can live under God's guarantee of being loved. With it should come the satisfaction of being an object for the Other and not having to encounter the lack in the Other.

Now, the Lacanian subject appears precisely at this point. Its division has to do with the bar that separates the signifier from the signified, the saying from meaning. This division made Lacan refer to the Cartesian subject as the subject that is not the cause of his thought. In "The instance of the letter in the unconscious" (2006e) Lacan situates this division between thought and being.

"I don't think" on the left and "I am not" on the right. "I am not" designates Lacan's formulation of the unconscious. The unconscious is not what we think, even if thought is unconscious, but what we say, although thought, in so far as it is uncertain as a thought of *what*, is implicated, for example, "what do you think you are saying?" Apart from that, "the unconscious is what we say" indicates that saying and thinking are distinct processes. Thinking remains silent. As a process, it is a narrative that fails to link the real of loss with speaking. It is where Wittgenstein stopped.

As for the level of being and thinking, since they have different causes, Lacan situated them as separate. On the right we have "I am

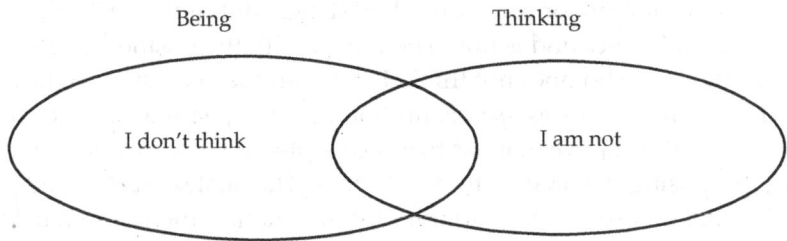

Schema 1.

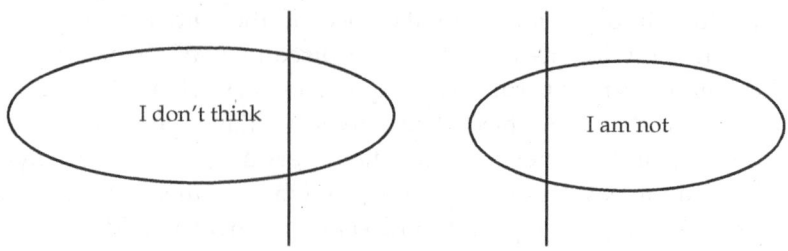

Schema 2.

not". On the left there is "I don't think". That's where the doubt is, maybe I did not get it right after all.

Where I am not it thinks. Where I do not think—am I? Either way the doubt remains and the guarantee is in question. Of course I get my diploma, pay my fees, attend the meetings but does all this guarantee my existence apart from giving me a symbolic function, a host of duties, responsibilities etc.? Somewhere there is a gap and what remains is the "not-whole", the position Lacan designated as feminine and not to be identified with the universal. So we return to the particularity of the *cogito* as a primary material of being. Thought, as Lacan followed Freud, is unconscious. Thought is unconscious and functions as a reminder of a failure to tie up the experience of the lost object with what never comes to its place in perception. In essence thinking is a wishful thinking doomed to stir delusion in the subject faced with the lack. In the 1970s Lacan speaks of thinking as a mode of jouissance, a satisfaction linked to the superego. The superego is characterised by the mode of imposition. At that point of his teaching Lacan conceives of thought as a satisfied delusion in the face of the lost object. In the 1950s Lacan is Freudian and speaks of thinking as a creative process in search for new dimensions of more or less assured existence. But in the 1970s thought becomes jouissance and is not to be linked with the position of the analyst as the one who does not think. For Lacan the analyst is on the side of "I don't think", or as *apensé*, unthought. It is just that this negation touches on the object *a* that has to be accounted for. Lacan accounted for it by proposing the analyst to incarnate it. The analyst supports doubt in the subject's search for certainty by incarnating the unthought that causes thinking. In making the object *a* cause thinking, Lacan condenses the analyst's position to what he says, to the unconscious speaking, interpreting, as Miller punctuated. Lacan shifted the emphasis with regard to the analyst's position from thinking to saying. He seems to be saying that in analysis it is better not to think.

What emerges from Lacan's schema are two lacks of not thinking and not being, which is how the speaking subject is constituted. The subject owes its constitution to two lacks, the lack in being, where "it thinks", and to "I don't think", where can be located the remainder of being as unrepresented yet present and imposing, just as in René's dream. We can situate the Lacanian subject as sandwiched between the lack of being, which is a fall of identification, $-\varphi$, and the fall of the little real as the object a, which is where Lacan located an analyst. When the object is situated on the side *of* the Other's desire, this object is called the gaze. But it is the voice object when it is in relation *to* the Other. I proposed that we approach thinking as a mode of a silent speech that nevertheless is made of the unconscious signifiers. Thought is a kind of mute signifier that is not raised to the level of the subject's articulation in addressing the Other because thinking does not make use of the voice object, that is to say of the loss in the subject's desire *for* the Other. And this would imply that thought is structured like a letter to the extent that the letter refers to itself and always says the same thing between those two lacks in signification. Articulation is not self-referential, as cannot do without the reference to the Other. Therein lies the helplessness of the speaking being, and where Freud recognised the origin of morality. Where does this relation to the Other place the voice as object, given that for Lacan the voice is not a physical voice, neither a sound nor a substance, but a lost object to be refound only at the backdrop of silence? I can recall here a case of a singer who having lost his singing voice did not cease looking for it. Which was what? It is not that he could not find it. As what was inscribed for him was the loss, the irreversible loss of his own voice, it was the voice that gave his desire a direction. The object voice is to be placed where the Lacanian object is placed, namely as a cause. The voice of a woman this patient loved was what animated him and made him listen to the Other to tell him what to do, or not, to be this or that, and the voice became the instrument of his desire in his relation with others. He would listen out for what in the saying of the Other gave him a task, an assignment to complete, he always followed the initiative of the Other, which was his alienation. On one level, I am not the cause of my thought, and my thinking follows the unconscious process. On another level, the object as lost causes desire.

It is not the Other as a place of truth and of signifier that causes desire but the object. What causes desire is the object with respect to the Other as desiring. Subject's desire is not without the Other's. That's the mystery you could say as it is no longer a secret. Augustine linked the voice with the gift of love from God provided he wanted to love what is known, thus giving meaning to the unknown (Leff, 1959). Lacan raised the mystery of the Other's desire to a new level, where meaning is not a response to the demand for love. Lacan showed us that love is not concerned with meaning but with speaking where the cause is. We can just as well love what is not known.

And this allows me to say that psychoanalytic clinic is not a clinic of meaning but a clinic of saying. In the beginning, the analytic clinic draws support from the letter, both the materiality of language *and* the function of speech in the primary experience of the *Nebenmensch*. The subject is not there yet to register it as subject, it is still absent or not yet present. At the end of analysis there is the letter with which we try to write to capture some of the real, which remains distinct from the mathematical symbol as letter. In the Lacanian writing the letters, a, \$, S_1, allowed him to write a matheme or a discourse. The subject is spoken first, supposed and pushed by the traces, echoes, residues of the letter in the body. Speaking does not follow from meaning but assumes direction through what resonates. The subject follows this direction, often as duped and deceived, because the subject is always supposed as subject by what is said. Jacques-Alain Miller says rightly somewhere that psychoanalysis is the only profession where the psychoanalyst does not say "what I meant to say was ..." meaning is not an answer, and speaking wants to say more. We could say that from the clinical perspective there is always more to say and that what in saying more remains unsaid, points in the direction of the symptom.

CHAPTER FIVE

Two sides of repetition

From infinity to a teardrop

The pleasure principle is one of Freud's oldest inventions. It dates back to his *Entwurf* where he situated it as the law governing the primary processes and as an essential function regulating the work of the psychic apparatus. It seems that at the dawn of psychoanalysis Freud invented infinity. By inventing the pleasure principle, Freud invented a principle that accounts for infinity in psychoanalysis. He then went on to return to the pleasure principle throughout his life. It became the foundation of the dynamic and economical aspects of his mental apparatus. Lacan took it up in his work on the unconscious being structured like a language. It also allowed him to raise the question of ethics of psychoanalysis.

But infinity in psychoanalysis is not the same as infinity in mathematics. A numerical sequence of natural numbers may run to infinity. The pleasure principle does not run into infinity. It fails. It is meant to do so, which is why it is called a principle. Freud would not be going back to the pleasure principle over and again throughout his work if it was not a sign of a failure. It is due to the failure of the pleasure principle to run to infinity like the algebraic sequence in mathematics that led him to discover another force and invent another principle, or a counter principle, namely the reality principle. Since the Freudian invention of infinity was not without a flaw, an invention of the reality principle was to make up for the flaws and limitations of the pleasure principle. Pleasure and reality give us Freud's earliest and most lasting coordinates in psychoanalysis.

How, then, do analysts account for infinity in psychoanalysis? The pleasure principle was invented by Freud to account for a discharge effect and a reduction of tension. In Lacanian terms this occurs in effect of the sliding of significations and the movement of the signifiers. Lacan redefined the pleasure principle in this way, namely as a reduction of the libidinal tension to such a minimum that is sufficient for the movement from one signifier to another. The pleasure principle assures the subject's existence as being represented by a signifier for another signifier. Lacan's definition of the signifier, and of the subject, would be inconceivable without the propeller of the Freudian principle. In other words, what the pleasure principle failed to account for, or indeed to provide, is a reduction and obliteration of tension to zero. In short, the pleasure principle is not a Nirvana principle. We can account for the work of the pleasure principle by taking up its logic as developed by Jacques-Alain Miller and formulate it in the following way. The value (x) of tension (t) would always remain higher than zero.

$$? > t(x) > 0$$

The existence of the minimal tension allowed Lacan to formulate the pleasure principle on the basis of and with reference to necessity. Necessity is the minimal tension or the minutest amount of force needed for the passage from one signifier to another. This minimal tension was conceived by Lacan not so much in terms of a *quantum* of libido but as a *quantum* that remains as a result of tensions arising from the conflict or conflictual investments of "I want", "I don't want" and so on for which the subject is the stage. Such a conflict includes therefore the investments in the work of defence mechanisms, like repressions, and in the construction of new meanings. For Lacan the real is the remainder from the trauma experience of encountering maternal *das Ding* and the jouissance of the Other. It is a remainder intricately present and persistent in the subject's speech as irreducible, like a teardrop that has remained between the lines of what Lacan called a "crisis of tears". Despite the invention of the counter principle, often compared to the superego in the British tradition, the problem presented itself for Lacan as that of irreducibility, that is to say, as having to do with the cause, with what lies at the heart of the pleasure principle and of the unconscious.

We could establish a link between Freud's economical account and Lacan's work on the ethics of psychoanalysis as relative to the signifier of the lack in the Other. The primacy of the economical view taken by Freud, which was for him a primacy of *quantum*, signifies, in the Lacanian terms, the primacy of the signifier that is in itself meaningless. Quantity implies meaninglessness. But the term should not be confused with the dismissive gesture of a modern politician who calls "nonsense" what he pleases not to agree with. In this sense *quantum* also implies tension and synchronicity, which is how Lacan accounted for the primacy of the signifier as having a meaning effect.

In effect, the synchronicity of the signifier and the irreducible remainder of jouissance—that is not structured like the signifier—brings us back to infinity. Synchronicity carries the signifier to infinity while the pleasure principle reduces the *quantum* of the remainder to the absolute minimum, which I called a teardrop. On the right hand side of the formula above the tension in the signifying apparatus remains just above zero. On the left hand side the tension rises up to a certain level that is not yet determined. It does not rise to infinity but every time it is resolved it goes up, infinitely, again. Infinity in psychoanalysis then is not the same as infinity in mathematics. Structurally, the remainder is always the same, always being structured not like the signifier. Economically, which is Freud's reminder, the remainder goes up and down, oscillating from just above zero to less than one, in a series of single strokes which is the work of the pleasure principle. This fluctuation allows to determine and keep afloat the anxiety that does not deceive and is not without the object, as Lacan said. If a dream does not reach its aim, it comes back, and after one dream there is another. The same dream may keep coming back, each time the pleasure principle reduces the libidinal tension by a fraction while the work of the unconscious carries to infinity. In the telling of the dream the subject becomes confronted with a speechless effect that remains at the heart of his speaking about the dream.

In this way, the pleasure principle introduces us to the dimension of duration which is a dimension of temporality where every failure to reduce tension to zero is followed by this tension rising again. Infinity, which remains integral to the circuit of the pleasure principle, can therefore be regarded as a mode of time of the unconscious. And this is how the analytic session is organised, as a series of sessions or moments in accordance with an agreed frequency, time, place, payment etc. In other words, the pleasure principle is set to work by virtue of a circularity that facilitates to beat out the unconscious tracks, called by Freud *Banhungen*, in the network of the unconscious. There is a beginning of a session and an end of it. This happens again the next time, and again the time after that. Whatever happens in the session takes place between zero and one. So, the analytic process as a series of sessions involves infinity although the process itself is not infinite. The subject's speech is organised according to infinity between what is speechless and what is said.

In this schema of circularity and succession, the Freudian invention of infinity in the form of the pleasure principle has all the characteristics of the Aristotle's concept of time. For Aristotle time is constituted as a series, and therefore as a discontinuity, of instants. There is an instant, a moment, followed by another and so on. A succession is therefore presented as a series of rests, a series of stoppages. A series of "nows" is also a series of break points or stoppage points. For Aristotle, time is a set containing all moments which for him are the parts of the whole. In this sense one could oppose Aristotle's concept of time to that of Cantor, which I will do elsewhere.

Such a series of sessions, of beginnings and ends, of openings and closures, is how Lacan defined *automaton*. It may be that in the series of sessions and in the series of stoppage points, the analytical process encounters an impasse of *automaton* where the pleasure principle rules supreme because the analytic process revolves around the production of sense. More and more sense leads to *automaton* in analysis.

The pleasure principle appears to be the hardest worker in the unconscious, as it continues to work to infinity. This infinitely hard work, this working itself to death, also allowed Freud to speak of the death drive, which is the limit the infinity poses to the pleasure principle. It is strange to speak of infinity as posing a limit. After all, infinity should be without limits. The pleasure principle also, as long as the subject is alive, should also be without limits and continue to work infinitely *ad infinitum*. And yet, despite what should be and is not the case, there is a limit that the pleasure principle carries with it. It has to do with the reality principle. In the structure of the unconscious the reality principle has a function of discontinuity and intervenes as a principle of discontinuity. It is doubtful, however, if it is a principle at all except for being a disturbing force that thwarts the work of reduction of tension only to increase it. This increase causes discomfort and pain. So the reality principle could be perhaps called the pain principle in distinction to the pleasure principle, except that pain is not a principle but an effect of default in the pleasure principle.

The manifestation of this flaw as pain is how Lacan described the pleasure principle as tending towards hallucinatory satisfaction. When the pleasure principle runs its course to infinity and towards hallucination, then it runs itself to death. This encounter with death in the form of the death drive results in pain. Then it is back to equilibrium.

Two infinities and the irreversible

The pleasure principle could also be called the principle of insufficiency. If one dream is insufficient to reduce the tension in the wish-fulfilment, there will be another and another. Each time the reduction is insufficient and, each time the production of the unconscious will lead to the increase of tension. So, we could say that the limit which the pleasure principle carries within it, even if it works itself to infinity, implies a limit intrinsic to the subject's place in the language. The limit, namely pain, namely hallucinatory satisfaction, implies what Miller called the unconscious as subject, *inconscient-sujet*. The limit to the inertia of the pleasure principle is manifest as subject.

The introduction of the unconscious as subject is another way of bringing the reality principle back into focus. But let's be careful here because the reality principle works not so much as a mastery over the pleasure principle but as its correlative. This is how Lacan presented it to us—as one being a correlative of the other—and that is why he referred to the opposition between the principles as an intersection. What is this intersection if not an indication that the place in which they intersect, the place where they cross, is the site of the irreducible real, the remainder of the two processes never really coming to an end?

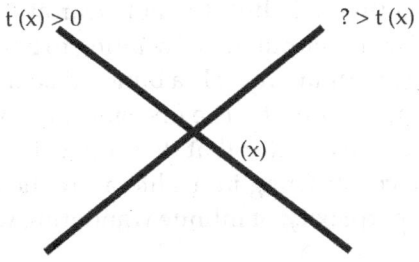

The Freudian infinity in Lacan's hands, the infinity of the pleasure principle and its limit, intersect at the point x. Let's call it the teardrop of the real. We can determine its value by placing it between zero and one, where one designates the libidinal *quantum* at the moment when the pleasure principle intervenes.

$$1 > S(x) > 0$$

This is where we are, one by one. The value of the remainder oscillates between zero and one. Moving from one signifier to another in accordance with the pleasure principle is what Miller called the unconscious as knowledge, *inconscient-savoir*. On the one hand, we have the unconscious as knowledge, which is the libidinal reference, the *Bedeutung*, the sliding of signification in search for a new, surprising solution only to stumble upon the old failed one, which is where the repetitive action or the *automaton* have their source. On the other hand, we have the unconscious as subject, the infinity of repeated strokes or the ones, one after one, in relation to what remains, the real, the unrepresentable "x". When in analysis the subject speaks about her belief in infinite love, this belief is manifest in a series of attempts to find satisfaction in love. And what does she do when she is not in love? She seeks the one to be in love with. For her love cannot be satisfied. In her discourse of stories of love, the pleasure principle intersects with the search for more and again and one more time, as once is never enough and never the way one wants it to be. This intersection of two infinities is sustained through her castration as not having enough which makes her uncertain about another love to come as the current one does not make her happy.

These are the two infinities in psychoanalysis. One has to do with circularity, with coming back to the same place, always at the same time, which supports transference, but which also touches on Freud's compulsive action. She has come to see me to find love that does not exist. It seems that the infinity involved in its search is not without a reference to the drive and its rhythms. But it is not clear at this moment which drive and how it orients her pursuit of wanting to be in love when she is not. The other side of infinity reveals a bundled action, a miss, a failure at reduction, and back to infinity. The first side is a story of guilt without a crime, of a debt to the creditor that does not exist. It is a story Kafka lived his entire life constructing in his literature the endless narratives of not knowing, of perplexity, of infinite wandering without ever facing the causes or its effects, of one downfall after another, of the body of suffering being somehow left to itself. In his life story the place of the law was never to help the suffering body to navigate out of the deep waters. Kafka's law is not for humans. It remained the inhuman law.

The limit at the heart of the infinite operation to reduce the displeasure brings me back to the unconscious as subject. Where there is pain there is a subject. And it is also linked to where Freud established the canon of his ethics: "where it was there I must go". This ethics might not have been of great use to Kafka but it is certainly illuminating to my patient whose search for someone to love without a break encounters an intermission in the form of expecting to be loved. Where there is a remainder there is also a way for the subject to follow the inverse ladder of her desire. And this of course touches on the fantasy that is supposed to speed up the process of finding what she is looking for.

The subject recalls a number of relationships in her life, and discovers that when she met her current husband, she felt as if she knew him all her life. This discovery marks a certain moment in the subject's discourse. It even appears as obvious to her and yet, at the same time, it surprises her. Referring to this discovery when she had met him she says she wanted to marry him, which she subsequently did. After all if you know someone as if you knew him all your life you want to marry him because it is as if you have already been married to him all your life. Now she realises she wants to divorce him. Things are not working out and she has had enough. Since she had enough of her marriage to him, divorce becomes a thought. But it is only through the thought of divorce that a question poses itself for her: how come she never noticed this? The discovery, not that she wants to divorce him but that she only now noticed she knew him all her life, reaffirms her in wanting to come to analysis to pursue the options available to her. The one of divorce remains as the most appealing one.

The master signifier "all my life", preceded by "as if", which Deutsch (1942) isolated as a mechanism of imaginary compensation in schizophrenia, seems to have an effect of taking her off the beaten track of *automaton*. It gives her an idea that perhaps there is another path and different way for her love life, for example a divorce. What is this "all my life" referring to? I leave "as if" to the side because the imaginary realisation of the subject at this moment points us in the direction of a mode of satisfaction. This satisfaction, this modality of jouissance, deserves no other name than the one brought to our attention by the teaching of Jacques-Alain Miller, namely as a jouissance of "once and for all". I do not know whether "once and for all" marks the formula of jouissance as such, but it is a satisfaction that by way of a fall or subtraction of satisfaction, disrupts the infinity of the one after one after one. "Once and for all" is a kind of satisfaction that wants to be the satisfaction of all satisfaction, the all-jouissance. But it turns out to follow the subject at every turn of her love life until the series of ones and of all-jouissances meet its last stroke—"all my life". Where is the knowledge by which this series can be sustained? "All my life" answers the question of infinity in analysis as suddenly collapsed into a single moment and a singular signifier with which the subject looks to the knowledge it calls for. For her this question is "what now?" The moment of discovery first appeared to the patient as necessary, as an inevitable kind of eternal moment, the never ending story of for ever and ever, that nevertheless can come down to just one, single stroke of time, now. Before it happened, before she married, before she even knew her husband to be, before the years passed by, this moment appeared as "once and for all", every time, for the rest of time. But once this moment has passed, and once "all my life" befell her, it marked a loss, an empty place where a thought of divorce becomes a lifeline, an option, perhaps a solution. A contingency was introduced. Then there are stories of abuse by her husband, retroactively followed by stories of abuse by her father who was partly present, busy with work, then present, all too present at other times. All these encounters, erratic, precarious are sexual encounters, traumatic in one way or another, and they come to this abrupt end, or at least a moment of realisation under the heading of "all my life".

The subject is caught, sandwiched, between "once and for all" and "all my life", the latter marking a stopping point to what she wanted from every relationship, even when not being in one. Whereas the former makes the mode of jouissance belong to the dimension of irreversibility of one passing to the other, the latter puts an end to it, appearing as a discovery. When one satisfaction is passed onto the next one, this mode of satisfaction appeared as irreversible. When it came to pass it became contingent. The irreversible here stands for the place proper of jouissance, its disparate place, but also a place that does not change. Jouissance as disparate to the subject held the subject incarcerated in the modality of time called the irreversible (Miller, 1999). Infinity at the core of the pleasure principle presented itself to us as a mode of temporality. Faced with the intersection of the infinity, as infinitely sending the subject to the same place, and its limit as disparate from the subject, we have encountered another modality of time, that of the irreversible. For the subject, loving, as continuous and relative to the fantasy of knowing her man all her life, came to constitute the irreversible dimension, namely the one from which there is no way out. Now, with the signifier "as if I knew him all my life", she is out of the trap, to go where? Anywhere, for example to see an analyst, which introduces her to contingency, to tell him about her men in her life, how she encountered them including the first one, her father. With the discontinuity on the horizon of her discourse, the meaningless appears. And in the face of what does not make sense there is a thought of divorce. The satisfaction of the irreversible became the habitat for the subject until she ceased to inhabit it. And this happened through the cut that marked the moment of realisation about the end. Now there are two paths or contingencies for her, either to continue with her love life in a different, discontinuous way, or to divorce from it altogether.

Time as real

The "all my life" mode of jouissance of wanting the same thing over and again from every boyfriend, her love life represents a dimension of the infinite that analysis did not leave intact. In fact, what the analysis posed, navigating between transference and the unconscious, was the order of repetition. Repetition is on the side of the subject who stumbles upon "it was" in such a way that it appears as "it is". Repetition remains linked to the unconscious as subject because the subject's mode of satisfaction arises from the irreversible passage from "it was" as for ever and ever, to "it is" that insists on rendering the former necessary and inevitable. And this is what Freud told us in his formula of time *Wo es war soll Ich werden* to which I keep returning. The "all my life" is in fact the *es war* as a future where as the subject in transference she was prepared to go to.

Despite the fact that the pleasure principle appears as the most *infatiguable* of workers and the hardest of labourers, something remains irreducible in this opposition to castration. In the subject's repetitive action love is on the side of hypnosis and the subject is asleep. The patient is caught in the *automaton* mode of jouissance and finds no way out. Then, there is a lucky find, a serendipitous moment when the subject awakes. It is an awakening *as* subject, marking the unconscious as subject and opening the door of contingency to an encounter with an analyst. In analysis her path soon leads towards the irreducible object and reveals the direction of "having" it, or not, without "being" it for another.

The modalities of time and of satisfaction I have just outlined belong to the dimension of the meaningless. The patient discovered it straight away, hesitating, seeking to make a new sense of the place she reached. They do not as such, one by one and one after another, make sense. The subject gets used to it because it is a mode of existing. These moments point to what Lacan called the real, the real jouissance in so far as it aims at the hallucinatory in the subject's speech. When Freud said that the unconscious is timeless he did not necessarily made it exempt from any mode of temporality whatsoever. In one sense the unconscious is timeless as it does not obey the laws of linear time and of continuity of time. But we can see that *es war* troubled him in this sense as it retained for him a dimension of temporality of the unconscious. Time has no representation in the unconscious or there is no representation of time in the unconscious. But there is a dimension of satisfaction in the subject's relation to the unconscious, which is a dimension of time. We could say that this is a real time, time as real because the experience of the real as unsettling and traumatic for the subject has a direct connection to the dimension of time as a duration, insistence of the past or as a series of encounters or as a cut. Temporality of the trauma is written in the body. But it is written not as a memory, which psychologists make us believe. Time as traumatic is written as experienced by the subject only through repetition that leads or brings the subject back to love, in psychoanalysis called transference. This is how Lacan formulated it in *Seminar XI* (1977).

The fact that Lacan thought of the formation of the unconscious in terms of synchronicity already shows us that timelessness of the unconscious and temporality of the real are different yet related things. For Lacan there is a link between the temporality as real and the ethics of the unconscious. This link has to do with the way he situated repetition, the concept of repetition, one of the four fundamental concepts of psychoanalysis, as adjacent to that of the unconscious. In fact, when editing *Seminar XI*, Jacques-Alain Miller marked this neighbourhood by entitling the first section of Lacan's *Seminar XI* "The unconscious and repetition" (1977). There is a trace which the subject follows, a trace which for Freud runs from the past to the future. But, although for Freud the fundamental reference of the unconscious is in the temporality of the past, for Lacan it is in the future. For Freud "it was" is in the past where the subject must come to be. For Lacan, this "it was" does not imply that it came to pass. On the contrary, "it was" implies that it will always be, that its future will not cease to be. And as it will always be, the time of the unconscious as subject is still to be made, to be struck, like a clock. Struck not as the Aristotelian clock of consecutive "nows" but as a Lacanian clock that strikes not on the hour but on the time of the subject, which is the cut.

Transference, deception, repetition

We can say that the irreversible, the traumatic time as real that runs into the future for the subject is situated between the unconscious and repetition. Lacan draws on the German etymology of the term *Wiederholen*, repetition—*holen*—"to haul, to pull, to draw" calls for a chance. Repetition is an invitation to a chance. "To draw lots" is an expression of chance, serendipity. Repetition is how the subject is pulled along the beaten track, how he is dragged, Lacan says, or pulled by the nose. There is nothing new in knowing someone all your life, but when the patient hears herself say it in the course of her discourse, that is to say when it is punctuated in analysis, there is a ring of surprise.

There are then two sides of repetition or two modalities of repetition which Lacan formulated in relation to the unconscious. On one side there is a repetition as traumatic, a repetition linked to the Freudian *es war*, of which the presence of the analyst is both a reminder and a remainder. And when, all in all, the subject attempts to make sense of the past event, this is accompanied by a failure, by a missed encounter and falling off the track of the pleasure principle.

On the other side repetition is the way for the subject to follow the trace of the unconscious. It is a trail of contingency and follows being tripped by the irreversible and the necessary. Contingency is linked not only to necessity but to a fall as necessary. In this sense repetition concerns the symbolic dimension *vis-à-vis* the irreducible cause, and has a power of an act, which is where Lacan situated it. In fact, Lacan even calls it "repetition in act". So it is on the side of the subject because for my patient it is not only repetition in act but in love.

Repetition in act brings the subject back to the cause which is the site of the irreducible real and the symptom. In his early work with the hysterics Freud opened the floodgates for catharsis. The cathartic method, rechristened by Spillrein as a "dangerous method", involved a purification through reiteration of the same. But for Lacan repetition is not a purification. Repetition is not cathartic as it does not reduce the necessary minimum that sustains subject discourse to zero. I would even say that in this sense repetition is even anti-cathartic because it reminds the subject of the irreducibility of anguish between 0 and 1. And this reminder reaffirms the bipartite structure of repetition.

The anti-cathartic tendency of repetition points us in the direction of sexual reality for the subject, which Lacan called transference. In effect, repetition brings transference to the point of demand in analysis. The demand in analysis can become a demand for analysis once the satisfaction of "all my life" is subtracted from and in analysis in transference. It would be unjustified to speak about a demand in and for analysis without the effect of transference, or without repetition in act and in love, given the latter, namely transference manifests itself, Lacan tells us, as an enactment of sexual reality. And what else is the sexual reality of the subject if not a mode of satisfaction according to which the subject is caught in relation to the letter of the drive seeking the same means of its entrapment over and over again?

The enactment of sexual reality, Lacan says, takes place under the conditions of supposition of knowledge. This is radically new. We know that the epistemological approach was for Lacan one of the main coordinates of transference, what he called subject supposed to have knowledge and knowledge supposed of the subject, which in analysis becomes a knowledge supposed to the analyst. And what is this point, this moment of supposition of knowledge to the analyst if not a place of intersection of two sides of repetition, namely the $S(x)$? And this allows me to say that there is a connection between repetition and transference, the connection made from the start, to the extent that it allows the subject to move from the position of a patient to that of an analysand, which is an act.

There are then two temporalities in psychoanalysis. One concerns temporality of the unconscious. Lacan called it "another temporality", finding as yet another way to respond to Freud's claim that the unconscious is timeless. This other temporality Lacan discovered is the one of opening and closing, the unconscious as pulsating, oscillating between two moments, one of a discovery and serendipity, and one of resistance. Temporality of the unconscious in this respect has to be distinguished from the temporality of repetition and of what is repeated.

Why did Lacan devote so much room in *Seminar XI* to repetition, finding its function elusive and even "most enigmatic", calling upon authors like Kierkegaard to find more clues, indications of its two sides? Why do we find repetition as almost omnipresent in the seminar, unfolding almost side by side of the unconscious if it is not because repetition constitutes a temporality that leads and introduces us to the unconscious?

In the end Lacan reminds us that repetition is linked to the real that does not lie, does not deceive, and at the same time, fails to reach an aim. Hence Freud's compulsion to repeat, where the neurotic subject's renewed attempt at the satisfaction in love fails, for, in Lacanian terms, it involves the desire of all, namely the desire for exception. This desire to be an exception, to be loved like no other involves a refusal, as in the case of my patient, to be everything her husband wants her to be, namely his mother, his cook, his cleaner, his accountant, and his teacher. For Nabokov all these demands and many others were satisfied by his wife in everyday life. But this is not the case of my patient who, having found her husband's dissatisfactions addressed to her, and jouissance spilling over the borders of subjective disparity, discovers she has known this all her life and now only divorce can save her from it. She no longer seeks a man to be in love with. She now comes to tell me about wanting to divorce him and to separate from all the men she has known in her love life. Repetition has to do with coming back to the same place, always returning to the moment she had passed through in the past, not when "it was" but when it will be, as Lacan says. Where the signifier "all my life" marks a point of loss and void, this animates her desire as transcending the repetition. On the graph of desire Lacan marked the first trace of the Other's desire as the signified of the Other. One can only repress it with the signifiers one has at hand: "all my life" → "divorce". With these two signifiers at her disposal she is now faced with a gap. First from repetition to transference, then from alienation to separation, are the two itineraries of her desire at this moment, each producing a gap. That's why transference can carry at this point an element of deception. The deception in transference overlaps the subject's supposition of knowledge which is a knowledge of sexual reality. Is it the sexual reality of the Other or of the subject? This is how we could link repetition to transference. To the extent that transference deceives, repetition does not.

CHAPTER SIX

The drive and its satisfactions

The drive's blindness

What can we say about blindness in psychoanalysis? The term is not unknown both in the clinic and as a depiction of the drive's work. It also designates a cluster of symptoms Freud dealt with in his work with hysterics. Today, the visual impairment poses no objection to the clinical treatment as it is not the blindness that is the cause of the symptom or of the demand for treatment. In the work of a Lacanian analyst it would be barely noticeable that the patient in the treatment is blind. On this occasion, I will focus on the blindness of the drive, its work, even if, but not necessarily, it appears to narrow down the scope of how things work in the field of vision and the play between the visible and the invisible. Last, but not least, blindness sends me to Lacan's work on the gaze that is to be situated in the field of the Other that as such is neither visible nor invisible. On the contrary, the field of the Other designates for us the locus of language and the place of desire to the extent that it is caused by this strange object Lacan called object *a* I have just been speaking about. Not only does it cause desire but also enlivens the subject that this desire supposes to exist in the first place. I am bringing these three categories of blindness to our attention. What I will therefore put to the side in this pursuit is the phenomenological treatment of blindness, and anything that may come under this term, especially as arising from Merleau-Ponty's work *The Visible and Invisible* (1968). Lacan's articulations of the drive take up Freud's vicissitudes to present drive's work as a mode of jouissance. It will no longer be paradoxical to say that from this perspective blindness can be best served in the work of the scopic drive.

Starting with the hypothesis that the drive is blind, let's try to situate the position of the subject as driven. It is a symptom, on the one hand, and the field of the gaze as object, on the other. The Freudian symptom is made of the drive satisfaction and the representation as repressed. But it is the blindness of Oedipus that made Freud see the pathway where he spoke of castration, to which Lacan added privation. As Oedipus makes his way from Thebes back to Colonus, his solitude acquires another dimension than the one when he had left it. In returning home Oedipus shows us that he knows where he is going without seeing his way. Blindness is no objection to an aim being achieved, and this works at several levels. The passage from Thebes to Colonus could be structured along the lines of the logical time and its three moments: Thebes or the time of seeing conceived as the first moment of blindness, then, already in Colonus, the time of understanding and the second moment of blindness, which Lacan marked by highlighting the words of Sophocles, μηφυνάι, better not to have been born. And finally, as Lacan was quick to remark, the third moment of blindness as constitutive of the time to conclude, namely to separate from the object gaze, for the only one who never had to pass through the Oedipus complex. Lacan makes this remark somewhere in the seminar on the ethics of psychoanalysis, and many found it amusing. But it also serves as a prelude to his later work where he redefines Oedipus. This paradox that refers to the position of the *exception* is crucial for us because it concerns the real in Lacan's new formulation. Hence the question that arises from this: how to construct the final days of Oedipus' journey as an end of analysis for the one who, unlike Freud and any neurotic, never has passed through the complex? This led Lacan to open a dimension of the beyond of Oedipus which Lacan continued to work on in the seminar on discourses as no longer being a question of prohibition but of the impossibility inherent in language.

Let's start by differentiating the eye and the gaze, which could be pursued in three stages: the split between the two, the emergence of the stain, the object gaze.

The split between the eye and the gaze was for Lacan an important point of distinction whereby it separated the psychoanalytical field from phenomenology. The visual field of *perceptum* and the field of the gaze as linked to the scopic drive may intersect but are not equivalent. It is where they part that interests me here. To the extent that the function of the eye is constrained to the field of the visible, it, the visible, appears as confined and limited. The visible is limited not only by the invisible, by what is still to be seen. The limit of the visible is not only discerned by what is invisible. Borges (1984) remarked that people associate blindness with blackness, the colour black, but his experience of blindness was that it is red. Borges perceived his blindness differently to the common assumption that differs from perception. There is a blindness in the field of perception because it is conditioned by the light which comes from the place of the Other. There is another modality of limitation of the visible that could be grasped when we approach the division between the eye of the observer and the subject whose conditions are determined by the Other of language. In this sense, an observation is already a set of conditions that implicate language laid down for the subject. Borges was able to articulate his experience because he knew how to see that was not the same for others. This was the structural basis on which Lacan constructed his mirror stage. The mirror stage aims to demonstrate the formation of the function of the "I" that stands for the subject as emerging from the Other as a place of language. This function of the "I" is distinct from the formation of the ego—that, strictly speaking, despite Strachey's suggestion, deserves no other name than "the me" or, precisely, what Lacan refers to as *le moi*—in relation to the mirror reflection that by addressing "me" allows me to say "I am". But this only occurs, Lacan shows, as an effect of reference provided by the parental Other holding the child or at least indicating "look, look, this is Johnny". The subject who says "I" is not the other of the mirror image and not the imaginary "me" that the image appears to address. The subject arises from the Other whose function is carried by the parent or the analyst, who initially introduces the child to the specular image as me, *le moi*, conjoining the one looker and the image. The "I" is not a name of the synthesis but a mark of distinction from the imaginary unity, and identification, thus formed. In some way "I" is the first disidentification from the identification with an image. That is the difference between the imaginary me and the symbolic function of the "I". The split between the eye and the gaze inevitably draws and relies on the difference between *le moi* and the subject.

From the mirror stage to the split between the eye and the gaze

What can be seen by the eye presents itself as a continuity that combines reflections and objects, interconnected in a more or less panoramic view, in accordance with the conditions of optics and light. Illusion is an integral element of this view for it is not up to the eye to distinguish illusion from non-illusion. Blindness of the eye, as subject to the optical conditions that Lacan illustrated with his vase and flowers in the optical schema, remains inscribed in the difference between what is seen and what is not, of which illusion is a part. The limit of the visible therefore, which is where I started, has to do with the blindness of the eye or a blind spot and this is how Lacan distinguished it from the gaze.

In this sense, to give the term "blindness" its proper place, let me isolate the blind spot in the field of vision. A simple exercise will serve the purpose. If we position the eye closely in front of the gap in the line while looking at the dot on the left, the line will appear as continuous.

•
▬▬▬▬▬▬   ▬▬▬▬▬▬

In its function, the eye, when confronted with a gap, renders the invisible visible. The blind spot shows the limit not only in the visual field but also in what Lacan called in "Some reflections on the ego" (1953) the congenital fault. To the extent that the eye is in its heart blind, it tends to approximate the visible elements and join them into a continuous view. It is a view from which the eye itself is excluded. The sexual function of this approximation shows us the true colours, not just one, of the term "imaginary" in the form of a fantasy of the phallic mother. This fundamental fantasy, whose status in the clinic seems as striking as the banality of Oedipus, aims to veil the subjective castration, namely subject's eagerness to phallicise the lack where the phallus is present only as absent. As for the function of the eye, despite its congenital fault, which is to be distinguished from a fault as symptom, it is constantly on the look out to complement the other, to fill in the gap in the other and by this virtue to give its bearer a sense of fullness from which the term *Gestalt* draws its full meaning. In perversion the subject is driven by the combination of denuding and stripping the Other bare to embarrassment and shame because the pervert's aim and game is to preserve his belief, and his position, as the object and jouissance of the Other. Once he succeeds in this, only then will he endeavour to provide a cover and to fill in the gap in the Other by complementing it and by pleasing it which is only a cover up. In neurosis, on the other hand, it is the subject as lacking and incomplete that will seek in the Other a complement and a tool with which to dress the lack.

The function of the lack in the structure, arising from the inconsistency of the Other as falling short of the guarantee to take the signifying chain to infinity, has to be distinguished from the optical fault. For it is the division between the two that gives birth to the subject as he follows the object gaze looking at him but not to be seen in the field of perception. That is why Lacan speaks of the subject as divided, split in the alienating myth of complementarity that governs imaginary formations. It is therefore not for the subject to see, or not to see, but to find his alienated position as divided between the field of the Other, where lurks the gaze, and the drive that aims at the satisfaction of soliciting it. Fantasy, to the extent that its structure offers the imaginary veil beyond which there is nothing, despite what Heidegger said about the existence of things, appears as the fourth term here. The way Lacan situates the formula of fantasy on his graph of desire shows that it is also the only time where the object *a* is mentioned there. The vector of desire points happily to fantasy when castration is refused. At least the graph tells us this. The practice confirms it in so far as there is fantasy after analysis. Crossing the fundamental fantasy, which is how Lacan once formulated the decisive step at the end of analysis, is not an objection to fantasy to continue to function albeit not in its fundamental dimension as a refusal of castration. In what dimension then? In this sense the subject's alienated position in relation to the master signifier in the Other precedes the construction of fantasy. According to Lacan the function of fantasy is to support the subject's desire as caused by the object to the extent that in fantasy the subject seeks ways to produce jouissance by way of imaginarisation of the object lost and by reinserting it into the libidinal circuit of satisfaction that may come from, but not only, looking and seeing. This brings me again to *Seminar XI The Four Fundamental Concepts of Psychoanalysis* (1977), where Lacan introduces us to the division between the eye and the gaze. What is it that the subject cannot see? Whatever it is, the satisfaction is experienced at the level of the hallucinatory effect over the object lost as I have previously pointed out with reference to Freud's early work. What cannot be seen is, of course, the lack because the lack belongs to the symbolic dimension of language. The lack is marked by the phallus, the signifier of desire, that is present as absent by pointing to the signifier of the lack in the Other. The phallus marks the lack. Its symbolic value consists in the fact that the lack owes its existence to the phallic signifier. The elusive presence of the phallus as an indicator of desire can also create comic effects in the visual field when the subject slips on it right before our eyes. In which case, because we always laugh at such moments, the so-called "blind spot" should be marked as a moment of a fall, and therefore as a minus or -φ, which renders it central to this whole picture.

The function of the stain

Let me move on now to introduce what Lacan calls the stain. Lacan isolates its function when he shows us a radically new way of looking at the painting. This novelty owes to his structural approach to psychoanalysis. The arrival of the stain in the picture marks the moment of the subject. To put it in one big step the split between the eye and the gaze, which is caused by the stain, is a moment of the subject coming to existence. How does this division, this split between the eye and the gaze come about? Elsewhere I tried to illustrate the function of the stain with reference to a scene in Shakespeare's *Othello*. For my purpose here suffice it to say that Desdemona and Othello, who love each other, encounter an obstacle that proves insurmountable. Iago suggests to Othello that she is unfaithful to him. He supports it by saying he saw Cassio wiping his beard with Desdemona's handkerchief. When Othello asks her lover to show him the hanky she says she does not have it. Othello rejects her feminine position of the one who does not have it, and is attracted by what Duras called "homosexual desire" that emerges for him through the handkerchief being used to wipe off man's bearded face. This object, the hanky, completely reorients the scene of love. It creeps in, unexpected, and makes the whole discourse on love revolve around it. It both belongs to the scene and does not, having the power to change desire's direction. It does not even have to appear as such in the picture but only as a crack in the scene of love. So there you are, the little blob, thrown in between the signifiers, shows us how the function of the stain can reorient the relations between the sexes.

I want to mention another example which seems to me of great relevance to Lacan's discovery. Lacan was looking at the Holbein's painting *The Ambassadors* and did not get distracted by the opulence of colour, clothing, and scientific objects around the two figures. He found at the bottom of the painting an object that did not make sense to him. Somehow the mysterious object does not belong to the painting and yet forms its pivotal part. The object, which Lacan calls anamorphic and to which I will have a chance to return later, was how Lacan went on to account for the function of the stain. The stain emerges in the scopic field and separates the visible from the invisible. The topology of the Moebius strip shows us how their opposition can change place without changing their relation that has the stain as an axis. The Moebius strip is a strip of paper both ends of which are joined together when one of the ends is turned 180 degrees. When you start on any given point and move your finger along the surface full circle you will end up at the point exactly underneath the one where you started. You can do this with the Moebius strip because it has one side. Two points, one in reverse to other, illustrate two functions of the stain.

Lacan articulates this function as having a topological structure, and we can easily disregard size, dimension, colour, etc. The stain can indeed emerge in the form of a blob that stands for a focus-point, a kind of a vanishing point in perspective. In other words, it is an operator in the visual field in which, while being removed from the play of the visible and the invisible, it structures their relations. The stain can thus be marked as $-\varphi$, as it opens the door to the object gaze—never to be seen but present. Lacan speaks about the can of sardines that we cannot see from the fishing boat but which can see us. This tin is indeed the gate to the object gaze. The can of sardines or Desdemona's hanky have a form of the stain in the scopic field, they both cover up a hole through which lurks the look and reveal it, opening it. The function of the stain is indeed twofold, to conceal and to reveal.

Following the edge of the strip, we are caught up in an operation of vacillation, covering on one side, revealing on the other, veiling and unveiling. The function of the stain appears to me as having the capacity to make the mirror stage collapse (Wolf, 2013). Lacan's work on the gaze in *Seminar XI* and on the scopic drive could be approached as the other side of the mirror stage, its negation and its collapse. Once the stain becomes part of the view, oscillating between its functions of veiling and unveiling, the subject's division is immanent. The subject exists as a bar between the two, between the little chink in the field of visual perception and the gaze. The object gaze as separated from the subject constitutes its proper division.

It seems to me that this radically new way of looking at the painting led Lacan to introduce us to the gaze as object *a*? The stain that covers the place of the gaze is what Lacan calls the point of intersection of the visual field and the field of the Other. Lacan is very precise here and designates this point of intersection as anamorphosis. It concerns the field of the Other. What does it mean? He locates the anamorphic object on the Holbein's painting to carry out and reverse the operation. Initially, the mysterious object at the front is merely a large dot, perhaps a smudge. But when looked at from the side angle, it assumes its proper, and scary, shape. How did the painter paint it, Lacan asks? The answer lies in the gaze of the painter—the way he looked at his subject matter is what we get when looking at the painting. In the case of the anamorphic object the painter is then in the place of the Other looking at the object in front of us—not from the other side, as it were, but from the place removed from view thus giving it to be seen. This oscillation between the viewer and the painter is therefore interlocked in a play at the heart of which is the impossible to see, the object *a*. This way of painting a picture, then, becomes reversed when we try to decipher it, read it in reverse, adjusting the eyes in relation to the object in the painting. And this is what Lacan calls the point of intersection of two fields, the scopic and the Other, the visual where the mysterious object appears, and of the gaze, the place from which the painter was looking.

The gaze and the logic of the couch

If we now raise the division of the subject between seeing and not seeing where he is looked at, which is the place of the gaze, to the level of the dialectic of demand and desire, what are we going to find? We will encounter the divided subject as caught between the demand to see what is behind the veil of the screen the painting represents, and the desire to be looked at from the beyond of the same veil. In this movement we see a demonstration of Lacan's formula of fantasy. A child likes to cover her head and eyes in assumption that she cannot be seen. Not to see implies to become invisible *to* the Other. We can say that seeing, and by the same stroke having one's eyes closed, is structurally inseparable from being looked at. And if so, there is a connection between the drive's satisfaction in the visual field and the desire of the Other from where comes the gaze. The connection is that because the scopic object is lost, satisfaction follows the same hallucinatory process I referred to earlier as described by Freud. As for the object in the field of desire that causes the subject to seek the lost object, it is the gaze.

The function of the stain for Lacan is to disrupt this misrecognised connection between the drive's object as lost and the desire's object as a cause. That's why I said earlier that the stain disrupts the specular harmony of the mirror stage's relation to the specular image. On the subject of scopophilia, Freud spoke about the satisfaction of wanting to be seen. We know from many examples that even covering one's eyes can aim at precisely that. Invisibility may doubtless present itself as the ultimate temptation for someone to come into full view. The entertainer Dame Edna, who is *de facto* a man dressed as a woman, wears on the stage the most glamorous and sparkling clothes. The moment he comes to view, greeted by loud cheers he often thinks to himself: "Alone at last". He knows precisely that the way to be left alone, and in this sense to become invisible, is to ensure that the shiny outfit serves well to bring him into full view in the eyes of the spectators.

Freud stresses that wanting to be seen should be approached at the level of autoeroticism. But Lacan goes further. The demand to be seen, to the extent that it involves the field of the Other, may represent a dissatisfaction and be represented by the signifier of dissatisfaction, in which case it is repressed. To experience the Other's look on me produces an anguish, which Lacan defined as a sensation that does not deceive. But this relation with the object as a look from outside also solicits a fantasy. Fantasy aims to bring back and restore—hence its imaginary status—what was lost, the scopophilic satisfaction. And when the child covers her face with a pillow to become invisible, this is also a moment of wanting to appear as an object to the Other. The anguish of being looked at, of being expected to renounce some of my satisfaction, is accompanied by a coming into an encounter with the lack in the Other. More specifically, appearing in the field of the Other as looking, which is the case of Dame Edna, leads to this lack in the Other being experienced as anguishing. It is not just about what the Other is looking at, wants from me and so on. It is also what/who exactly is looking at me? How does the Other as incomplete and lacking, look at me to claim a pound of my jouissance, come to address the subject hiding her head? How can this gaze be identified, flashed out, so to speak, if not by the voice? This is the way Lacan is going, it seems to me, having added both the object gaze and voice at the level of desire of the Other. The relation with the object gaze thus leads to the emergence of the voice that is addressed to whom if not to the Other from whom to solicit the gaze, both being situated on either side of desire? The voice as the signifier of the lack in the Other comes to confirm and regulate the subject's relation with the gaze by, as it were, catching me in the eye.

I recall a moment in analysis of a patient who was troubled by the view of the couch. She would ask whether she would have to lie down one day and if this was for her. At some point she answered her questioned by deciding she was ready and I invited her to the couch which she accepted. But this was not without anguish which she confirmed stating that now she would not be able to see me. I said she would be able to hear me and that I will continue to listen to what she has to say. The couch is contingent. It is not necessary when it imposes itself on the subject in the field of vision, which it does. But when it does come into view, it becomes somewhat unavoidable which is what happened here. In the first moment, the couch appeared to her as a little crack in her perception that was a bit disturbing as well as arousing curiosity. Sitting on the chair and speaking was not enough for her. In the second moment, the couch opened the relation with the gaze, which implied the Other's desire. By taking a step towards the couch, which the analyst supported, she now reversed her anguished relation with the gaze. She came to the place from where she was looked at, which evoked some long forgotten scenes, and by this stroke separated from the object gaze, repositioning herself as a subject. But this was only possible through a new relation with the signifier, namely the one that in signifying signifies nothing but pure, at least we assume, desire for difference.

You recall that in the mirror stage, the child's imaginary formation, her eye catching the body image, becomes cemented through the Other mediated by the voice. The subject's fantasy provides an answer to the question how the Other sees me, and with it, what the Other wants from me. And this is how Lacan defines fantasy as supporting desire. In fantasy the subject attempts to restore the losses by means of the object *a*. But since in the place where there should be an Other as desiring, there is an object *a*, the subject in the fantasy will be situated in relation to this object. To achieve what? Lacan calls the object *a* an effect of the loss of something essential in subject's love life. The object a is an effect of castration. If the object a at stake in the fantasy is the gaze, then it is because my desire as caused by the object, sought to solicit the Other's acknowledgement of my existence in the first place that I am responded to with the voice as soliciting the Other. One could call this loop hearing-oneself-speak but there is more to it as Lacan shows. The look as causing subject's desire, and the voice as coming from the Other, which in effect marks the separation between the object gaze and the Other, thus stand at two ends of the loop called desire as Lacan drew it on the top of his graph. That's why the third moment in the patient's shift to speak from the couch touches on the voice, which in this case is the signifier in its most primitive dimension, namely as what is heard. It concerns her that she would not be seen. Will she be heard? What does that imply? It implies the presence not of the analyst but of the analyst's desire. This third moment appears to be marked by the subject taking the place of the gaze where the couch was looking at her and, following the analyst's invitation, coming to occupy this place while vacating the place she has just occupied. Nothing has changed in the shift at this level. To put it differently, the swapping of places relative to the gaze only produces a change if this passage concerns her position in relation to desire. Whose desire if not the one of the analyst and, subsequently, and through the recognition of her voice, her desire? If this shift is not without anguish it is because it is not without the object, amplified by the uncertainty of what the Other wants from her. The object gaze did not disappear as it was never in sight anyway but it changed places and is no longer attached to the Other as looking. Where is it attached then? Is this the last word on the logic of the couch? It is a logic of contingency that implicates a shifting of positions relative to the gaze of the Other but not without the analyst's desire that comes into view, so to speak, when the voice enters the scene or as hearing her speak. If Lacan speaks of the analyst's desire, which is his invention, it is because he is telling us about the analysand's desire too. These three moments or steps echo the emergence of the stain as Lacan brought it to our attention, and in which he led us to have some grasp of the object a perhaps the oddest object of all. Not every step in the passage to the couch follows this logic. Sometimes an analyst asks his patient to take the place on the couch in which case we could perhaps speak of a push-to-the-couch. But this passage seems to be inscribed in the logic of transference where some knowledge of the object a is supposed of the analyst, or towards the analyst, at the moment when the subject's position underwent what Lacan called rectification.

The drive as a "mythification" of the real

It seems to me as inadequate to try to reduce fantasy to the wish to be seen. And that is not even because seeing masks what is impossible to see, revealing the fundamental dimension of blindness in the visual field, but because fantasy is supposed to make up for this impossibility. Fantasy is supposed to produce jouissance at what is not there. Lacan gave fantasy a very precise formula, scooping it out from the generalised field of satisfaction to which Freud testified with his notion of *Befriedegungserlebnis*. Lacan placed in this formula the subject as divided in relation to the object *a*.

$$\$ \lozenge a$$

In this relation is supposed some compensatory mending of this division, causing jouissance at bringing back the lost times. Lacan tries to refine this nostalgia by resetting the compass pointing in the direction of what does not exist, which gives fantasy its true name. And this is where the drive comes in. Fantasy appears to conceal the real whose failed evocation at the level of the symbolic lands us in the face of the Other's desire, and more precisely in the face of the signifier that signifies nothing save the desire for difference. For this reason let's take a closer look at the relation between the fantasy and the drive. Jacques-Alain Miller advanced Lacan's elaboration of fantasy by calling the fantasy a mask of the drive. In the fantasy involving the object gaze, the scopic drive is masked, and this has an effect of jouissance.

The consideration of the fantasy as a mask of the drive can be further highlighted by Lacan's remark about Oedipus in *Seminar XVIII From an Other to the other* (2006h). Lacan says there that although Oedipus finds the answer to the Sphinx's question, he does not know what this answer is an answer to. We could say that finding the truth does not always imply that we also grasp the contours of the real. The truth gives us an inkling of the locus of jouissance which, although the answer is *anthropos*, marks a path on which castration will have been realised. In fantasy we do not know what the drive it masks is a drive for except following the satisfaction it attains once its aim has been achieved. One

THE DRIVE AND ITS SATISFACTIONS 141

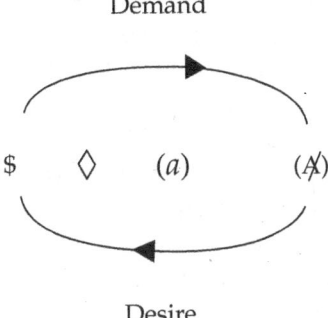

Schema 1.

constructs the fantasy based on the drive achieving its satisfaction in one way or the other, which is its aim. We can construct an orientation for the subject given the jouissance as produced by the drive and the object direction where the fantasy takes the subject. As we know it was oral and anal for Freud, to which Lacan added scopic and invocatory.

In the schema above the subject is in relation to the object *a* that is an effect of castration. This relation in Lacan's matheme of fantasy, is flanked by demand and desire, and shows how the subject comes into existence by separating out from the Other in the dialectic of alienation which entails the relation of demand and desire. The dialectic of demand and desire led Lacan to the topology of two conjoined toruses, which is where it is best demonstrated. The schema above attempts to condense that dialectic in the form of the circular movement in the midst of which can be found the object *a* that belongs neither to the Other nor to the subject.

Continuing with his return to Freud, Lacan reminds us some years later, in the text "On Freud's 'trieb' and the psychoanalyst's desire" (2006f), that for Freud drives are our myths. What is a myth? A myth is what carries a reference to the real. That's why it captivates us. It is therefore not to be dispensed with as the party politicians would wish but to be reckoned with. The real is the reason why we are concerned with the myths following them and being enchanted by them. It is only because of this reference that myths, of antiquity or modernity, appeal to us and even captivate us. The drives are a particular modality of myths as resting on the real. They "mythify" the real, Lacan says. We could say that the myths are the mask of the real. The drives allow to recreate the subject's relation to the object as lost. That's why Lacan can say that the gaze comes before seeing. This is crucial and Lacan's discovery of the stain serves as its support. The gaze contains a reference to the scopic drive where the object is lost. It is the gaze, Lacan tells us, that forms the conditions of seeing. We could thus speak of the drive's blindness, its cyclopic quality. What comes before seeing, what conditions it, is a loss that through the stain determines the contingency of seeing. But wouldn't this amount to saying that the signifier, in particular the signifier of desire is the condition of speech?

After Lacan introduced the stain as decisive in the problematic of the gaze and the scopic drive, there is a link to be made to the work of the unconscious in the same *Seminar XI*. Lacan presents the unconscious as pulsating, as interchangeably opening and closing, uncorking the gap and obturating it. What happens at the level of the drive apart from it being masked and mythified? By considering the unconscious as a pulsation Lacan invites us to take notice that it is not without an echo of the drive and its vibrations in the body that produces an effect of division. What does the drive do? It divides the subject. The pulsation of the unconscious consists of two instances, its opening at the time of a mistake, and its closure at the moment of its signifying representative being repressed. This dynamic of the unconscious, this fluctuation between opening and closing, is not without an echo of the drive whose work seems dominated by two elements although Freud speaks of four components. The drive is somewhat teased to come out of itself to seek the object that is always lost and in effect to end up with a hallucinated satisfaction at not having found it. It is an outward movement. The drive goes out of itself and in this movement of going out of itself it returns to the pit of its vanity having produced what Lacan will call later a round of demand. I am anticipating here Lacan's topological reading of Freud's work on the drive. Lacan will introduce language and the work of the signifier through demand as a response to needs. There is not much an infant has at his disposal except for the cry and jerky movements of his body. That's where they are interpreted and read, and that's where the Other of language comes in. At some point the cry becomes transformed into the demand that in addressing the Other from where it came, serves to facilitate the satisfaction of a need. In the heart of the dialectic of demand and desire, which Lacan topologised, the latter becoming a reminder of what has not been satisfied, we can find the fantasy as drive's mask. And as a myth. Myths are names of satisfactions, names of jouissance, which includes representations of animals. Desire in turn comes into existence as eternal negativity caused by the effect of the lost object and chiselled from the Other's desire. It flares up, rises, hovers, call it what you like, there is no drive satisfaction there to stand on. It arises out of the lack and as a lack. Is the object *a* real or imaginary?

The pulsation as a movement of alteration has topological and therefore structural implications for the clinic. In neurosis, the stain, clearly supporting the object in fantasy, has a duplicitous function catching the eye in the trap of *fascinum*. It can take on a form of a remainder that does not come off like the blood stain at the start of Macbeth. Or it covers the Cyclop's eye. Either way, it does not wash. In psychosis, the stain does not divide but becomes an object of persecution.

This is how Lacan proposes to dispose of Merleau-Ponty's claims to consciousness that in the field of vision is quilted to the master all-seer which is in fact the master signifier S_1. Lacan gives us an example by quoting from Valéry's poem: *seeing oneself seeing oneself*. In it we can find a true fulfilment of the Eastern promise in which consciousness grasps itself in the way Freud elaborated it in his "On narcissism: an introduction" (1914c). In this text Freud stresses the function of being-watched and relates it to the way in which philosophical insight operates. Freud gives us here a paradigm of the paranoiac work in the course of which thinking operates in the space between being-watched and watching oneself. With it, and in relation to the scopic drive situated between the grammar of the active and passive voices, Freud introduces the death drive as central to the imaginary relation.

Blindness as symptom

And this brings me back to the problem of blindness. There is a Borgesian blindness of light and the blindness of the drive. What then is there behind the visible? Behind the visible there is nothing. Behind the mask there is a void. But behind the veil there is also a death drive. Freud found the gaze unawares in the representation of Medusa. It is the mask of the death drive *par excellence*. Medusa is the petrifying gaze that cannot be seen, and until Perseus finds the way of locating her wandering horror in a specular image no one knows where she creeps in. What brought Perseus to confront Medusa if not what lies beyond the object gaze and what concerns the Other's desire? It is wrapped around fantasy that supports it. The subject navigates between the Charybdis of the Other's demand through which the Other exerts the expectations, the influences, and the Scylla of desire founded on castration, the promised land, you might say. Before I get there the question poses itself for me: what am I for the Other whose demand I have taken as my compass and whose desire is my ultimate goal? What does the Other want from me, setting me on this journey in the first place? These questions mark a certain limit in the passage. Each of them is a mask and a veil beyond which lies concealed, what? Only the inverse side of the mask, the inner lining or its reverse side that Moebius strip always helps us to grasp. Lacan called it *l'envers* which does not render "the other side". Odysseus knew when to pluck up his ears crossing the fantasy towards the reverse side of his knowledge. These are our little points of orientation with regard to fantasy as what marks the end of the road for anyone who flinches from crossing beyond. Beyond what if not the refusal to recognise the Other's castration at which point it becomes clear that we navigate not on the mythical waters of the drive but follow the vectors of the divided subject on the graph of desire as Lacan designed it?

Freud did not doubt that the visual field is organised by the unconscious. He did not doubt the significance of the concept of the unconscious organisation that structures the subject's relation in the world. In 1910, Freud gave an account of a hysterical symptom formed by the subject in the scopic field. In the article "The psychoanalytic view of psychogenic disturbances of vision" (1910i), Freud says that although hysterical blindness is a form of refusal at the level of perception of light, this blindness is not an anatomical fault. We could even say that it is because the unconscious is structured like a language that the refusal to see can be organised as a symptom. Thus, Freud, although not having any linguistic evidence before his eyes, goes on to speak of blindness from the perspective of the dialectic of representations. In this he distinguishes the symptomatic, Freud calls it "hysterical", blindness, from that of the unconscious. The subject can "see" in the unconscious, namely associate between the past visual perceptions and their articulations. Having established a causal connection between symptomatic blindness and autosuggestion, he gives up the latter as a *cause* of impaired vision. The hysteric may go blind not because of the inner autosuggestion, which is a work of an ideational representation

Lacan isolated as *Vorstellungrepräsentanz*, but because of a dissociation. What is dissociation in this sense? Freud asks how it is possible that a suggestion may lead to a formation of a belief in one's impairment of vision. A couple of years later, in 1912, in "A note on the unconscious" (1912g), Freud tries to answer this question by bringing into consideration a post-hypnotic effect that may leave anyone blind, deaf, and so on. The unconscious for Freud gives us this possibility that may be realised in the symptom formation. Having then discarded the idea of the symptom of blindness as an effect of an autosuggestion, Freud proposes a hypothesis of dissociation of the representations or indeed signifiers in the unconscious structured like a language. With a little help from Lacan we can formulate this dissociation as a disjunction between the drive representations, namely the articulation of demand, and that of desire, namely the signifier of the *lack* in the Other. Speaking of drives implies the subject is already caught up in the dialectic of demand, he is in demand, as it were. In this sense the drive as caught in demand is always satisfied, which implies the satisfaction of a symptom, for example of blindness. If the drive is always satisfied, indestructible and unconditional, it is because its circuit always achieves the aim, going out to capture the object, encircling it as if it was the real one and, satisfied, ending in the hollow marked, in distinction from other hollows, by a rim. Just as the drive always misses the object, it is always satisfied having looped around its semblance as Lacan showed us on his little schema in *Seminar XI* (1977).

The drive, as a kamikaze of the mental system, does not directly determine the object *a*. It encircles the object and determines its place. Since the primary object is lost, the loop of the drive determines the place of the object in desire. But it is not the object of the drive, say the anal object, that causes desire. What causes desire is the object of desire. The object *a* as that which arises from this determination causes desire and as semblance sets fantasy into motion. Lacan was asked, by Safouan, about the difference between the object of the drive and the object of desire. Lacan replied by distinguishing the love object, "I love the lamb stew" or "I love caviar", from the object of desire. To love something or someone does not imply that we desire it. The difference between loving a woman and loving your dog being that the latter, while following you everywhere, does not ask any questions. According to Lacan, and relative to the difference between the drive and desire, the oral object is not the same for both. To love your seafood is not to desire it. What

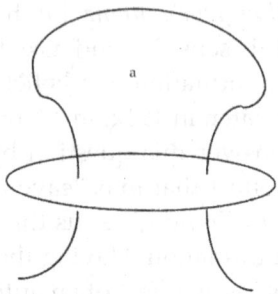

Schema 2.

causes desire is the object of desire, namely that I do not want any. The butcher's wife loves caviar but does not desire it. At this point Lacan adds that this object that causes desire is, *de facto*, the object of the drive. In what way? The drive encircles the object cause of desire. What makes the difference is not the object but the fact that desire never closes in on it, never reaches satisfaction over it. In some way, once the desire is animated and set in motion, Lacan says "agitated" by the drive, this object becomes redundant for desire while causing it all the time.

What then, we could ask, agitates the drive? What sets it into motion given it is a partial drive, for example, a scopic one, that is always seeking the satisfaction around the visual object? Is it teased out of its hollow by the object or is the drive aroused by what comes to its proximity in the field of perception as the discourse? The drive may be jouissance, a drive-jouissance, but it is not, as Lacan often stressed, an instinct or some divine inertia of *élan vital* flowing through the flesh. If Freud did not speak about the drive in terms of castration, it is because for him castration centred on the phallus. But Lacan spoke about castration in relation to satisfaction called jouissance, the drive-jouissance not being the only one. Lacan isolated jouissance as a body excitation that is passed on from the Other, on the verges of the messages, settling like magnetic dust alongside the drive rims. So he spoke about the remnants, leftovers of the impact of language on the body, on the holes in the body. As an effect of the impact of the signifier, the drive-jouissance is teased out to encircle the object that also serves to cause desire but has a different status in its circuit. And this brings me back to the problem of Freudian dissociation in the case of blindness. It would be justified, it seems to me, to speak of a dissociation between the drive

THE DRIVE AND ITS SATISFACTIONS   147

and desire, between the always satisfied drive and never satisfied desire. Demand is to be situated in the heart of this disjunction, as it acts there as an intermediary. It names the child's needs and incorporates the drive. The Freudian symptom is to be formed on the basis of the dissociation of the drive, whose satisfaction can always be substituted for another satisfaction, from the articulation. After all what is not articulated remains invisible, occulted from the field of vision. As for satisfaction, the leopard print on the fabric is as pleasing to the eye as on the animal skin, and the imitation gun can frighten you as much as the real one.

But although there is no difference between the two as the satisfaction is always the same and the aim or the circuit remains the same, something awakens the partial drive. And what awakens the oral drive is not the scopic object. What calls the drive out of its hollow is the signifier that facilitates variations of satisfaction Freud called the life of need. Through repetition, the satisfaction of a need isolates and narrows down the exteriority of the object, say a nipple, around which satisfactions revolve until the object can change and the satisfaction of sucking now encircles a dummy or a finger. So the object has changed whereas the satisfaction remained the same. The scopic drive follows the same logic of *ananke* although no link to the life function has to be present. In the end what is life, and so called "self-preservation" if not a life of a function itself whose eternal repetition serves best our survival as a social group by resisting the forces of death?

Freud develops the hypothesis of dissociation between the aim and the object by putting forward a thesis of a dominant idea that overshadows other representations, dazzling them so that the link between perception and its articulation is broken. We can call this break a disjunction although it is not clear why a disjunction of this kind should lead to blindness unless we can speak of a substitutive formation such as a symptom. The dominant idea that organises the symptom is of course the repressed one. The cause of blindness, as Freud elaborates in his article, is not the drive or the object in the scopic field. Its causality, which clearly reminds us of Lacan's psychical causality, has to do with the symptom and the repressed signifier that dominates the whole construction. The phenomenon of being dazzled is linked directly to the disjunction between the master signifier and the chain from which it was isolated.

In the end it is the return of the repressed that installs blindness as a symptom. What comes to the fore for us in this examination of the drive is the dissociation between the drive's aim, namely its unceasing satisfaction, and the object that has to be given up as substance, and refound, indeed reanimated as a cause of desire. The dissociation in question appears to boil down to the disjunction between drive-jouissance and the lack in the Other through which desire can be recognised. Somewhere between them there is a difference between baking a cake and eating it.

Discourse as an echo of the drive

Although the work of the unconscious is not without an echo of the drive their disjunction constitutes the material explanation of the causes of blindness. The drive becomes manifest as a production of satisfactions, namely of jouissance as caused not by a single occurrence of the signifier but by its circularity and repetition as a body *work*. The illustration of the drive that fits our purpose here is the workout of the body in the gym. No object or love is needed for the workout to achieve its aim because none can interfere with it. In this sense, the drive is indeed a separate entity from desire, love, even from ignorance as at this level it is not a learned ignorance but a blind one, disparate from knowledge. The knowledge of the drive, as it were, of the drive-jouissance, and of the production of satisfaction, will have to be approached therefore from the position of the signifier as lodged in the Other. And this is crucial for Lacan who extracts from the Freudian drive his own claim of the sexual reality, putting it into play with transference and demand. Other than that the drive is a merry-go-round without an operator.

Lacan took up Freud's idea of repression as a conflict of imposition and domination of one representation over the other. On this point Lacan speaks of the master signifier, S_1, as opposed to the signifying chain, S_2, by way of the subject's alienated production of sense. The signifier that is most insistent and dominant becomes repressed because, in Freudian terms, it would produce an excessive affect that consciousness could not handle. This is where we take notice of the repression that founds the symptom such as impaired vision. On another level, the production of jouissance does not cease in the service of needs and well after and beyond their fulfilment. The question we need to pose concerns the locality of tension with respect to the opposition between the pleasure and reality principles. It is of concern to both Freud and Lacan but from slightly different perspectives. This conflict benefits from the unconscious and from the production of the chain. The signifier as coming from the Other, produces jouissance called phallic to the extent that the phallus governs the difference between presence and absence. That's why I said that the drive-jouissance is not the only one. The phallic jouissance is another one, and that is still not all.

Towards the end of his article on the causes of the symptomatic blindness, which is a partial impairment, a refusal, otherwise called repression, to connect the repressed and consciousness—which, as we recall, is the site for the acrobatics of thinking—Freud introduces and distinguishes for the first time the ego-drives and the sexual drives. He is inspired not only by his clinical experience but also by Schiller whom he quotes as saying that all human inclinations fall under two "hunger" and "love". It is worth noting that Freud recognises a whole range of sexual satisfactions that run along the human development from childhood to adulthood and that are not related to the sexual organ. But he reserves castration solely with reference to the penis. Among the sexual satisfactions can be found scopophilia. This link would be Freud's final word regarding scopophilia were it not for the fact that at the end of the text he brings back the connection with the organ, and relates neurotic blindness to a sexually charged experience of having seen what we are not supposed to see. And he mention the story of a naked Godiva riding across town with all the inhabitants closing their shutters. And he who disobeys is punished by becoming blind. In the same vein Freud connects the hand that carried out masturbation with an inhibition to play a musical instrument. Is blindness an inhibition? Or is it a symptomatic effect of the failure to perceive the phallus where it is not, which allows us to mark castration, $-\varphi$?

Lacan was interested in the link between subject's drive and articulation, which is why he placed it at the top of his graph of desire. Seeing, like any other chain in the unconscious, is primarily governed by the pleasure principle. It is organised by the movement of the signifiers that suppose the subject as nonsubstantial in their shifting in the chain. In this way the subject is able to move in the field of perception, pushed around by the appearances and their effervescence to which it was subjected in the first place. With the sliding of the signifiers the tension decreases whereas the reality principle generates it. When the demand on the viewer "to see", or the prohibition to look, is excessive, and the associations unfold slowly and lazily, the tension will grow. Freud himself uses the term "excessive demands". It is in relation to the demand that the neurotic symptom is formed. And Freud describes repression as akin to the condemnatory judgment in the field of logic.

According to Freud, the visual blindness is thus organised around the tension between drive-representations. What Lacan highlights in his reading of Freud's work is that this tension arises not only from the opposition of the pleasure and reality principles but from *das Ding* as extimate to the work of the pleasure principle. But this should not mislead us by opening the back door to sublimation where *das Ding* is a kind of prototype of the object. Blindness as symptom, that is to say as the too-much of jouissance of seeing, which turns into partial impairment, undergoes, as I have said, a different vicissitude, that of repression. When a partial paralysis of the body, whether blindness or stiffness of the arm etc., comes to play, the hysteric, as Lacan once remarked, is on strike. This implies not only the mechanism of repression but that in its work a refusal to give is interlaced with a cooperation with the other. These two elements of refusal and of cooperation, of yes and no, point to repression as underlying the hysteric being on strike. As one of drive's vicissitudes, repression is a destiny of the symptom. For Freud symptom is a destiny of the subject. In *Beyond the Pleasure Principle* (1920g), Freud will say that no substitutive or reactive formations and no sublimation will be able to remove the persisting tension of repression. In other words, the dominant signifier, to use Lacan's term, will never give up on the compulsion to attain the same satisfaction over and over, which, as Freud says, would consist in the repetition of a primary experience of satisfaction. The stress on the repetition of the primary *Befriedegungserlebnis* constitutes for Freud the mechanism of repetition that Lacan raised to one of the four concepts of psychoanalysis as I elaborated it in the previous chapter. This repetition must therefore also have a locality, a place or *topos*.

The significance of *das Ding* comes into view again. Lacan approached it at the metahistorical level, first as that which is inconceivable in the mother, and then as a dark pit of horror for the subject, its real neighbour beyond any signs of familiarity. This connection between Freud's *Nebenmensch* and Lacan's ahistorical and absolute Other appears as the first attempt to give *das Ding* a place and a reference. *Das Ding's* true place rests between the inside and the outside of the subject, which is why Lacan called it *extimate*. For Lacan the Thing is the real without limits, that is to say the real as an internal extimate.

Now, it is over twenty years before *Beyond the Pleasure Principle*, in 1888, in the study "Hysteria" (1888b), where Freud states, and the relation to scopophilia is of importance here, that what constitutes the primary experience in hysteria is dissatisfaction. In other words, in hysteria, the amount of satisfaction expected from the hysteric is always greater than what can be attained in articulation, which in turn becomes folded into what is called a refusal to give. For Freud the hysteric just does not have the body for "more". The dissatisfaction is experienced as a mortifying jouissance but refused as a gift of satisfaction for the Other. She keeps it to herself, so to speak. With respect to the gaze, the demand for the hysteric to be seen spills over the satisfaction of not being seen, namely on her missing on the satisfaction of her image as a whole. A woman's narcissism in relation to the mirror image in this respect follows a different vicissitude than the man's. And this is what Freud does not consider in his introduction to narcissism (1914c). The dissatisfaction of missing on her image as a whole in the gaze of the Other can displace regressively the hysteric's demand for love to the field of *das Ding* and its ravages on the outskirts of speech. And this is what Lacan sometimes refers to when he asks whether it is me or the thing itself speaking. "It speaks" epitomised for Lacan the thing speaking. We encounter it in the clinical experience and hear about its sublimations in literature. Whether it is the Furies swooping on Orestes or the witches in Macbeth, the primordial jouissance of *das Ding* swings between the drive's hallucinatory satisfaction and the foreclosure of the Woman.

Last time the pleasure principle was at the centre of my inquiry into Freud's mental apparatus. I want to take up its function at the level of perception. The function of the pleasure principle in the field of perception is to allow to maintain such a level of libido that some constancy is possible in the production of the signifying chain. In the hysterical symptom of blindness, the pleasure principle is replaced by the reality principle. This marks the moment of the representative of the image being repressed. Thus the return of the repressed in the symptom will make its entry in the form of a fixation of a signifier to an image that mediates the real of anguish. In other words, there is a connection for the subject between *das Ding* as the real of the drive and the stain whose function is to both point to, which is the giving-to-be-seen, and to veil it like the screen in Plato's cave where the happy shadows continue to gyrate.

On the schema below we can see Lacan's schema of the drive that he designed specifically to show its circuit which is its jouissance. The movement from the signifier S_1 to S_2 encounters a disjunction between the aim and the object of the drive. These are the elements with which Lacan will later construct his discourse. In his formula of discourse the dominant signifier and the object *a* are never on the same side but on the opposite side in relation to each other. That's why Lacan entitled his seminar on discourse *The Other Side of Psychoanalysis* (2007), the eminent translator rendering *l'envers* as "the other side". While the aim of the drive is always achieved, which Lacan shows in its circuit, its unstoppable circulation, the passage from S_1 to S_2 is never achieved due to repression that touches on the primary experience of satisfaction. This passage is barred and impeded by the fact that repetition presents itself to the subject as a disjunction between the primary satisfaction and what is supposed to substitute for it, the object in love or in transference, namely knowledge of what went wrong.

The Freudian symptom appears on the border of the drive going out of itself and achieving its goal which is satisfaction. The drive moves in units of one after one after one. It is essentially incomprehensible. What brings it to the subject's attention is the experience of repetition and how the drive's circulation gets caught as the demand of the Other in the loop of desire. Through the entrance of language the baby's cry receives an interpretation and significance which in turn introduces repetition. The drive remains submerged in the body. For the subject, symptoms are modes of jouissance.

Strictly speaking Lacan never tried to represent the drive but to shrink its echoes in the production of discourse. Lacan incorporated the drive into desire first, and then, the drive into discourse. The drive echoes in the discourse as well as appears on the graph of desire as demand of the Other as incomplete, inconsistent, which is the place of the signifier. Drive's work, as Lacan formulated it for us, contains the insignia of the discourse of the unconscious where the drive does not submit to the signifying network, we could say refuses to be pacified by it. Fantasy as the subject's relation to the object *a*, the lure and the bait of the object lost reveals to us the mythical dressing of the drive, its

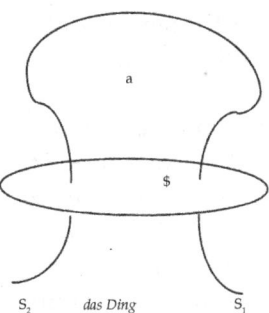

Schema 3.

mask and semblant. While the symptom is always satisfied, the fantasy always asks for more jouissance, and never the way it is experienced or used to be experienced and so on. These might be the variables of fantasy.

The clinic of the symptom and of the sinthome

This presents itself to me as a crossroad, a junction of the symptom and fantasy. In the Lacanian orientation we are always at the junction of the symptom and fantasy. Lacan was working on the logic of fantasy at the time when he was compelled to advance the way in which an analysand would testify to the end of analysis. This was never achieved before him. He constructed a mechanism or a procedure he called the pass. Under this term Lacan designated a passage or a crossing, and he put an emphasis, not without reason, on the crossing of the fundamental fantasy the experience of which could be testified to other analysands who carry the same momentum. What does Lacan mean by the fundamental fantasy? At the time of his work on the pass in the late 1960s, Lacan already elaborated the fantasy of the phallic mother and the ways of veiling and denying the Other's castration. What he designated by the crossing concerned the passage of the subject crossing over to the place of the object *a* where desire is caused at the moment when castration is realised. The change of the position of the subject follows the effects of loss and castration where the object *a* that supports fantasy is produced. The lack in the Other is only revealed in the subject as a result of castration, which is the moment when a question arises as to whose castration, the subject's or the Other's. Lacan called the place of the castrated Other the signifier of the lack *in* the Other, $S(\cancel{A})$, and named it a mystery. Why did he call the desire of the Other the most mysterious element in psychoanalysis? Is it because the speaking subject can only access the Other as desiring through castration? And, secondly, is it because the Other, which is not a secret, is incomplete and inconsistent? On the graph of desire, the crossing of the fantasy leads through the point of castration, $\$ \lozenge D$, all the way up and round to what he calls then an "x", the signifier of the Other's desire. In this sense crossing the fantasy proceeds from the renunciation of jouissance which facilitates the movement of the subject across to the place of the object *a*. If the castration is refused or if the loss of jouissance is refused then the subject is stuck in fantasy. It all appears like a game of snakes and ladders at this moment. Here is the way towards the lack in the Other as inconsistent, and here is the fantasy. If the inconsistency is refused, it is back to consistency of the fantasy. Jacques-Alain Miller stresses in his commentary on Lacan's *Seminar XVIII From an Other to the other* (2006h) that fantasy's consistency veils the inconsistency of the Other. Why? Because when the Other appears as demanding a full payment we are in fantasy. And this allows me to say, which Lacan seems to imply, that the drive of the Other is a myth. In other words, the drive is a way of mythifying the inconsistency of the Other. Jouissance of the Other is a semblance. The drive fictionalises the real, which is what mythology is infused with, which is to say imaginarises the real. It is in this sense that the drives are mythical for Lacan, and that the drive is indestructible for Freud. It is indestructible because the inconsistency of the Other, which is the place of repressed signifier, is indestructible. In fantasy, the object *a* has a function of complementing the subject and, when the Other's inconsistency becomes refused, when God plays dice or could not care less if two plus two equals four, as it was for Descartes or Einstein, fantasy in the Lacanian sense of "fundamental" appears at work. In short, however simplified this game of snakes and ladders on the graph of desire may seem, once we are in the upper level of the graph, there are only two ways from thereon: *either* the long way of the inconsistent and desiring Other *or* the shortcut to the fantasy.

On the graph of desire, the route Lacan called crossing of the fantasy is the long one because it involves the fall of jouissance in castration. But it can be the shortest one just as well. In other words, the crossing marks a cut at the point of passing to the place marked by the object *a*. I say "place", *topos*, because it is a position. The analyst assumes this position, which is how Lacan marked it in the analyst's discourse in which the analyst acts *with* the object *a*. On the one hand, Lacan spoke of the crossing of the fantasy he called fundamental. On the other hand, the end of analysis can be designed around the symptom, and more specifically an identification with the symptom, taking it beyond analysis so that it can serve to prop up the subject on his life journey if the social bond does not offer an alternative. And this was the case of Oedipus the father who did not have to go through or cross the Oedipus complex. In short, at the end of analysis one does not dissolve the symptom or depart from it but take it with you wherever it is you are going after the end of analysis, for example to the Lacanian school where there is work to be done in accordance with the symptom.

Freudian drive remains constant in its aim. I said earlier that the drive is blind or blind-folded. This can be illustrated by the game "blind man's buff" or "blind nanny" as children call it. In the game, which you must have played at some point, the blind-folded player tries to catch other players. The fun is not only to catch them but also to chase them as well as in not being caught. There can even be a sense of disappointment when you catch another player as if this was not the objective. A little illustration of drive's work.

In *Seminar X Anxiety* (2014), Lacan invites us to imagine the following: imagine that one night you go to bed as you always do every night, and just when you are about to go to sleep a strange shape, a praying mantis appears in the window. This is how Lacan illustrates the head-on encounter with the real, pure anguish, whether it be mantis, demon, Dracula or, indeed, their Freudian paradigm, *das Ding*. The question that emerges from this encounter concerns the relation to the desire that comes from the Other. And Lacan, who elaborated its place in detail on his graph of desire, is very precise here as this question is addressed to no other but the ego as the imaginary formation and therefore of the highest importance: *Que vuoi?* Or what do you want from *me*? Or what do you want from my image? It is *das Ding* as impinging on the image that causes the Medusa effect. Nothing can be more unsettling than a creature that does not speak, an unspeaking being, which is where the nocturnal creatures are to be found. The analyst therefore must find his way between day and night.

The question is how to work in analysis with the real of the drive as indestructible and always satisfied, the drive that is a myth of the consistent Other, from which remains a traumatic trace, the undeletable.

Two uses of the clinic emerge here, the differential clinic of the symptom and the clinic of *sinthome*. If the differential clinic rests on repression that is guaranteed by the phallic function, how do we distinguish from it, with respect to the field of vision, the clinic of *sinthome* in which we deal with the foreclosing effects? Freud's clinical legacy is the clinic of the symptom. What Lacan inherited from Freud is a clinic of the symptom and of the repressed. However, towards the end of his teaching, what we have come to call the "later Lacan", he supplemented the clinic of the symptom with another clinic, that of *sinthome*. It is an old term for symptom Lacan found under the patina of time and put it into new use that varies from the symptom in the Freudian sense. *Sinthome*, first of all, is a homophony of *saint-homme*, which is an allusion to Joyce, and to *Saint-Thom*, Saint Thomas Acquinas, whom Lacan chose as one of his references when posing the question of the end of analysis. Lacan was interested in the jouissance of a saint, in what the saint really wants, what makes him tick, in a different way than they were seen by the Catholic Church. And Lacan disappointed many by saying the saint is not on the side of the good, of the benevolent.

We can distinguish in psychoanalysis two clinics with regard to the symptom. In the classical, Freudian approach the symptom is a compound, a combination of sexual satisfaction called jouissance, and of sense, *joui-sens*, which is a bit flimsily translated into enjoy-meant. The symptom formation presents the subject with a metaphorical variable that, sliding along the path of the symptom, substitutes one sense for another. Freud gives examples of men and women performing compulsive and ritualistic actions that replace the original, traumatic encounters with the real. In this sense the symptom is both a failure before the traumatic jouissance in the language's impact on the body and a success to find a way to substitute that failure with an alternative mode of satisfaction that is less imposing and exhausting. But it is only a provisional success as the symptom pushes the subject to repeat actions and appears stronger than the subject, stronger than me. The clinic of the *sinthome* involves writing and therefore writing's relation to the body. Lacan presented it originally when he was working on the topology of the Borromean knot in relation to Joyce. *Sinthome* describes a supplementary device or *suppléance* that provides the subject, not only psychotic, with a minimal manageability of existence, as writing became for Joyce. In the face of the foreclosure of the signifying operator Name-of-the-Father, and of an incapacity of phallic jouissance, which brings significations to a halt, what assumes a paramount importance in relation to language is the dimension of writing and of the letter. On the one hand, the letter is a place of anchorage for the drive jouissance, and on the other, it provides a small variation to meaning in relation to the signifier. We could say that in the clinic of *sinthome* as a result of the phallic incapacity and a search for the name, jouissance is pinned to the letter. One could compare this process to that of collecting distinct species of living beings like insects or butterflies, which are also non-speaking beings. So I called it pinning jouissance to the letter. Earlier we spoke of reading desire to the letter. Now we are speaking of pinning jouissance to the letter, which is a different thing. This provides the subject with an alternative formation where the significations are immobile. The only signifying dynamic that remains can be shown in the relation between the letter in the visual field and the signifier in the auditory field.

At the end I would like to take up briefly a clinical case presented by Marie-Hélène Brousse, and published in 1998 in the *Psychoanalytical Notebooks*. It is about a woman who had an encounter with the real at the level of visual perception. Walking at night she saw a skin of a dead animal at a distance which petrified her. Of all things visible and invisible, the dead animal punctuated the crack in the visual field, almost like the stain for the eye. She thus became introduced to *das Ding*. In effect, we are told, jouissance produced at that point, the overbearing satisfaction of being caught in the field of the gaze of the Other, found its locality by fixing, almost gluing the subject to the signifier *peau*, skin. What emerged from this terrifying experience for her was a letter constituted in this knot of the real and the symbolic. The woman went on to spend a considerable amount of time writing *peauemes*, and devoted herself to poetical creation with great passion. This pursuit, however, was not without foreclosing effects, as the phallic function did not mobilise significations but rather brought to the fore the function of writing as a way of keeping jouissance knotted to the letter. The patient was not psychotic, Brousse says, which shows that the clinic of *sinthome* can also be applicable in neurosis. In this case we could situate the *sinthome* at a junction of the symptom and fantasy. What happened to the subject amounts to being smitten by the image of the skin that nevertheless served as a complementary object to the subject as divided in this experience. The *sinthome* in this sense combines the effects of the variable of jouissance in relation to the object *a* in fantasy with the effects of the symptom as always satisfied, always finding "enjoy-meant" in writing one poem after another.

Reading this clinical vignette reminded me of Freud's early remark about the processes of reading as more complex to that of writing because of its links with speech. Let's see if we can put it use. In his work on aphasia in early 1890s, Freud presented us with the schema in which he links reading and writing at the level of the visual image, that is to say as the letter, which is constitutive of the word-presentations that in turn are linked to sound images. Freud established a connection between the auditory field as represented by the signifier and the letter as pertaining to writing and reading in the visual field. This connection places reading as far more complex a process than writing. Freud obviously indicates that reading is connected to the Other through the signifier that comes before writing. From this perspective, the connection between the signifier *peau* and the image of the cadaver opens another link, which Brousse elaborates, namely that of the desire of the Other. Although the woman has now become a successful poet pursuing her life writing and publishing *peau-âimes*, the signifier *peau* emerges not only as a knot at the moment when she was struck by the real image. It also has a value of signification in relation to the Other in so far as the beginning of her writing career is not without a mark of her father's desire to perform well at university exams. She fails to satisfy his demand and becomes poet instead.

What is interesting in the *sinthomatisation* in this case is that primarily, *peau* is the signifier and only later assume a status of the letter. The terrifying encounter with the real image is more on the side of a subjective division than a psychotic perplexity. In the way the letter *peau* supports the subject's life, nevertheless gives *sinthome* its rightful place of a crutch, a device without which walking could end up in falling. And this would suggest to us that the woman was subjected to a foreclosing effect as the signifier S_1 is solitary and does not suffice by itself to carry the phallic signification along the metaphorical substitutions or by the father's desire of his daughter's academic success alone. What seems striking to me is that it is the letter, not signification, which provides a vehicle of support for the subject. What can we say about the letter? First, that it is self-identical. As self-identical it itself becomes a *sinthome* where the *joui-sens* finds a stable mooring. It also has a function of a device that operates in the visual field where the scopic image of the dead animal and of letters are knotted. On the other hand, the cadaver has a function of the Lacanian stain that both veils and uncovers the evil of the gaze, which takes place by means of and through uses of the letter. And she becomes successful enough to enable her to continue her search for the name.

It seems that the skin has an anamorphic quality for the patient. Initially it was a blob in the dark, a mysterious and a meaningless shape concealing a look. But then it turned into a shape with the name *peau*. Is this enigmatic shape on the side of the signifier or of the letter? Because of her father's desire the subject relies on both albeit it is writing that mainly orients her subjective destiny. It is a destiny of a symptom in the Lacanian sense, because it takes us beyond the differential clinic of neurosis and psychosis. For example, it is impossible to decide subject's position without the delusional phenomenon that in the cases of Schreber and Joyce was decisive in distinguishing the clinic of the *sinthome* from the one we call differential. As for the latter it has drawn from the enigma of Oedipus in which Freud found the yardstick of neurosis. Lacan found him striving for knowledge after having crossed the field marked by the object gaze in the most radical way.

Oedipus beyond Oedipus

There is something uncanny about the way the gaze remains present for Oedipus and how it accompanies him after he becomes blind. The gaze has now become his guide. Not sooner does he reach Colonus than he begins to experience the look from afar, the look of the Theban eyes he left behind. Putting Lacan's inversed logic of the mirror stage into use, we could say that the only thing he cannot see are his eyes. Not seeing his eyes is at the exact opposite of the spectrum of seeing himself seeing himself, the Valérian theme Lacan evoked for us in *Seminar XI* (1977). At the same time the eyes can see him, which is where Freud situated what he called the dissolution of the Oedipus complex. But Lacan goes on to refind Oedipus beyond the complex and the *Ich-ideal*. And for this purpose Lacan goes beyond the Oedipus as a legislator of family laws and a regulator of the paternal name and of maternal ideals. The real Oedipus Lacan finds at Colonus goes beyond the complex and its dissolution, and presents itself as the real of the body knotted to the language of the drive. Blindness obviously does not kill and the castration may well appease his troubled life by giving him another one, life as real outside the scopic field.

Let's situate this life as real in the psychoanalytic experience. It is clear that the clash of the pleasure and reality principles does not reduce libido to zero. It is this failure of the pleasure principle to accomplish its course, and as responsible for the decrease of libido, that bears the marks of life. Life both refuses this failure and supports it. Life remains ambiguous. In his later teaching Lacan no longer speaks of the symbolic or imaginary life but calls it real. From the 1970s life is marked for Lacan as real. And we recall what Lacan teaches us about the real, that it is impossible and that it makes impact through traces and remains between presence and absence. When Lacan returns to the Oedipus of Colonus, because the Oedipus of Thebes is not the only one, the scene spills over with life that remains ambiguous to the end. How does this ambiguity drive Oedipus on and where is it taking him, given his attempt to cross the field of the gaze? Obviously seeing is not a condition of the drive that is blind from the start to the end, and Oedipus merely came to realise that at the moment of encountering blindness. Life spills over beyond this infliction. Why not to say that Oedipus is the very embodiment of the Lacanian stain from *Seminar XI*? Does he not in his ambiguous life still continue to bother us and to divide us, even to tease us? Does he not anguish and terrify us but also appease us, sending us in the direction of more and more life? In the *RSI* seminar of 1974, Lacan speaks of life as no longer following the symbolic trail of signifiers. This is surely a reference to Freud's sexual drives. Life also dealt a blow to the imaginary spectrum from which the subject saw life as a life of the body image. This new definition of life emerges in Lacan's last years of teaching, and I found it punctuated in the distinction Jacques-Alain Miller makes between life and the living.

He proposes to couple life not with truth but with knowledge. Life and truth are no longer allies. Are life and knowledge better bed fellows? In a certain way, life cannot stand knowledge. Life seems to say: "I do not know and do not want to know". In fact, and this is what I have found in Lacan's reorganisation of the *RSI* (Real, Symbolic, Imaginary), life sheds knowledge like a skin. It is not exactly what he said of Joyce which I will take up later. Life shedding knowledge marks the end point for Oedipus. He comes to realisation that life can do without knowledge, finding knowledge superfluous. Life remains blind. As for the knowledge of life it is caught in the body of the Other. The subject's knowledge of life can thus become an admission of the refusal to know life as real. This is because the refusal of the knowledge of life, while being caught in the signifying chain, solicits *Thanatos*. The death drive brings us back to the imaginary as there is no knowledge of death. In the last days of Oedipus, life flows in and fills in the lack of knowledge of death. For Lacan death was a matter of faith, of believing in what allows to sustain life. One must believe in what is beyond knowledge of life to make life sustainable. For the Oedipus of Colonus life has become a surplus, a bonus of jouissance. In this sense, life refuses to know and, as real, is refused. This is the double refusal, highlighted by Miller, that forms some vague dialectic with the real. In the last hours of Oedipus' life, there is an appeal to life as real, namely to life as life. This appeal is refused for the subject of knowledge or for the father as loved by his daughters.

At the very end of *Oedipus at Colonus* (1986) Oedipus parts with his beloved children, walks away alone as if life was already finished and done with. His position of standing alone, even all alone, marks this life as finished and done with. Life became a void that guides him towards life. Of course we must not forget that Sophocles' deliberations about life caught between birth and death catch him unawares at the age of ninety five when castration outruns perhaps its analytical use.

At the end then the gods call him, saying he is holding them back and they must move on. Life does not stop for the gods. Oedipus' departure is tied to this call from the real. This is, more or less, the end of Oedipus of Colonus, although the dramatic effects of the translation exceed those of the original. For Lacan the gods are on the side of the real, the same side as that of life in its double refusal. In other words, the gods are not on the side of the Other from where comes desire, language, truth. Life as real remains caught up in this double refusal because no living person has gone through the experience of death. One can only believe in death but no one really knows how Oedipus died. So it is now back to us, one by one, how the real of jouissance is refused and how it refuses. For Lacan, the agency of knowledge is no longer in the symbolic. Since no living person can speak of death there is at the end, thanks to the messenger who conveys it, the enigmatic impossible to tell. He obviously does not tell us everything. From the time of the riddle of Sphinx to the time of blindness, Oedipus has come to realise that there is knowledge he does not know, what Lacan calls an "unknown knowledge". If for Lacan the gods are on the side of the real then they do not belong to the field of the law of the Other, which Lacan already signalled taking up Antigone. It is one more reason why to say that what remains for Oedipus is a surplus of life and more life.

Perhaps Oedipus became a saint. Who knows? But if so, there is no church to give him the beatification. He no longer has to face up to Desdemona's handkerchief or to Lacan's can of sardines or to the praying mantis or to Holbein's skull that puzzled Lacan and made him introduce the anamorphic object. Oedipus of Colonus may have become a saint without a church but not without an orientation in relation to life, which is how Lacan thought of the saints. Let's take a note of the passage above. From becoming an embodiment of the stain that disturbs our field of vision and divides us as subjects to becoming a saint at the moment of crossing the field of the gaze, reuniting with life that does not stop. Let's mark this passage as from *stain* to *saint*. According to this anagrammatic and surprising writing there is a connection beyond the grammar that belongs to the symbolic order sanctified by the Name-of-the-Father. Lacan was interested in the real beyond the law, unregulated, outside the Other. And in this respect he was interested in the jouissance of the saint, say of Saint Thomas, or Saint Oedipus, asking what the saint really wants, what guides him, what the coordinates of sainthood really are. Lacan also said that he himself tried but failed. As analysts we all fail, one by one, leaving it to Oedipus who never had to go to analysis. Lacan made this amusing remark and in this way put some emphasis on the exception. Concerning the jouissance of a saint, the one Lacan raised to the level of a hero who does not become affected by the betrayal, standing all alone as he himself ended up doing, we should not be duped by the Church fathers. For centuries they made us believe that saints are servants of the universal good, altruism, and all that. Freud already explored this in his topographies. The lives of saints may show signs of some good deeds, yes, but their desire shows ambiguity, and history points to transgression. A saint is by and large a trouble maker, sometimes a crook or a thief. Look at Augustine, Francis of Assisi, etc. The latter almost caused the whole Church to collapse, showing himself as a true revolutionary rather than a conservative knave of a politician Lacan spoke about. In effect, the saints are more of redeemed villains. What makes them different from a redemption of an average criminal is that it is not proscribed by the authorities. The redemption of a saint is not a rehabilitation programme readapting a freed criminal back to reality. Whose reality? In this sense, the sainthood of a saint is not authorised by the Other. It may be bestowed centuries later but that is immaterial. The central point of a saint's life as a redeemed life is that his redemption does not come from an authority of the Other. In other words, the saint authorises himself, so to speak, that is to say he does not *draw* authority from anywhere and renders life his authority. And he is not in a bad company, given one can also find there an analyst and a woman. This is what Lacan said when he posed the question about what makes an analyst. He did not shift authority from the Other to some self-satisfactory folly, as it is sometimes misunderstood or implied. He made the analyst and the saint partners. At least briefly. He could only do that by rendering the saint the real's partner. But how does one become the real's partner? How does a saint or an analyst or a woman become the partner of the real that is outside the law and does not honour any partnerships? Either you *saint-homme* or you are staying-home, *stai-n-homme*, to pun the difference. Inevitably, the saint derives his reconciliation from his life as a life that includes irredeemable drive. He derives it from life *in vivo*, as it is lived and enjoyed as persevered. Lacan said that this perseverance marks a cessation of the symbolic authority of the *pater*. Does Oedipus disappear in the end, does he live on?

CHAPTER SEVEN

Superego and the logic of guilt

Heidegger and "as if all"

We have shed some light on the relation between the drive and desire. This allows me to make the next step and follow Lacan's elaboration concerning the relation between desire and guilt. To do that I want to bring back the reference to the discourse of philosophy because the mastery it offers serves the purpose of my endeavour here. It is not by accident that philosophers are said to be the guardians of silence. Silent in speech, silent in writing, they well conceal, one by one, the experience Freud placed as pivotal in the dynamic of neurosis. How do we speak about the philosopher's jouissance if it is jouissance, as Lacan states, the philosophers do not speak about? How conceptually vociferous must a philosopher become in order not to say anything? This was no doubt the case of Wittgenstein who in reply to the silent desire of the Other responded with a commandment of silence. The discourse, indeed the ethics of psychoanalysis does not advocate silence. Whereof one cannot speak thereof one must say the impossible, would be an analytic prescription if it were to offer any but it does not. There is no need for that because, instead, the subject can simply rely on the register where he can settle his score with his neighbour. Or can he? How then do we speak of being of the other without speaking of jouissance and how to speak of love while speaking of guilt and debt? These are my main axes here.

To start it will suffice to say that in psychoanalysis truth fails to fall silent and it is not possible to muffle it which is when it speaks, in fragments and between the lines. And it is because of this analytic experience of truth that Lacan showed us that the ethics of psychoanalysis is not on the side of silence. In the analytic experience truth has a singular, particular modality of the subject's truth. Nietzsche highlighted that dimension when he put into question the symptomatic side of the so-called "universal truths". While he paid the price he exposed something of the dimension of the subject's real as operative in philosophical discourse. But it did not take him any further than stating that the real of the symptom in play conceals a psychological problem behind the guise of ontology, as Klossowski noted. Freud placed the truth in the unconscious so that it could surprise us when we least expect it. For Heidegger the experience of truth, *aletheia*, revealed itself as unconcealment, which in his ontology of Being had concealing effects. For this reason it is not surprising that many expect that once his silence over the life-long love for Hanna Arendt comes into light in the publication of their correspondence, this will reveal the truth about Heidegger.

It is in this vein that I propose to read Jacques-Alain Miller's remark that there is not a single line in Heidegger's work that is anti-Semitic. If Miller indeed tries to imply that every line in Heidegger's opus has, if not such a meaning then such an implication, it is because there is not a single line in his work that is about love. Heidegger's style and mode of inquiry into the meaning of Being promotes a *modus operandi* that aims at a certain totality which, since it profoundly neglects the particularity of the subject, produces a semblance I will call "as if all". There is no more precise guideline to the rural world of Heidegger's ontology than the yardstick of "as if all". I say "rural" for the reasons given earlier, namely in order to punctuate again the nostalgic character of a Heidegger's meditation that yearns for the "natural", to wit prediscursive dimension of the relation with Being that remains trapped in the dimension of the imaginary. This term, or these terms if one also includes nostalgia as a retreat from desire, and the ontology of *Gestalt* of being-whole as Heidegger's master reference, are the ones Lacan did well without. Lacan's interest in language and the analytic experience led him to question philosopher's insights in order to isolate the logic of the signifier, and in this case the logic of the signifier *is* and its copulas. What I would like also to single out from his *corpus* could be called the silence about love with the proviso that it is as if he was speaking about nothing else.

Lacan took being to stand for the jouissance of the body. It is the being of the body that was sexed by the Other, and therefore the sexual body. To take Being as the supreme good, whether for Parmenides, Aristotle or Heidegger, is to mistake it for the asexual. And Lacan expressed his surprise that even to attempt to contemplate in Being, in the jouissance of the body, the basis for the verb "to be", that is to say, to give it a value of the signifier, is to keep it in the enclosure of the master discourse, as I mentioned before. You will hear here the discourse of the master, *m'être*, the resonance of the very theme of Heidegger's pursuits as subject, namely the "being-me" in which the ego and the other's image are stuck at the level of imaginary identification. Was it this that made Freud flinch at the prospect of "love the other as yourself"? What never made Heidegger distract was this dimension of "as if all" that gives every line an aspiration for totality under the appearance of there not being a single line about love.

Dasein's *alienation and being guilty*

Let's start with *Dasein*. In Heidegger's discourse it appears as a unique, singular, authentic, substanceless mode of existing that has no other temporal dimension except for its having-been, *Gewissenheit*. And you will see straight away that *Dasein*'s extreme isolation and its ownmost potentiality-for-being is what makes it a kind of semblant of the Lacanian subject. It is therefore not inconceivable to regard *Dasein*, the *Dasein* that welcomes and embraces its *fatum* of being-thrown-into-the-world, as most intimately, that is to say extimately, linked to the Other of language, for it is first and foremost an alienated *Dasein*.

But if we nevertheless accept Heidegger's existential offer of *Dasein*, he will show us some years later that *Dasein*'s existential solitude in the face of death will assume another, very specific sense to become the most powerful instrument of his political rhetoric. This alienation is for Heidegger an expression of the fundamental guilt which is to be distinguished from conscience. As alienated, *Dasein* has to drop its identifications, its master signifiers incarnated by what I would call the *vox populi*, the common voice as distinct from the singular voice of conscience, in order to authenticate its own existence whose possibilities begin at the moment of dealienation, which is also separation. Thus *Dasein* is always already entangled in the signifying structure of language.

I am interweaving some of the themes in Heidegger with Lacan's work here and there but the limitations of this exercise are already obvious. In its attempts to dealienate itself from the Other, *Dasein* must try to reclaim what is properly its own. It must, Heidegger says, venture to the rural land of Being that it had once inhabited. In short, it must follow the trace of its tale to recover what had pre-existed it, which is the pre-discursive dimension of being. The path of *Dasein* is marked by the compulsion to repeat and runs a whisker away from the edge of Freud's death drive. It is in this sense that we could speak of a strange return of, and a belief in, the jouissance of the Other, which *Dasein* is supposed to reclaim as its own. Freud marked this territory as pertaining to the myth of the primordial father. The connection between such an aspiration that Heidegger sets for *Dasein*, and what Freud elaborated under the term of "superego", is quite patent. No agent in the structure enjoys more than the superego. In effect, the project of *Dasein's* return to the prediscursive landscape of being amounts to a search for the lost or never experienced jouissance.

Dasein's primary position, Heidegger tells us, is that of *Schuldigsein*, the fundamental being-guilty. And this position should not be dissociated, as Freud defined it, from the structure of obsessional neurosis as revolving around the primary experience of pleasure. When Lacan takes it up, he points to the neurotic's relation to the object that produces an excess of pleasure and orients desire towards avoidance, indeed concealment. Let's take a note of that. The obsessional neurotic is led to conceal his pleasures because his experience of them frightens, even terrorises him as if he had to confront some imaginary "totality" of the Other, or the Other as "being-whole", although what he encounters in this anguish is desire. This "as if all" dominates his subjective ethics and appears to him as a modality of jouissance that exposes his castration, namely his lack or more precisely his want-to-be. Let me take it a bit further.

In order to dealienate itself from the *vox populi*, from the common garrulity of the mass media or the generalised blabber of empty speech, *Dasein* seeks the key to its possibilities. These can only be attested by the voice of conscience. The term, let's stress, appears as secondary to the *Schuldigsein*, and only emerges when *Dasein*, seeking its authentication, comes to face its finitude, its death. Therefore, the voice of conscience appears as crucial, for it provides a testimony to the fundamental guilt which is not to be surpassed. This is what I found in the crucial passages of *Being and Time* (1962). To the extent that *Dasein* wants to have a voice to break loose from the alienating other, it is an effect of the primordial guilt or debt, which is also the ontological condition of *Dasein*'s ethical position. But this wish-to-have-conscience is also indicative of the ego-ideal, namely a lack in the other. Let's not doubt about what Heidegger has to say, when he contests the lack, about the fundamental ontology of guilt and ethics of the superego. The ego-ideal as the master signifier that comes from the Other is the very principle of subject's alienation and of a demand for love. It is therefore the calling of the voice, the voice of conscience, which testifies to the want-to-be.

The fundamental being-guilty is for Heidegger the basis of *Dasein*, which is also the neurotic's secret, revealed under the term of wanting, wanting to be and wanting to have conscience. It is therefore from the perspective of the secondary term of the voice's testimony, the lack that Heidegger refuses, that we are able to shed some light on the *Schuldigsein*. This is how Lacan approached the problem when he situated the subject between guilt and desire. Lacan defined guilt as a way of giving up on one's desire or turning away from it. This would be another way of denying the subject's lack by passing a blame to the other, to the fellow man, the next-door-neighbour, the *Nebenmensch*, who else. And this is what we must stress, *Schuld* or debt makes the subject deny the lack in the other.

From this moment the problematic of the fundamental *Schuldigsein*, being-guilty or being-in-debt, ramifies into the ontology of *Dasein* and the ontic of jouissance. The former concerns the structure of speech or the subject's relation to the lack-of-being, which is precisely the position of alienation in so far as what escapes sense is always displaced, always elsewhere, disguised as an object in the place of the lack. As for the ontic of jouissance, it touches on drive-satisfactions whose reserve, as Nietzsche stated in *Genealogy of Morals* (1968), represents the very economy of *Schuld* and credit, which is also the shortage or imbalance in the debtor's relation to the creditor. And Jacques-Alain Miller stressed that this debt of jouissance belongs to the order of necessity, as it does not cease to be inscribed. In this sense, the debt supports the symptom in neurosis. What is important here is to determine the status of the Other—the Jew being the one against whom there is not a single line in Heidegger according to Miller—and whether this Other exists making us guilty one by one or whether it is the Other as desiring and therefore lacking as Lacan introduced it. This is what interests me.

The fact that Heidegger contests the lack as an element of structure, and instead assigns it to the order of what he calls "present-at-hand", leads him to assert the subject's position as that of the denial of the lack of a lack. This is where guilt comes into being. Guilt emerges as a primary position of the subject as divided between alienation in relation to the master signifier and the lack-of-conscience.

It is not my task here to do the philosopher's job of providing an *apologia* of *Dasein*. I am concerned with its contingency and the ethical consequences Heidegger's ontological meditation had for his relations with the *Nebenmensch*. As contingent, *Dasein* does not have to exist. What makes it exist comes from the anguishing anticipation of death and from its unceasing indebtedness in relation to the symptom. This was already suggested by the lack-of-conscience as a kind of "reality" that differentiates *Dasein* from the *vox populi*. This differentiation, realised in the anguishing anticipation of death—or in anguishing loss of something that concerns life—allows Heidegger to speak of "another voice". This other voice is not a substitute for what is lacking but an additional entity that concerns the Other. It is this other voice or the voice as coming from the Other that for Heidegger remains silent, has always been silent, and could thus be approximated to thought. We must distinguish this silence from the silence of the Lacanian voice as object *a*. The Lacanian object voice remains silent because it does not belong to the field of speech. An object *a*, although it has no substance, can be heard against silence. But it can cause the Other to speak, to order and to impose instructions upon the subject which can only be carried by the voice, as Freud already noticed. The search for the voice can turn into the search for the Other that exists to set us free, the voice of the father and even of the mythical, primordial father of the Freudian horde, which is supposed to come to us from beyond of what is lost and what is lacking. Somewhere Heidegger calls this voice as singular and ownmost. And Heidegger attributes to it a quality I would call *salvational*. It will re-emerge in his interview, published posthumously, where he no longer makes any secrets that it is all in the hands of God.

The sense of guilt, demand and desire

With this introductory commentary on Heidegger's being-guilty as a fundamental condition of human existence, I can now return to Freud who was the first one to come with a theory of guilt in the modern civilisation. To recall the rudimentary fact from *Civilisation and Its Discontents* (1930a), let me state that the deployment of the superego, which was Freud's second theory of the origin of the sense of guilt, depends directly on the identification with the father.

Freud tells us that the legacy of guilt has two sources, the myth of the primordial father and the work of the reality principle. The latter, Lacan says, allows for an isolation from reality. This means that the reality principle makes up the reality of the subject. It is an anguishing reality, difficult to reconcile with because something of the order of life is at stake for the subject. But while the anguish concerns castration and something of the order of life, there is always uncertainty whether it is a castration on the side of the subject or on the side of the Other. This Other, Lacan is talking about, and he already developed it in *Seminar V* and *Seminar VI*, is the Other whose castration renders it incomplete, lacking. We can find it in the upper part of the graph of desire he elaborated there. The incomplete Other, or the lack in the Other, is marked as S (A̶), which should be read: the signifier of the lack *in* the Other. This gap in the Other becomes the way in which, anguished as he is confronted with the desiring Other, the subject has to come to confront his own reality, which is first and foremost the sexual reality. As we know Freud used a mythical example of the primordial father to introduce the Other as such, that is to say as real and as unreal at the same time. And this is how Lacan spoke of the drive, as I said on the previous occasion, as having a real effect, giving the dimension of the drive the status of the myth. While the real of the drive cannot be denied it cannot really be represented within the order we have come to call symbolic. Freud considered the father as an exception, which Lacan used in the tables of sexuation as the one that is outside the set of the castrated speaking beings, men and women, as those who are subject to the phallic function. We could say that the primordial, mythical father of *Totem and Taboo* (1912–1913), is the father who has it all, the power, the women, etc. He stands for the only Other whose decompletion is successful. While enjoying all women he forbids others access to them. This clearly is Freud's response to the subject's position in obsessional neurosis. The father of jouissance is eventually murdered by his sons who take his position, the difference being that this position is now marked by the birth of guilt. They now have to confront the dead father who becomes manifest and will for eternity remain an incomplete Other. This means in effect that one owes him, as Freud's Ratman did, that a portion of jouissance always goes towards the Other. One for you and one for me. The symbolic debt to the Other can only be formulated to the extent that it concerns the dead father or the Other as incomplete.

Why is it that when someone close dies the subject feels a sense guilt? It is as if he had a part in the demise of a friend who died. His lingering, if surprising, sense of guilt commemorates the friend's presence and participation in the subject's life. His guilt is a product of that departure. And now, after his death, I am left with the symbolic debt that is impossible to pay because nothing is owed. But this symbolic debt nevertheless takes a form of homage, memory and support to the living, each marking the epitaphs for those who remain. Humanity owes the burial and funeral rites to that symbolic debt that Freud called the unconscious sense of guilt. But Freud is precise to distinguish between guilt that is not suffered as a result of committing a particular deed, in which case he speaks of remorse [*Reue*], and the one suffered in relation to the external authority, which is Freud's first theory of the origin of guilt. It is the former, his second theory of guilt, where guilt is suffered as the departure and loss of the loved one, which Freud links to the subject's identification with the father. According to Freud every time someone close dies, the guilt that follows bears a symbolic connection to the primordial father as killed by his sons. In this sense, we are all children of the Big Castrator that does not exist.

If patricide is Freud's response to obsessional neurosis, the so-called dissolution of Oedipus complex responds to the hysteric's position. It is how Freud introduced the function of the superego. Melanie Klein (1988) elaborated superego as belonging to the pre-Oedipal stage of development. One wonders why the child's aggressivity in the pre-Oedipal stage should be explained in terms of the *ÜberIch* if the ego, *Ich*, is not yet formed. It was Lacan who shed light on this issue when formulating the mirror stage (2006a) and the source of narcissistic aggressivity that logically follows from the former. Klein devised the term "maternal superego" that embodies mother's jouissance, which Lacan refers to in his earlier teaching. Lacan found the term useful as it allows us to distinguish the remainder of the mother's jouissance that is not subject to the Oedipal solution. Freud's superego is post-Oedipal, whereas Klein's superego is pre-Oedipal. It relates to the mother's jouissance as unsatisfied so that to satisfy it the ground has to be cleared of any intervention by the symbolic father and his prohibitive "no". The maternal superego, the sister of ravage, is therefore a "no" to the "no" of the father. It attempts to foreclose the symbolic effects of the prohibitive law introduced by the father to pacify the child's anguish, and anger, at the unsatisfied jouissance of the mother. In Lacanian terms the maternal superego should be referred to as the maternal jouissance, the satisfaction in dissatisfaction, if I could put it this way. Klein's idea of the superego gives us some indication of the maternal contamination of the Oedipal process, which Lacan found of use.

Lacan went on to elaborate the superego at the level of the Other as a place of language that impacts on the body, leaving traces there from the start. Initially, Lacan marked it on the lower part of the graph of desire as the signified of the Other, namely as what remains concealed from the signifier and from the Other. The signified of the Other epitomises for Lacan the introduction of the Other as such, namely as the superego, even the maternal superego in so far as it has to do with the real transmitted on the verges of the demand. This is the unrefined, primary form of demand and interpretation the mother, or the father, gives to the child's cries and calls. It can be found on Lacan's graph of desire as represented by the vector $s(A) \rightarrow A$. This superego at the level of the signified of the Other appears as a meaning, as what the Other means, at the level of demand as a signifying chain, in opposition to the signifier S given by the Other, as Lacan says in *Seminar V* (1998a). The child is told: "Do it", "Eat your meal", etc., and that's that. It is an instruction, and as an instruction it carries a meaning in which a satisfaction is demanded. For Lacan the appearance of guilt is inseparable from the effects of the signified of the Other of demand, such as an instructing parent who demands that things are so and so, on the child. Lacan intertwined guilt closely with desire, which is why any indication of guilt in the Lacanian clinic comes suffused with the indications of desire as unsatisfied. For this reason guilt should receive all attention it calls for as this might lead to some form of fading of desire to which guilt is a signpost. Demand, in turn, is always satisfied. When we demand something we demand a satisfaction and we get it. You expect to be treated so and so and you address this demand to your colleague or to your child. But what you are asking for or demanding is satisfaction. This satisfaction is conditional upon the articulations in the signifying chain so a message is addressed. To whom if not to the one who is supposed to oblige? In this way demand, for example in obsessional neurosis with which I will deal separately, differs radically from desire in which lies inscribed a lack of satisfaction, refused or deflected when demanded, which can be indicated by a sense of guilt whether as a feeling of having done something wrong or of the causes of loss of love not being explicit. Desire leaves the outcome of the demand undecided and open. If the subject is subjected to the demand and expected to act in a certain way, it all depends at what level this expectation is received, demand or desire.

For Lacan the neurotic guilt and desire are inseparable and we can find guilt in the upper part of the graph as encircled by desire. This connection between guilt and desire appears to come from the law. Guilt, which Jacques Alain Miller calls "polymorphous", and for a reason if you follow Freud's polymorphous perversions in *Three Essays On the Theory of Sexuality* (1905d), appears to be a violation of the law of the demand and of what is expected, namely its refusal. Desire, on the other hand, points to the beyond of the law, for example to the beyond of rules of language, grammar, etc. In the end Lacan responded to this exigency by speaking of the *lalangue* that is a language without law. Both guilt and desire therefore have a tangential, if not unfriendly relation to the law, a relation that involves a recognition of a disarray, of an insufficiency and of something not being right at the moment of dissatisfaction. Superego as maternal tries to impose this dissatisfaction *as* satisfying by way of an instruction, although following a rule does not have to be pleasant or satisfactory. But then the function of the law is not to generate satisfaction but to introduce an order, for example a symbolic order where the Name-of-the-Father organises the exchanges of the signifiers and the distribution of jouissance. Both guilt and desire are the registers of recognition of the disarray of the real, for example a demise or a loss, or something not being right, in the symbolic law as organising the world we are part of. And it is in this sense of the law malfunctioning or leaving much to be desired in its functioning that Lacan placed guilt and desire as distinct indicators of this disharmony.

Freud's paradox of the superego and the windmill of jouissance

In his formulation of the superego Freud presents us with a paradox. Once the Oedipus complex has been dissolved, and the voice-of-conscience assumed as a substitute for the father, the renunciation of the drive satisfactions did not diminish its ferocious impact but fuelled it. Freud says that every renunciation of the drive now forms a dynamic source of conscience and every fresh renunciation produces the increase of the severity and intolerance of conscience. I always found this paradox puzzling. But guilt has also another source, and that is why Freud speaks of the unconscious sense of guilt, *Schuldgefül*. We should not confuse *Schuldigsein*, being guilty, with a lingering feeling of guilt, *Schuldgefül*. It may sound surprising but for Freud guilt is correlative to love. If in *Civilisation and its Discontents* (1930a) he tells us that conscience is a tension between the superego and the ego that asks for punishment, he does so to define the nature of what is "bad" that might have generated such a tension. But for Freud the sources of what is called "bad" should be sought nowhere else than in the subject's fear of the loss of love, which is one of the facets of castration. Here then is the link between the superego and the fear of castration to which it is a response. The fear of loss of the love-object solicits punishment and sets the subject in pursuit of jouissance that is forbidden, Lacan says, to the speaking subject as such to make up for the fear of loss. Superego is called up to fill in where the jouissance is forbidden. Superego states that we should have satisfaction all the way and enjoy to the death. The demand of punishment, which at another level opens the dimension of fantasy, has as a source that of the superego. And the superego sustains guilt.

Here then we have a little circuit. The fear of loss of love is the fear of castration to which superego responds by commanding that we enjoy without limits to the death, and suffer, to make up for no signs of love, and this supports the unconscious sense of guilt whose origins are polygenetic. One of these origins lies in the subject's attempt to conceal the lack-of-enjoyment [*manque-à-jouir*] by refusing to speak about the jouissance at stake where being-guilty is proposed as fundamental rather than as a product of an alternation from jouissance as prohibited to the subject as such, to the jouissance of prohibition. This refusal forms the basis of the social discourse. In this sense, what takes us away from guilt by lessening its overbearing weight, is not an increased subjection to the superegoic agency of prohibition, because that is where jouissance is churned up, but an admission of the Other as desiring on the border between being and lack, which has effects of equivocation. If equivocation is used for interpretation it is because such an interpretation aims at the object *a* as the one that awakens desire.

And this is Lacan's answer to Freud's paradox. The fear of loss of love implies that some of the libidinal satisfactions have to be given up and castration taken on board. Freud was astonished nevertheless that despite some marks of renunciation to lift guilt in the subject, the accounts were still not settled and the debt remained unpaid. Freud dealt with it in his commentary on the case of the Ratman. Why then the unconscious feeling of guilt lingering on? Why is it that the practice of temperance and virtue that guided the *ascesis* of the holy men, the sages, the philosophers for millennia, brought them, one by one, more satisfaction by refusing it? How come that these minimalist practices were not only insufficient to lift guilt but even amplified its resonances? Is this the case of less becoming more? Lacan's early formula of jouissance as prohibited to the speaking subject as such, refers to the subject as represented by the signifier. But there is a jouissance as implicated in the subject's discourse where it is topologically knotted with it as extimate. Guilt, in Lacan's response to Freud, arises as a result of turning away from the knot of jouissance as intricate to the subject, and for this reason turning away from desire. But this process is not straightforward. From this perspective desire marks subject's destiny as extimately entangled in the knot of jouissance. Lacan will elaborate this in his commentary on Antigone to which I will come back later. The knot of jouissance as intricate to the subject is an effect of Lacan's approach to the superego as a place where jouissance is insisted on, indeed commanded. The guilty subject is trapped in the windmill spinning from the prohibition of jouissance and the jouissance of prohibition. Hence the schema below.

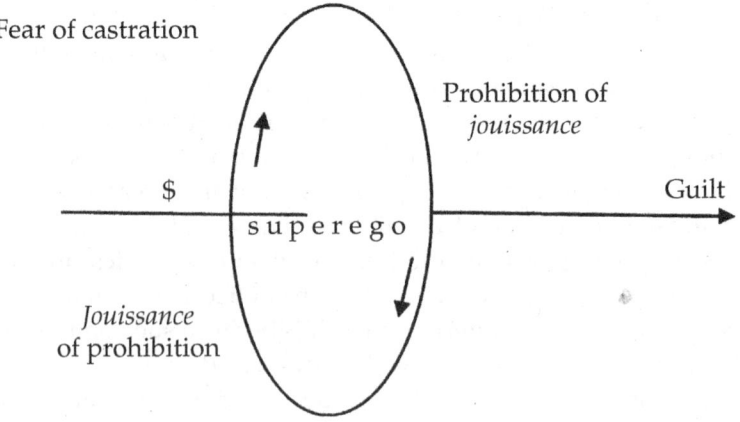

Schema 1.

This double negative of the windmill of jouissance was the signature of the superego Lacan called ferocious. Obviously the swapping of places makes no difference to its ferocity. At one point jouissance is tied to what is forbidden to the subject, at another moment it is tied to the transgression of the forbidden, which in turn becomes the subject of social discourse and its relation to the law. Lacan even went on to ask in *Seminar VII* (1992) about what jouissance makes us transgress the prohibition of jouissance. If this may lead to produce a superegoic effect of being-guilty, it resonates in everything Lacan has to say about good and evil in relation to the subject, namely about the good and the Thing as the subject's coordinates.

Lacan's treatment of guilt goes beyond and eclipses the patricide that Freud placed at the centre of the Oedipal universe and from which he did not flinch. He approached the question of guilt with emphasis on the status of the superego as the beneficiary of the renunciation of libidinal satisfactions and the place of the castrating father as an agent of jouissance. He left us with a paradox that Lacan took up as a knot that gives basis to the discourse. It is not as an effect of the command of the superego that jouissance can be dropped and renounced. Its renunciation materialises as an effect of loss of love which translates the supposed jouissance of the Other into the hollow that the Other has always been, namely the desiring Other, the mysterious and unequivocal Other of desire to which the object *a*, belonging neither to it nor to the subject, is both a clue and a cause. It is through the knot of the real and the symbolic that Lacan opened the dimension of desire as disharmonious with reality. But he did not introduce desire as fundamentally the desire of the Other, from which the subject takes its place, without Freud. What kind of Other has Freud given us from the beginning? It is the most present and proximate Other from where desire, sometimes received as hatred and sometimes as love, unfolds, namely the *Nebenmensch*. This allows me to write the following schema 2.

We can see here the proximity of guilt and desire as Lacan situates them. When the subject follows his desire, this involves disharmony with reality due to the lack in the Other, its inconsistency. Or if the subject flinches, it is back to guilt effects. The link between the signifier and jouissance that is forbidden to the speaking subject as such, presents itself as a knot which for Freud imposed itself as an unease and discontent in the world called civilised, *Unbehagen*, being foreign at home. The Lacanian knot, tied in to the very fibre of the Freudian civilisation

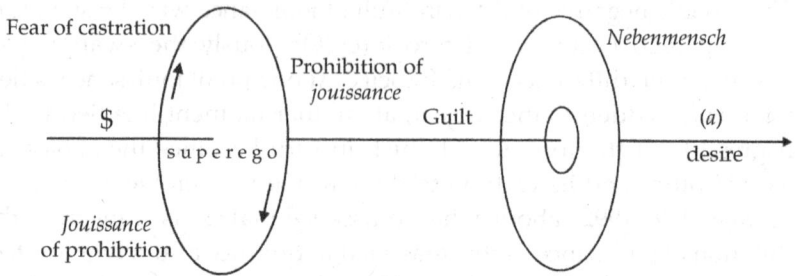

Schema 2.

as discontent, brings in what is most distant yet nearest, alien yet familiar to me, the *Nebenmensch*. And this has been my preoccupation with regard to the claim of being-guilty lying at the core of our being.

We can say that the presence and proximity of the *Nebenmensch* in Heidegger's discourse did not cease to implicate him and his interests at every possible level, sexual, ethical, and political. This *Nebenmensch* is very important and present for Heidegger, not only in *Being and Time* in relation to *Schuldigsein* as being guilty, but to those neighbours like Husserl, his Jewish mentor and predecessor, the chair of philosophy in Freiburg at the time. But, above all, there was Hanna, his beautiful Jewish student and a lover at first sight, on and off for decades, that's what happens to great loves, who did not cease to question her Judaic roots in her own right, while Martin was flirting with the leader. And last but not least there was of course Martin's wife, the sworn anti-Semite as portrayed in a book by Elizabeth Ettinger (1995). Heidegger's symbolic indebtment to his fellow men and women seemed greater than he dared to say in his lifetime. Any serious student of Heidegger's work should include this excellent book into their reading list.

Being-guilty and shame

Not a word of love was Heidegger's way of work in the course of which he made up for its deficit by weaving an impossible nest for the subject as guilty, the one who gives up on his desire. He made up for "not a word about love" by acting in accordance with jouissance that is silent because it is forbidden to the subject as such. Accordingly, he threw his fellow professor Husserl out of the university for being this or being that, while making a pact with the leader, the father of all fathers, and his henchmen. Freud's lesson of the primordial father and the patricide did not remain unnoticed. Heidegger was not the last professor who was throwing his fellow peers out of academia. In Britain today we hear every now and then about a senior academic being suspended on the spot. And although this is not related to race, sex, etc., the carefully designed script for expulsion echoes the conditions of segregation that include the jouissance of outrage of those in power who act on the confusion between beings and speaking beings. One then says it is a normal practice. Lacan's excommunication would require a separate chapter.

And this leads me to evoke what I find one of the most resonant themes in Lacan's teaching on the subject of love. Jouissance, Lacan says relatively late but one can hear him say it much earlier, is not a sign of love. Does this mean that jouissance, although it is not a sign of love, makes up for "not a word about love"? It never ceased to come to him from Other, in this case from the one who never ceased to love him until her death. The semblance of love in *Being and Time*, together with the semblance of not being anti-Semitic, led Heidegger in the direction of another concept of community, and humanity, namely of "being-with-others", as he called it. It was a community of those for whom being-guilty serves as a fundamental reference, and in this way provides the necessary coordinates for the type of act where consequences bear no relevance because guilt is implied *a priori*. If this teleology smacks of cynicism, one must distinguish here Lacan's desire as a basis for acting without impunity, that is to say starting with castration relative to the loss of love. But what on earth did my uncle mean, this eloquent and so well-read old man, when he said to me: "If the Jews say they were chosen by God, that's fine, so they should leave us alone"?

Acting in accordance with one's desire and with impunity is Lacan's response to Heidegger's presupposition of guilt as a motive to act criminally. Guilt and responsibility are mutually exclusive. Lacan based his act on following subject's desire, seeking an impossible fulfilment even if on the way, as in the case of Antigone and Creon, there is a law that stands in the way. The law as symbolic order stands in the way of another law of the fault in the Other where flow the rudiments of the subject's desire in which can be recognised the beyond of death, which Creon obviously refused. And the beyond of death resides in the construction of the funeral and burial rites as signs Antigone followed, and which I have just spoken about, where the homage and epitaph serve as the place of separation. And this is where Lacan situates responsibility in psychoanalysis. It comes with an act in accordance with the subject's desire that transcends the imaginary qualification of the good or bad of your dead *Nebenmensch*. Guilt is the true alibi of the refusal of responsibility and of denial of the Other's castration. Is it my fault then? No, it is your desire.

Sharing jouissance with others appears to be Heidegger's proposal, but how to share jouissance with your neighbour without putting your own into the pot? Lacan answered this question with his formula of discourse. How to share jouissance, provided this communion does not include my own jouissance, my ownmost? This is how Lacan situated the function of the good. I have reread the relevant lessons of Lacan's *Seminar VII The Ethics of Psychoanalysis*, and am focusing here on the ethics of the unconscious that deals with the jouissance of the body. This innermost jouissance of being that Heidegger mistook for *Schuldigsein* is shame. Nevertheless the logic of guilt that I have been elaborating here, takes notice of shame as that which is innermost for the subject. Shame is the primary exposure of the subject to the Other, his or her first appearance to the Other. It is an affect that precedes anguish but is correlative to it. The subject put to shame is no longer represented by the signifier. We could say that the subject in shame is a naked subject, alone with jouissance but without a signifier. The signifier as subject's representation serves not only to represent it but also to veil it, to cover it. Veil is a sign of shame. Without the symbolic, and sometimes literary, veil the subject is pierced by the gaze of the Other. In this case the subject in shame takes cover in the night, hides away from the social, runs miles from the garrulity of the common market into the solitudes of alienation Heidegger found so familiar. Whereas shame pushes us to take cover, guilt points in a different direction, that of obligation and duty. Desire, in turn, incurs responsibility for acting without impunity. Here, then, we have three ways in the face of the real, the denuding jouissance at the moment when it surprises us, putting us at unease, caught as a foreigner at home, which according to Freud forms our civilisation. The problem of immigration, today and tomorrow, starts here.

The subject in shame can be described as speechless. Not so with guilt where speaking and representing are very much part of the subject's outfit. Perhaps in this sense guilt, and Heidegger's being-guilty in particular, is the tailor-made means for the subject to cover his shame as the most hidden jouissance. The question arises whether it is made to appear as non-existent, namely as semblant, or whether it does not appear.

With the function of the good, Lacan also set out the conditions of segregation that underlines immigration. It is in the name of the good of the other that Heidegger approaches the semblance of love, not saying a word about it, under the name of segregation, supremacy, societal division and whatever goes with it. Envy plays a part in the conditions of segregation, you are there and I am here, we are obviously not in the same place. Envy—which etymologically carries *invidere*, to "look askance"—supposes the jouissance of the Other and places *Dasein* as guilty between the prohibition of jouissance and the jouissance of prohibition. We are at the end of cul-de-sac. If there is a way out from this vicious circle it has to do with love, namely with a loss of love. But it is not clear what kind of love. Loving the other as myself is evocative of an image of the other and this in turn appears as an imaginary trap in which the image is incarcerated. Lacan linked this image to the ego, "the me" [*le moi*], because its formation takes shape from it. The ego is cast in the likeness of the mirror image of the other, and this was how Lacan tied it to the barrier, to the limit of the Thing I dare not cross because it concerns my ego. Lacan's choice of words here is not accidental, so I will follow them. What does Lacan mean when he speaks about the barrier of the ego? To cross the barrier of the ego that moulds the image of the other that I should love is another way of linking it with the crossing of fantasy. And fantasy, the perverse fantasy Lacan was referring to, concerned the abominable yet admired a figure of Marquis de Sade. Sade was a man without any sense of guilt because all he was interested in was to put everyone to shame. He acted in accordance not with his desire but with his jouissance as shame itself, exposing himself as subject and shaming everyone around him. But he was not entirely speechless, as I implied earlier, not as a subject because he found a different way to cause shame in others. It was through writing. And in doing so, in writing that had to be necessarily obscene and blasphemous Sade admitted some measure of guilt and debt to the Other. While putting the subjects to shame, he also found his own refuge under the cover of writing. To put it in Lacan's terms, Sade's act to seek refuge and cause scandals did not amount to crossing the barrier of jouissance but rather to reaffirming a bond with it. It was at this point where Lacan tried to grasp the function of fantasy when he gave the well-known formula of $\$ \lozenge a$, a position of the subject who uses object *a* to produce jouissance.

This led Lacan to speak about the crossing of the barrier of jouissance in terms of passing to the position of the object *a* as a cause of desire. What is the satisfaction the obsessional subject finds in being-guilty if not the practice of the good for the benefit of the other without crossing the barrier of jouissance? And when you hear an announcement in a public place that such and such a restriction would be imposed on you *for your good*, today called "safety", you know what is happening and that this has nothing to do with responsibility. What is guilt if not a retreat of the ego from the desire of the Other in the belief in the jouissance of my neighbour as the seat and cause of all evil? What, in effect, is being-guilty or being-in-debt if not a precise expression of that retreat from desire replaced with a belief in the consistent Other? Freud presented it to us as a myth of the primal father, and Heidegger refound it in the figure of the Father of all fathers.

And it is not surprising that Heidegger situates the being-guilty outside law. It means that the primordial *Schuldigsein* stands as *a priori* to every form of transgression or breach. In short, it precedes any dialectic of transgression-compliance, obligation-repayment, debt-credit. The voice of conscience, in turn, becomes, it has to be said, complementary to and complicitous in being-guilty. Heidegger's voice of conscience aims to arouse guilt by making a bond with others such that *Dasein's* "being-with-others" amounts to making them guilty too. We are all partners in crime, it is just that there is no allegation. Such would be the logical loop of *Dasein's* primordial *Schuldigsein* as *a priori* to any law whatsoever. I am trying to highlight the difference between putting the Other to shame by denuding my jouissance as unrepresented and reduced to the one which is my innermost, which shows the logic of the Sadean fantasy, and, on the other hand, making the Other guilty, as Bataille called it. At this moment guilt and shame are clearly distinct. How does the subject become guilty? By being put in the position of owing, of obligation, and therefore of being supposed to have. Freud's Ratman gives us an undeniable example of such a neurotic guilt. The way Heidegger treats guilt, and the way the Ratman pulls it, so to speak, shows us how to make the Other exist by decompleting it, supposing it to have in its possessions what is owed and what should be paid back. For Heidegger, this Other, this *Nebenmensch*, with whom he is logically and ethically entangled, is the Jew, Husserl for one, his mentor to whom *Sein und Zeit* was dedicated. The Other is to be decompleted by being deprived of the part I as subject assume exists as his, namely his jouissance, happiness, even suffering, possessions, privileges, and so on. We can see that Heidegger's position aims at the paternal One outside the discourse because the latter implicates the real knotted to the subject and the ways in which his jouissance becomes produced, distributed and how it changes hands, so to speak, so that the dialectic of obligation and repayment, debt and credit, can be reduced to their symbolic terms. The terms of discourse, however, imply from the start the point of subtraction, which is the point of entry, namely a loss and renunciation, which for Lacan are the signs of love.

The ethics of a double agent

In the end I would like to deal with the paternal one, the point on which Heidegger's meditation on being-guilty appears to me to conclude. Heidegger's appeal to the father appears consistent with his considerations of the *Schuldigsein* serving as a basis of the politics of silence. Is the silence about jouissance the same as the silence of the signifier? Does the signifier here imply the voice, no longer the voice of conscience, but the voice in the Lacanian sense as an object that in fantasy the subject listens out for to follow the instructions and to obey? In the end we are confronted with the solitary signifier, *Dasein*, that faces up to death as what Heidegger calls "absolutely ownmost" and "unsurpassable", while supposing a unity of potentiality-for-being-a-whole for which it aspires. Where the *Nebenmensch*, the neighbour, the other, the woman, the Jew is in sight, *Dasein* hides in its primordial state of "being-guilty" and remains in debt. Throughout *Being and Time* (1962), but in particular in the decisive passages I have focused on, *Dasein* does not part from being that signifier all alone Lacan called "dominant" and presents itself as One. But now we can ask: is it *Dasein* or *Das Ein*? There lies the subject's politics of silence about jouissance, in its proximity to death. This is a well-known motif Freud explored in depth in his analysis of obsessional neurosis and the neurotics' passion for death. Heidegger gave us a "being-for-death" which for Lacan was the limit of desire. But here, death is treated as the most intimate possession—as that which no one can take away from me, as Blanchot aptly put it—and therefore as a form of commodity to be appropriated. In this sense, Heidegger turned death into the hallmark of the subject to be found in the analytic experience of obsessional neurosis.

There is a point of convergence of the One signifier and of the love of the all-mighty father. The appeal to the leader as the father of all follows from the belief in the One as supreme and therefore superior to the Other. *Das Ein* can in the end only be coupled with itself. The being of the One as one and the same makes it one. So now we have two neighbours, a good one and a bad one. On the one hand, we have the One of the signifier, a notion Lacan will take up later on in his teaching, and, on the other hand, there is a belief, on the imaginary level, that being one and the same holds an unfulfilled promise of being-whole. This is where Lacan places the bar on the subject as divided—never to be whole except in fantasy. With two neighbours one on each side of *Dasein*, let's now take up the logic of the "double agent" Lacan touches on in his *Seminar XVII The Other Side of Psychoanalysis* (2007).

The history of espionage is full of it. On the one hand, the agent allies with the enemy and is paid for it, which is his work, his good, his profession that represents his interests. But it is not for the money, the agent says, that he works, but to fulfil his mission, which is his belief in the ideal, for which his pay is a commission. Then people speak of betrayal, of the agent betraying their national ideal for his own as they suppose the agent to represent their good in the first place. And, what I find striking is that it works, one to the ideal, one to the pocket. Then, to make the next step, it turns out that something in the agent's relation to his ideal, for which he is commissioned by the enemy, remains unaccounted for. It slips through the calculations and escapes as a remainder. The agent holds on to it as something dear to him but soon becomes ready to exchange it too. At this point, Lacan says, the agent is compelled to *agence*, to process, this remainder, too. What is not included in the agent's first operation in relation to the other of the enemy, becomes included, as a remainder of satisfaction, in the second operation, hence the double agent. The double agency involves a semblance by means of which the agent makes the enemy believe he works only for them, while at the same time, with whatever is unaccounted for, he sells the enemy's secrets to his own country. That's another way of speaking about the subjective division. There is always something of his being, of his jouissance that is unaccounted for. The double agent successfully capitalises on what is left over from his "guilty conscience" over spying for the enemy. We might say at the end that a single agent is an idealist and a fool. The double agent by contrast is a perpetual liar who, wherever he turns, no longer has anyone to tell the truth to, even if he believed in it, which he no longer does. This relation to truth as unbelievable guides the double agent from one side to the other and back as what really represents him is the unsayable. He represents what Lacan called *cannaille*, a knave or a scoundrel. Lacan spoke about it not only with reference to the political life of his day but as having a broader implications.

The relation between the subject's fundamental guilt and a denunciation of his neighbour follows the same logic. What escapes subject's first testimony of the neighbour's guilt, or what remains outside the trading exchange with whoever is his partner of the day, re-emerges as reversed in the second testimony. Whatever was not included in the first denunciation of the neighbour, can be added as a little surplus in the second one. Either way the subject refuses castration for hurting another, which implies his refusal of responsibility for believing in truth and being duped by it. Why? Because he is always already guilty. And because he is guilty *a priori* to any dialectic of harm, its recognition and making up for it, he is also ready to harm another who, on this account, must be guilty too. This indeed can be found in everyday discourse of the party politicians but it comes from somewhere. The question I am raising here is not whether Heidegger professed the logic and the ethics of the double agent in his theory of *Schuldigsein* and in his flirting with the One as superior to the Other. Incidentally, and topologically speaking, the relation of superiority is a reversal of the primacy of the Other as the place of truth to which the West seems attached and of which the Orient does not seem to have much use. It is only the subject who always has to pay for his truth. The question I am raising is whether the assumption of the subject's fundamental guilt is already an anticipation of and a connivance at a crime against another. In the discourse of psychoanalysis the fault has a dimension of castration resulting from loss. It paves the way for the symbolic debt that Lacan linked to love. And he did that by pronouncing his famous aphorism that to love is to give what one does not have. Love follows and derives from castration and, therefore, has an intimate relation to privation and not having. Lacan speaks of not having alongside the lack-in-being, and places desire as a relation of being to the lack. Guilt was the reverse of desire in so far as it comes from the belief in the jouissance of the Other. And it is worth making it more precise by saying that guilt arises from a belief in jouissance as a leftover that is unaccounted for. Why must it be accounted for? Lacan called it *plus-de-jouir*, the surplus jouissance that is one of the products of castration. Here, again, we see how less becomes more.

If castration is admitted there will always be a reminder of satisfaction irrespective of the number of agencies waiting to capitalise on it. From this perspective capitalism's foundations combine the assumption of primordial guilt and allow the wealthy to roam free while endlessly processing the surplus because, as Lacan says, they never pay enough. But there is another approach to the surplus. It starts with the question how to recycle it.

The primordial guilt, that echoes what Lacan called the lure of the fault, allows me at this point to stress a disjunction between the one of the signifier and jouissance produced in the discourse. Although jouissance is forbidden to the speaking subject as such, there is no discourse without jouissance. Lacan advanced his position in relation to this disjunction after giving us a precise formulation of discourse as a bond of social relations where the Other is addressed in a number of ways. What is not accounted for in the subject's satisfactions is externally included in the discourse. It is the object *a* as a product that accompanies social exchanges and agencies that mediate them. The neurotic can go to quite a length in his strife to recapture the lost jouissance, and he requires the object *a* for this purpose. Fantasy is a useful tool to support this quest. And if he fails, if he fails as subject to trace the place Freud called *es war*, "it was", he is resigned to renounce it as always-already lost. We could say that in this case, he has given up on his desire. And this is because he believes he owns what is not his of which potentiality-for-being-a-whole, as one of *das-Ein*'s incarnations, is a precise representation.

The experience of guilt in the psychoanalytic clinic has nothing to do with the ontological guilt as *a priori*. That's why Lacan situated it as a neighbour of desire albeit it is not through guilt that the subject accedes to desire. The subject has already acceded to it, which is why Lacan stresses in quite a radical sense that only when giving up on it the subject ends up as guilty. But this does not mean that desire exists *a priori* either. Lacan merely punctuates that desire is initially and foremost from the Other, and that its cause has to do with the object that supports desire through fantasy. I am referring to the upper part of the graph Lacan called the graph of desire although in another sense it is a graph of the subject's relation with the Other's desire through castration. What Lacan brings to our attention is that the subject is only guilty when he turns his attention away from the Other's desire and begins to relish his solitude, namely alienation, in denial of being in the world because of the Other's desire but for some other reason, for example guilt.

The experience of guilt in psychoanalysis has nothing *a priori* about it when the subject brings to his sessions the heavy burden that weighs down on him in his relation with the desire of the Other. The analyst's desire, the term Lacan invented, serves to recognise the analysand's sense of guilt as a contribution to his discourse. Learning about his analysand's desire, he follows closely every indication he may give of his guilt and shame. The neurotic is compelled to smuggle into his discourse the blame with which to make the Other guilty. By this stroke, he demonstrates his belief in the Other as whole and complete, namely as existing to guarantee the social order, human rights, etc. And that's what the Other, as a place of truth, can provide. And what it provides becomes a sign of the lack of the guarantee from the Other of the Other that does not exist. What incarcerates the neurotic, what ties him down to the path of the masochistic jouissance, is a horror of having to keep it by hiding it from the world. It is the horror that Lacan resonated with error. The fault in the structure and the division of the subject are already expressions of the error having been made. Guilt is a product of the subject's passage through the field of the Other when he turns away from his desire.

The neurotic's relation to the other appears as that of mortification, so evident in the Ratman, as he is confronted with God who is always dead. The neurotic subject spends his life flogging the dead horse which in the history of psychoanalysis acquired a different meaning than the one supposed of the universal discourse, namely of proverbs. In short, it is in relation to what Lacan called lack in being that we can situate *Schuldigsein*, the primordial being-guilty in Heidegger's discourse, as being-in-debt or as owing at the moment when the voice of conscience demands the repayment. If *Schuld* signifies just that, namely a debt, then there is nothing the neurotic can enjoy more than the obligation to search for the anonymous creditor that does not exist. And let's note that it is in this way that Lacan defines envy as a modality of jouissance that is useless for the subject.

This is how Heidegger situated the existential foundations of morality which provides a striking difference to the findings of Freud who designated them around the term he found indispensable for the subject, namely that of *Hilflosigkeit*, helplessness. In analysis the subject encounters *Schuldigsein* as a symbolic debt of jouissance to the Other, the dead Other of jouissance. But does this not amount to saying that in the face of being-guilty/being-in-debt that open before *Dasein* its authentic possibilities, it is *das Ein*, the One that appears to us as an "as if all"? "As if all" and, *ergo*, "as if One". The connection to the one of the nation, the one of the fathers, will become more explicit and pronounced in Heidegger's work. It is at this point that I would like to evoke the expression of Lacan from the *Seminar XI*, "the dark God". It is a term that gives meaning to the sacrifice and its fascinations. With being-guilty as its alliance, the *fascinum* finds here a fertile soil. What Lacan designated by the term of sacrifice was to adequate the Thing to the signifier. Has not Foucault given us some of the most spectacular examples of punishment in history where the body and the signifier are to become one and the same Thing? If a sacrifice is a means to seek in the body the proof of the Other's existence, Lacan's evocation is a resounding one. To show the renunciation of the adequation of the Thing to the signifier, Lacan makes reference to Spinoza as the one who brings to the fore, and highlights as man's essence, desire. This will subsequently become Lacan's link to guilt. The link of the *fascinum* to the sacrifice supports the logic of the double agent as a process of capitalisation of the waste. Must nothing go amiss? We need to distinguish the terms of sacrifice and renunciation here, which should be clear by now. To sacrifice is to take the subject for a thing, to renounce points to the subject's castration. Speaking of Spinoza, Lacan thinks of a Jew detached from the tradition, and Spinoza was obviously not the only one. Heidegger's failure to distinguish between the two terms brings him closer to the Other in the Christian tradition than Spinoza or Freud. It is in this light that we should read Heidegger's words, published posthumously (Wolin, 1991), that only God can save us.

"As if one" is possibly the last hope of the philosopher who was not the one who tried to render all as one. The Lacanian subject stands in the way of such a rendition and of such a totalisation. Even so, Lacan was well aware that the time of social segregation and racism was in the offing. Is the idea of unity with the *Nebenmensch* a limit-point at which the impossible liaison between jouissance and desire go no further than the satisfaction of the death drive? Lacan will go no further than this, situating the death drive in relation to the master signifier that insists and dominates the subject's history and with the history of the drive where the limit-point puts, so to speak, a noose of the death drive on the neck of the signifier. And since we speak of being, we need to stress the term "partial" drive.

REFERENCES

Aristotle (1941). McKeon, R. (Ed. & Trans.) *Physics, Book IV*. In: *The Basic Works of Aristotle*. New York: Random House.
Augustine (1961). Pine-Coffin, R. S. (Trans.) *Confessions*. London: Penguin.
Augustine (1991). Rotelle, J. E. (Ed.), Hill, E. O. P. (Trans.) *The Trinity*. New York: New City Press.
Badiou, A. (2003). Feltham, O. & Clemens, J. (Trans.) *Infinite Thought*. London & New York: Continuum.
Beckett, S. (1938). *Murphy*. London: Picador.
Blanchot, M. (1981). Davis, L. (Trans.) *The Gaze of Orpheus*. London: Station Hill.
Borges, J. L. (1984). Weinberger, E. & Reid, A. (Trans.). Blindness. In: *Seven Nights*. New York: New Direction Books.
Brousse, M. -H. (1998). Voruz, V. & Wolf, B. (Trans.) Hysteria and *sinthome*. *Psychoanalytical Notebooks*, 1: 67–78.
Charraud, N. (1999). Dachy, V. & Menzies, H. (Trans.) Cantor with Lacan (1). *Psychoanalytical Notebooks*, 3: 117–131.
Cole, J., R. (1992), *The Olympian Dreams of Youthful Rebellion of René Descartes*. Urbana and Chicago: University of Illinois Press.
Dawkins, R. (2006). *God Delusion*. London: Bantham Press.
Descartes, R. (1973). Haldane, E. & Ross, G. R. T. (Trans.) *The Philosophical Works of Descartes*. Volume 1. Cambridge: Cambridge University Press.

Detienne, M. (1996). Lloyd, J. (Trans.) *The Masters of Truth in Archaic Greece.* New York: Zone Books.

Deutsch, H. (1942). Some forms of emotional disturbances and their relationship to schizophrenia. In: *Neuroses and Character Types.* London: Hogarth.

Ettinger, E. (1995). *Hanna Arendt Martin Heidegger.* New Haven & London: Yale University Press.

Focchi, M. (2008). Senia, G. (Trans.) A spectacular health. *Lacanian Ink, 31*: 63–85.

Foucault, M. (1977). Sheridan, A. (Trans.) *Discipline and Punish.* London: Penguin Books.

Freud, S. (1888b). Hysteria. *S.E., 1*: 37–59. London: Hogarth.

Freud, S. (1905d). *Three Essays on the Theory of Sexuality. S.E., 7*: 136–248. London: Hogarth.

Freud, S. (1910i). The psychoanalytic view of psychogenic disturbances of vision. *S.E., 11*: 209–218. London: Hogarth.

Freud, S. (1912g). A note on the unconscious in psychoanalysis. *S.E., 12*: 255–266. London: Hogarth.

Freud, S. (1912–1913). *Totem and Taboo. S.E., 13*: 1–161. London: Hogarth.

Freud, S. (1914c). On narcissism: an introduction. *S.E., 14*: 67–102. London: Hogarth.

Freud, S. (1917e [1915]). Morning and melancholia. *S.E., 14*: 237–258. London: Hogarth.

Freud, S. (1920g). *Beyond the Pleasure Principle. S.E., 19*: 1–64. London: Hogarth.

Freud, S. (1930a). *Civilisation and its Discontents. S.E., 21*: 59–146. London: Hogarth.

Freud, S. (1939a [1937–1939]). *Moses and Monotheism. S.E., 23*: 3–137. London: Hogarth.

Freud, S. (1950a [1895]). Project for a scientific psychology. In: *The Origins of Psycho-Analysis. S.E., 1*: 253–4. London: Hogarth.

Heidegger, M. (1956). Lacan, J. (Trans.) Logos. *La Psychanalyse, 1*: 59–79.

Heidegger, M. (1962). Macquarrie, J. & Robinson, E. (Trans.) *Being and Time.* Sections 54–60. London: Basil Blackwell.

Heidegger, M. (1984). Krell, D. F. & Capuzzi, F. A. (Trans.) Logos (Heraclitus, Fragment B 50) (pp. 59–78). Aletheia (Heraclitus, Fragment B 16) (pp. 102–123). In: *Early Greek Thinking.* San Francisco: Harper & Row.

Jakobson, R. (1987). *Language in Literature.* Cambridge & London: The Belknap Press of Harvard University Press.

Klein, M. (1988). On the theory of anxiety and guilt. (1948). In: *Envy and Gratitude.* London: Virago.

Lacan, J. (1953). Some reflections on the ego. *The International Journal of Psychoanalysis, XXXV*: 11–17.

Lacan, J. (1977). Miller, J. -A. (Ed.), Sheridan, A. (Trans.) *Seminar XI: The Four Fundamental Concepts of Psychoanalysis*. (1964). London: Penguin.
Lacan, J. (1990). Copjec, J. (Ed.) Hollier, D. Krauss, R. & Michelson, A. (Trans.) *Television*. (1973). New York: Norton.
Lacan, J. (1992). Miller, J. -A. (Ed.) Porter, D. (Trans.) *Seminar VII: The Ethics of Psychoanalysis*. (1959–1960). London: Routledge.
Lacan, J. (1994). Miller, J. -A. (Ed.) *Le Séminaire: livre IV, La relation d'objet*. (1956–1957). Paris: Seuil.
Lacan, J. (1995). Grigg, R. (Trans.). Proposition of 9 October on the psychoanalyst of the school. (1967). *Analysis*, 6: 1–13.
Lacan, J. (1998a). Miller, J. -A. (Ed.) *Le Séminaire: livre V, Les formations de l'inconscient*. (1957–1958). Paris: Seuil.
Lacan, J. (1998b). Miller. J. -A. (Ed.), Fink, B. (Trans.) *Seminar XX: On Feminine Sexuality, The Limits of Love and Knowledge, Encore*. (1972–73). New York: Norton.
Lacan, J. (2001). Miller, J. -A. (Ed.) *L'Etourdit*. (1973). In: *Autres écrits*. (pp. 449–495). Paris: Seuil.
Lacan, J. (2006a). Miller. J. -A. (Ed.), Fink, B. (Trans.) The mirror stage as formative of the *I* function as revealed in psychoanalytic experience. (1949). In: *Ecrits*. (pp. 75–81). New York: Norton.
Lacan, J. (2006b). Miller. J. -A. (Ed.), Fink, B. (Trans.) Position of the unconscious. (1960). In: *Ecrits*. (pp. 703–721). New York: Norton.
Lacan, J. (2006c). Miller. J. -A. (Ed.), Fink, B. (Trans.) The Freudian thing or the meaning of the return to Freud. (1955). In: *Ecrits*. (pp. 334–363). New York: Norton.
Lacan, J. (2006d). Miller. J. -A. (Ed.), Fink, B. (Trans.) Seminar on "The purloined letter". (1956). In: *Ecrits*. (pp. 6–48). New York: Norton.
Lacan, J. (2006e). Miller. J. -A. (Ed.), Fink, B. (Trans.) The instance of the letter in the unconscious or reason since Freud. (1957). In: *Ecrits*. (pp. 412–441). New York: Norton.
Lacan, J. (2006f). Miller. J. -A. (Ed.), Fink, B. (Trans.) On Freud's "trieb" and the psychoanalyst's desire. (1964). In: *Ecrits*. (pp. 721–725). New York: Norton.
Lacan, J. (2006g). Miller. J. -A. (Ed.), Fink, B. (Trans.) Science and truth. (1966). In: *Ecrits*. (pp. 726–745). New York: Norton.
Lacan, J. (2006h). Miller, J. -A. (Ed.) *Le Séminaire: livre XVIII, D'un discours qui ne serait pas du semblant*. (1971). Paris: Seuil.
Lacan, J. (2007). Miller, J. -A. (Ed.) Grigg, R. (Trans.) *Seminar XVII: The Other Side of Psychoanalysis*. (1969–1970). New York: Norton.
Lacan, J. (2013a). Fink, B. (Trans.) *On the Names-of-the-Father*. (1963). London: Polity.
Lacan, J. (2013b). Fink, B. (Trans.) *The Triumph of Religion*. London: Polity.

Lacan, J. (2014). Miller, J. -A. (Ed.), Price, A., R. (Trans.) *Seminar X: Anxiety.* (1962–1963). Cambridge: Polity.
Leff, G. (1959). *Medieval Thought: St Augustine to Ockham.* London: The Merlin Press.
Lehrer, R. (1995). *Nietzsche's Presence in Freud's Life and Thought.* New York: SUNY.
Merleau-Ponty, M. (1968). Lingis, A. (Trans.) *The Visible and the Invisible.* Evanston: Northwestern University Press.
Miller, J. -A. (1991). Jauregui, J. & Laporte, M., (Trans.) Ethics in psychoanalysis. *Lacanian Ink,* 5: 13–27.
Miller, J. -A. (1999). Twitchin, M. & Margolies, E. (Trans.) The disparate. *Psychoanalytical Notebooks,* 3: 99–110.
Miller, J. -A. (2001). Dachy, V. (Trans.) Jacques Lacan and the voice. *Psychoanalytical Notebooks,* 6: 93–104.
Miller, J. -A. (2003). Voruz, V. & Wolf, B. (Trans.) The analytic session. *Psychoanalytical Notebooks,* 10: 9–25.
Nietzsche, F. (1968). Kaufmann, W. (Ed. & Trans.) *Genealogy of Morals.* In: *Basic Writings of Nietzsche.* (pp. 439–599). New York: Random House.
Nietzsche, F. (1974). Kaufman, W. (Trans.) *The Gay Science.* New York: Vintage Books.
Nietzsche, F. (1984). Hollingdale, R., J. (Trans.) *Twilight of the Idols.* London: Penguin Books.
Perel, E. (2006). *Mating in Captivity. Sex, Lies, and Domestic Bliss.* New York: Harper Collins.
Plato (1973). Hamilton, W. (Trans.) *Phaedrus.* London: Penguin.
Roudinesco, E. (1990). Mehlman, J. (Trans.) *Jacques Lacan & Co. A History of Psychoanalysis in France 1925–1985.* London: Free Association Books.
Sartre, J. -P. (1956). Barnes, H., E. (Trans.) *Being and Nothingness.* London: Philosophical Library.
Saussure, de F. (1983). Harris, R. (Trans.) *Course in General Linguistics.* London: Duckworth.
Searle, J. (1971). Flew, A. G. N. (Ed.) The verification of linguistic characteristics. (pp. 241–244). Hensen, R. What we say (pp. 204–220). In: *Philosophy and Linguistics.* London: MacMillan & Co.
Sophocles (1986). Fagles, R. (Trans.) *Oedipus at Colonus.* London: Pelican.
Vollrath, H. (1991). Doane, A. N. & Braun Pasternack, C. (Eds.) Oral modes of perception in eleventh-century chronicles. In: *Vox Intexta. Orality and Textuality in the Middle Ages.* Wisconsin: The University of Wisconsin Press.
Wolf, B. (2013). Intricacies of the gaze: love, jealousy, envy and shame. *Psychoanalytical Notebooks,* 27: 135–144.
Wolin, R. (Gen. Ed.) (1991). Alter, M. P. & Caputo, J. D. (Trans.) Only a God can save us: *Der Spiegel's* interview with Martin Heidegger. (1966). (pp. 91–116). In: *The Heidegger Controversy.* London: MIT.

INDEX

aletheia 72, 166
alienation and separation 64–66
amor studentium 90
anamorphosis 136
Antaios 98
Antigone 24, 162, 176, 179
anxiety 25
apensé 16, 112
Apollo 41–42
Aquinas, Saint Thomas 71, 156
Arendt, Hanna 19, 166, 178
Aries 73
Aristotle 17, 22, 24, 55, 57, 65, 99, 107, 118, 167
Artemis 73, 76
atheism 28
Augustine 15, 88, 90, 93–94, 108, 114
Austin 94
automaton 118

Badiou, Alan 12, 20, 54
Bataille, Georges 182
Beckett, Samuel 14
Befriedegungserlebnis (experience of satisfaction) 82, 84, 140, 150
Being 57
Beoufret, Jean 53, 60, 76, 102
Berkley, Bishop 15
Blair, Tony 11
Blanchot, Maurice 18, 183
blindness 129, 131–132, 160
  symptom as 144, 150
Borges, Jorge Luis 131
Borromean knot 157
Brentano, Franz 14
Brousse, Marie-Hélène 157–158

Camus, Albert 15
Cantor, Georg 17, 118
castration 32, 46, 133, 154, 175
cathartic method 126

cause 55
Cavell, Stanley 94
Charraud, Natalie 20
Commandments 25
contingency 50, 125
Copernicus 69
couch 138–139
Creon 8, 24, 179

Dasein 69, 167–168
Dawkins, Richard 28–29, 39, 43
demand 34, 147, 150, 173
Descartes, René 15, 63, 106, 109–110
désêtre 52, 63, 71
desire 17, 30, 33, 37, 90, 133, 174
    hysteric of 38
    Other of 52, 59, 64–65, 82, 113
Detienne, Marcel 73
Deutsch, Helen 121
Ding, das 48, 74–75, 83–84, 151, 156
discourse 152–153
dominanta 45
Dostoyevsky, Fyodor 15
drive 140, 142–143, 145–146, 148, 152
    death drive 143, 161
Duras, Marguerite 134
Dwelshauvers, Georges 7

Edna, Dame 137
Einstein, Albert 15
Emma 61, 102
envy 181
Euclid 17
extimate 151

father
    imaginary father 48
    Name-of-the-Father 26, 30, 45, 91, 157, 174
    real as 171
fantasy 133, 138, 140, 144, 153–154
fascinum 188

Ferenczi, Sàndor 28
Fliess, Wilhelm 35
Focchi, Marco 3–4
Foucault, Michel 188
Freud, Sigmund 6–8, 14–16, 18–19, 22, 25–28, 30–31, 33, 35, 49, 52–53, 69, 72, 74, 82–84, 90, 94, 108, 110, 112, 115, 121, 126, 143, 149, 158, 163, 171–172, 177, 187–188

Gaia 98
gaze 159
God 94–95, 110, 188
    death of 28–29, 31
    deceiving as 63
guilt 28, 31, 33, 171–172, 174, 176, 179–180, 182, 186–187
    debt as 169

hainamoration 47
Hamlet 32
Hannibal 12
Hartmann, Karl von 7
Heidegger, Martin 15, 19, 53, 57–58, 60–61, 65, 68, 76–77, 102, 133, 166–170, 178–180, 182, 188
Henson, Richard 94, 101–102, 105
Heracles 98
Heraclitus 57, 61, 69, 77
Hitler, Adolf 11
Holbein
    Ambassadors 135–136
Hume, David 15
Husserl, Edmund 178, 182

identification 31, 33, 60
ignorance 24
imaginary 60, 92, 161
impossibility 39, 41
infinity 17, 116–117

interpretation 16, 89
Invention of Lying 62, 66

Jacobson, Roman 87
Jerusalem 47
jouissance 4–5, 15, 17, 32, 44, 84, 112, 122, 147, 167, 176
    of the Other 32–33, 37, 103, 133, 156
    phallic 157
    surplus of 161
Joyce, James 83, 104, 157, 159
Judas 12

Kafka, Franz 120
Kant, Immanuel 14, 93
Khan, Ghengis 12
Kierkegaard, Soren 127
Klein, Melanie 172
Klossowski, Pierre 166
knowledge 2–3, 24, 32, 37, 76, 87, 160
    and belief 29

Lacan, Jacques, throughout
lack 31–32
lalangue 74
language 75–76, 99
Laplanche, Jean 7
lapsus 100
Laurent, Eric 48, 110
Lazarus 96
legein 58–60
Lehrer, Ronald 28
Leibniz, Gotfried 17
Lethe 73
letter 81, 89, 96, 157, 159
Levi, Bernard-Henri 48
libido 32
lie, lying 62
life
    real as 160

logos 54, 58–59, 61, 69
love 8, 32, 36–37, 39, 41, 45, 67, 109, 175, 181, 185
    and speech 34–35
    and hate 47
    truth of 54
    and knowledge 108

Macbeth 143
Magritte, René 76
manqué à être 59
master 46
Masters & Jones 72
meaning 106–107, 109, 114
Medusa 143
Merleau-Ponty, Maurice 53, 130
metonymy 100
Miller, Jacques-Alain 16–17, 26, 36, 50, 67, 76, 84, 96, 106, 110, 113–114, 116, 119, 122, 124, 140, 161, 166, 169
mirror stage 131, 138
Monfort, Simon de 12
morality
    origin of 35
Moses 27–28
Myth 141

name 94–95
    pluralisation of 48
Nebenmensch 26, 67, 83, 87, 91, 107, 178, 183
negation 39, 85
neurosis
    hysteria 151
    obsessional 14, 26, 168
Nietzsche, Fredriech 13, 27–29, 166, 169

object *a* 21, 29, 39, 45–46, 67, 69, 75, 138–139, 175, 186
    cause as 37, 72

gaze 131, 137–138
  remainder as 48, 76, 117
Odo of Ostia 88
Oedipus 14, 84, 130
  Colonus at 159–162
Orestes 151
Other 28, 31, 46, 96, 110, 137
  inconsistent as 154–155

Pan 41–42
parlêtre 59, 77
Parmenides 68, 167
passion 35
Perel, Esther 35–36
Perseus 143
perversion 133
Phaedrus 94
phallic object 47
phallus 32, 40, 50, 134
philosophy 12, 14–15, 18–20, 27, 53
Pirandello, Luigi 15
Plato 7, 22, 54, 94–95, 99, 102
Pleasure Principle 115–116
privation 47
Potter, Harry 46
protos pseudos 61, 98, 102
psychoanalysis 1, 25, 28–29, 43, 77, 99, 107
  ethics of 33
  pure and applied 4
  secret as 47–49

quantum 116–117

Ratman 182, 187
real 56, 73, 102–103, 106, 124
Reality Principle 116
relation
  sexual 36–39, 45
religion 25–28
repetition 123–127
repression 39, 148

responsibility 69, 178
Rolland, Romain 27
Roudinesco, Elisabeth 53

sacrifice 25, 32–34, 188
Sade, Marquis de 33, 181
Safouan, Mustafa 145
saint 24, 35, 156, 162–163
Sartre, Jean-Paul 53
Saussure, Ferdinand 87
Schiller 149
Schliemann, Heinrich 6–7, 73
School, Lacan's 22
Schreber 159
Schuldigsein 168–169, 182–183, 185
science 29, 69, 104
Scott, Dun 15
Searle, John 94, 96–99, 105
semblance 40, 102, 154
session, analytic 17
Shakespeare
  Othello 134
shame 180
sicut palea 71
signified 80, 87, 100, 173
signifier 12, 59, 84–85, 91
  master signifier 65, 73, 121
  of the lack 44, 66
sinthome 156–158
Socrates 94–95
speech 89
  and writing 94
Spinoza, Baruch 50, 188
stain 160–161
  function of 135
Stalin, Joseph 11
Stein, Gertrude 7
structure 105
subject 13, 18, 31, 50, 59, 73
  divided as 66, 111
  foreclosed, as 77

happy as 63–64
superego 33, 175
    maternal 172, 174
symbolic 60, 171
symptom 13, 150, 152
Szasz, Thomas 12

Tao 26
Thatcher, Margaret 11
time 120–122, 124–125
    another temporality 126
thinking 15–16, 18–19, 112
topology 106, 134
transference 37, 86, 90, 126
truth 3, 13–14, 54–55, 72
    cause as 56, 62, 73

unconscious 6–8, 10, 16, 25–26, 30–31, 44, 54, 76, 99–100, 102–103, 106, 111, 124, 142

feeling of guilt 176
knowledge as 120
subject as 119–121

Valéry, Paul 39, 143
voice 92–93, 113, 138, 170
Vorstellung 86
    vorstellung representäntz 86

Weltanschauung 14
Winnicott, D. W. 13
Wittgenstein, Ludvig 111, 165
woman 68, 71
    veil, as 40
writing 100

Zen 26
Žižek, Slavoj 7